AF424272

COMMERCIAL LAW

LECTOR HOUSE PUBLIC DOMAIN WORKS

This book is a result of an effort made by Lector House towards making a contribution to the preservation and repair of original classic literature. The original text is in the public domain in the United States of America, and possibly other countries depending upon their specific copyright laws.

In an attempt to preserve, improve and recreate the original content, certain conventional norms with regard to typographical mistakes, hyphenations, punctuations and/or other related subject matters, have been corrected upon our consideration. However, few such imperfections might not have been rectified as they were inherited and preserved from the original content to maintain the authenticity and construct, relevant to the work. The work might contain a few prior copyright references as well as page references which have been retained, wherever considered relevant to the part of the construct. We believe that this work holds historical, cultural and/or intellectual importance in the literary works community, therefore despite the oddities, we accounted the work for print as a part of our continuing effort towards preservation of literary work and our contribution towards the development of the society as a whole, driven by our beliefs.

We are grateful to our readers for putting their faith in us and accepting our imperfections with regard to preservation of the historical content. We shall strive hard to meet up to the expectations to improve further to provide an enriching reading experience.

Though, we conduct extensive research in ascertaining the status of copyright before redeveloping a version of the content, in rare cases, a classic work might be incorrectly marked as not-in-copyright. In such cases, if you are the copyright holder, then kindly contact us or write to us, and we shall get back to you with an immediate course of action.

HAPPY READING!

COMMERCIAL LAW

SAMUEL WILLISTON,
RICHARD DUDLEY CURRIER,
RICHARD WILLIAM HILL

ISBN: 978-93-5614-391-3

Published: -

© 2022
LECTOR HOUSE LLP

LECTOR HOUSE LLP
E-MAIL: lectorpublishing@gmail.com

COMMERCIAL LAW

BY

**SAMUEL WILLISTON,
RICHARD D. CURRIER,
AND
RICHARD W. HILL**

PREFACE

THE Institute standard course of study in "Commercial Law" is not intended to make lawyers, but simply to impart to bankers sufficient knowledge of law to enable them to act in accordance with established legal principles, and refer doubtful questions to a lawyer. It is not usurping the functions of a lawyer for a banker to know his legal rights and responsibilities. The banker who does not appreciate the importance of this knowledge, eventually learns from experience, sad or otherwise, that he has neglected an important part of the training necessary to carry on his business with safety and confidence. This text-book is based on the splendid work, originally prepared for the Institute, by Samuel Williston, Weld Professor of Law in Harvard Law School. To this original matter, however, much new material has been added, cases have been cited, and new chapters on Master and Servant, Estates and Trusts, Bills and Notes, and Torts and Crimes added. The work of preparing "Commercial Law" has been done jointly by Richard D. Currier, President of the New Jersey Law School, and Richard W. Hill, member of the New York Bar and Secretary of the American Institute of Banking. The main purpose of this book is to teach bankers to recognize the danger signals in law, when they appear, and thus be able to distinguish between law and law suits.

INSTITUTE PLATFORM

RESOLUTION adopted at the New Orleans Convention of the American Institute of Banking, October 9, 1919:

"Ours is an educational association organized for the benefit of the banking fraternity of the country and within our membership may be found on an equal basis both employees and employers; and in full appreciation of the opportunities which our country and its established institutions afford, and especially in appreciation of the fact that the profession of banking affords to its diligent and loyal members especial opportunities for promotion to official and managerial positions, and that as a result of the establishment and maintenance of the merit system in most banks a large number of Institute members have through individual application achieved marked professional success, we at all times and under all circumstances stand for the merit system and for the paying of salaries according to the value of the service rendered.

"We believe in the equitable cooperation of employees and employers and are opposed to all attempts to limit individual initiative and curtail production, and, insofar as our profession is concerned, are unalterably opposed to any plan purporting to promote the material welfare of our members, individually or collectively, on any other basis than that of efficiency, loyalty and unadulterated Americanism."

CONTENTS

WHO IS A BANKER?

A SUCCESSFUL BANKER is composed of about one-fifth accountant, two-fifths lawyer, three-fifths political economist, and four-fifths gentleman and scholar—total ten-fifths—double size. Any smaller person may be a pawnbroker or a promoter, but not a banker.—George E. Allen.

COMMERCIAL LAW

INTRODUCTION

DEFINITION OF LAW.—The term "law" is used in many ways. We speak of moral law, law of gravity, divine law, and the like. In each case we are making proper use of the term, but in no instance are we using it as we shall use it in this book. To illustrate: You find a beggar on your front porch when entering your house late at night. Suppose he should ask you for food and lodging for the night. Although there is no other house within five miles of your home, you refuse to take him in, or do anything for him. As a result he contracts pneumonia from exposure, because he is not able to proceed further. You would, nevertheless, not be liable in the sense in which we are using the term "law." But, you say, in an extreme case of this kind, it is one's duty to act. We grant it, but to be accurate, you must preface your proposition with the statement, "under the moral law" or "under divine law it is one's duty to act in such a case." However much it is to be regretted that moral or divine law sometimes does not harmonize with "law" as we shall treat it, we must, nevertheless, recognize that fact. Law, as viewed by the jurist, and this is the way we, as students, are to consider it, is defined by Blackstone to be "A rule of civil conduct prescribed by the supreme power in the State, commanding what is right, and prohibiting what is wrong." Referring again to our illustration, is it not easy to see that it would be impracticable in the present condition of society for the legislature of California, for example, to pass a law which should, in that State, constitute "a rule of civil conduct" commanding that every one "shall be his brother's keeper" and for a violation thereof "shall be imprisoned for one year, or fined one thousand dollars, or both." However much we recognize the obligation of moral law, jurists and legislators cannot ignore the fact that society is composed of ordinary human beings, still far from perfection. Assuming, although perhaps it is doubtful, that it is within the power of the legislature of California to pass such an act as has been suggested, there are not courts enough in the whole United States to decide the cases which would arise in New York City alone in attempting to apply the provisions of such an act. On second thought, then, it is not such a startling proposition for us to learn that "law" is not synonymous with the same term when used in referring to natural law, moral law, and the like. Much has been written on the essential nature of "law" as we shall use the term. The time-honored definition of Blackstone, which we have quoted, is confessedly imperfect. The last clause, "commanding what is RIGHT, and prohibiting what is WRONG" has been much criticized, and Mr. Chitty has modified it to "commanding what shall be done, and what shall not be done." Today, to attempt to buy a bottle of light wine at a hotel does not seem to many of us intrinsically WRONG, but legally, under existing laws, it is, and so perhaps Mr. Chitty's modification of Blackstone's definition does bring out the correct idea more clearly. For our purpose, these two definitions are sufficient.

THE SYSTEMS OF LAW.—There are two chief systems of law in use among civilized peoples today, the Roman or civil law, and, the English or common law. The Roman, or civil law (Roman law is spoken of as civil law, from the Latin "civilis," belonging to a citizen) as its name implies, originated in Rome. As the city of Rome developed into the Roman Empire, its law became that of the ancient world. It was finally codified by the Roman Emperor Justinian, in the year 530 A.D., and was eventually absorbed, from the twelfth to the eighteenth century, into the law of modern Europe. It is the basis of the systems of law used in the countries of continental Europe, Central and South America, and all French, Spanish, Portuguese, and Dutch colonies or countries settled by those peoples.

COMMON LAW.—The common law had its roots in the customary law of the Germanic peoples of western Europe, and was developed by the English courts from the thirteenth to the nineteenth centuries. Like the Roman law, it has spread all over the world wherever English-speaking peoples have settled, and founded colonies. The common law now prevails in England, Canada (except Quebec), India, except over Hindus and Mohammedans in certain instances, and the principal British colonies, except those in South Africa. The United States is largely an English settlement, hence the common law prevails with us, except in the State of Louisiana, where the influence of the French and Spanish settlements still remains and makes the basis of the Louisiana law the Roman law, and in the Philippines and Porto Rico, where the law was Roman when we took those possessions from Spain in 1898.

THE SOURCE OF LAW.—Where does this rule of civil conduct we are to study come from? At first blush, the superficial observer might suggest some legislative hall where it is created by a legislative body, a perfect product, to be imposed on men and women as the guide in their every act in civil life. The slightest reference to historical jurisprudence will convince us that this is not the true source of the law. Mr. Justice Holmes of the United States Supreme Court, in his classic, "The Common Law," indicates the real source of law when he observes: "The life of the law has not been logic; it has been experience. The felt necessities of the time, the prevalent moral and political theories, intuitions of public policy, avowed or unconscious, even the prejudices which judges share with their fellow-men, have had a good deal more to do than the syllogism in determining the rules by which men should be governed. The law embodies the story of a nation's development through many centuries, and it cannot be dealt with as if it contained only the axioms and corollaries of a book of mathematics. In order to know what it is, we must know what it has been, and what it tends to become. We must alternately consult history and existing theories of legislation. But the most difficult labor will be to understand the combination of the two into new products at every stage. The substance of the law at any given time pretty nearly corresponds, so far as it goes, with what is then understood to be convenient; but its form and machinery, and the degree to which it is able to work out desired results, depend very much upon its past."

WHERE TO LOOK FOR LAW.—Knowing the source of law does not necessarily tell us where to look for the law. Today, in the United States, we have three primary sources to which the lawyer goes to seek the law on any particular point. First, the Constitution of the United States and the Constitution of the State in which he is to ascertain the law, including the statutes which have been enacted by Congress and by the State legislature under those constitutions. Second, the decisions of the courts, particularly those of the United States courts and of the State where he wishes to learn the law, and, if need be, the decisions of other States. Third, text-books and treatises on the branch of law to be investigated.

ILLUSTRATION.—Let us suppose you wish to ascertain the law concerning a question that comes up in your own daily life. Take two problems. First: We will assume you keep a clothing store, and an infant, twenty years old, purchases a suit of winter clothes. His income is $1000 per year. He already has two perfectly good winter suits. A week after purchasing this suit, he returns it and demands his money back. You wish to know whether you have to give it to him. If you should look in the Constitution of the United States, or of the State of Vermont (assuming this to be a Vermont contract), you would find nothing that would give you any help in answering this question. If you should look through all of the acts of Congress and the laws passed by the legislature of the State of Vermont, you would find nothing to give you any help. If, however, you should look in the decisions of the courts, both of the United States and of the State of Vermont, you would find cases, probably many of them, covering this particular situation, and you would find the rule to be laid down as law, that an infant (and by an infant we mean anyone under twenty-one years) is not liable on his contracts, except for necessities, and then only in a quasi-contractual action for their reasonable value. Applying the law to the problem, you would be obliged to admit the legality of the infant's claim, and if you did not refund the money to him, he would be entitled to sue for it in a court. Three winter suits are clearly not necessaries at one time for an infant with an income no greater than $1000 per year. This is a comparatively simple problem. Now let us take another case somewhat more difficult. You live in New Jersey near the plant of an airplane manufacturing company. Machines are constantly being tried out, and they circle over your premises within four or five hundred feet from the ground. You have several children who are using your back yard as a playground and you are much alarmed, fearing that an airplane may fall in the yard and kill or injure a child. You wish to ascertain your rights. You look in the Constitution of the United States, and of the State of New Jersey. You will find nothing in either about airplanes. You look in the acts of Congress and the laws of the legislature of the State of New Jersey. You will find nothing there to help you. You look in the decisions of the courts, both of the United States and of the State of New Jersey. You will find nothing there. You look in the text-books, and, except in the most recent, in all probability you will find nothing there in regard to airplanes. You may search the recent legal publications and you will find articles discussing in a purely theoretical way this interesting topic. You study recent legislation and you will find stray instances of attempts to deal with aerial matters. For example, Connecticut has a statute on airplanes. In fact, your whole search will be most interesting. All you will find, however, is not law in New Jersey, but is simply theory, based on common law principles or statutes having no force in New Jersey. Should you then conclude that you have no rights, that the law cannot help you? Perhaps not. If you turn to treatises relating to the ownership of land as developed in the English common law and as applied by the courts in the United States, you will find that the word "land" is often used as practically synonymous with realty or ground or soil, and you will also find that it includes everything attached to the realty or growing on it. As is commonly said, land has an indefinite extent upward as well as downward, the old books using the Latin maxim: "Cuius est solum, eius est usque ad coelum usque ad orcum." (To whomsoever the soil belongs, he owns also to the sky and to the depths.)

There are three houses in a row on Smith Street, Nos. 1, 3 and 5. Mary Jones lives in No. 1, and Sarah Green in No. 5. They are friends, and accordingly arrange to stretch their clotheslines from their rear second-story windows across the back yard of No. 3. Under common law principles, this is a trespass upon No. 3. Should Mary Jones and Sarah Green continue to do this for the required time, usually twenty years, they would acquire by prescription a permanent right to stretch clotheslines over lot No. 3. When the owner of lot No. 3 wished to erect a ten-story building covering all of his lot, he would be seriously interfered with by the right acquired by his two adjoining neighbors. He could have protected himself by proper action in a court when the offense was first committed. Could not, therefore, the court take this principle of the common law as to the ownership of land and apply it to the airplane case? If the owner of lot No. 3 could prevent the owners of lots Nos. 1 and 5 from stretching clotheslines across his land, could you not prevent the airplane from crossing your land, although it is five hundred feet above the surface of the soil? Twenty years' continuation of that practice would interfere with your ability to build a Woolworth building twenty-five years from now should you desire to do so. It is simply taking an old principle of law recognized for centuries, and applying it to new conditions. This is what we mean when we say that the principles of common law are capable of indefinite expansion; that the common law is always growing, or, as Mr. Justice Holmes puts it, it is the product of "the felt necessities of the time." As soon, however, as you have secured an injunction from the court preventing the airplane factory from practicing its machines over your land, all of the other property owners in the neighborhood of the factory decide to protect their rights, with the result that no airplane can leave the factory through the air. Does this mean that the airplane factory must move, and probably be subjected to the same annoyances in its new location in a short time? We are coming to realize that airplanes are necessities. When a necessity and a principle of law cannot exist side by side, something must be done to remedy an intolerable situation. The illustration here used presents what in the course of a few years, undoubtedly, will become an intolerable situation, unless remedied in some way. It has been suggested that we must modify our principles of the ownership of land, and give airplanes the right of free passage over the land of any person, when a certain distance in the air, far enough up to cause no great amount of danger or annoyance. Such a change in the law would have to be accomplished by the State legislature or by an act of Congress for such territory as Congress has jurisdiction over. No doubt, legislation along such lines may be expected soon. It will be simply a repetition of a situation created by a leading case in New York in 1902.

In Roberson v. The Rochester Folding Box Company, 171 New York 538, the suit was brought on behalf of a living person, a young lady, to restrain a flour company from putting her likeness upon prints advertising its flour. Mr. Justice Parker, writing the opinion of the court, held that there was no principle of law which would authorize the court to issue an injunction restraining this unauthorized use of a photograph. This created the unfortunate situation in the State of New York of allowing anyone to make use of another's photograph without that person's consent, for advertising or other purposes. The court, in its opinion, admitted the unfortunateness of the situation, observing that "The legislative body could very well interfere and arbitrarily provide that no one should be permitted for his own selfish purpose to use the picture or the name of another for advertising purposes without his consent. In such event no embarrassment would result to the general body of the law, for the rule would be applicable only to cases provided for by statute. The courts however, being without authority to legislate, are required to decide cases upon principle, and so are necessarily embarrassed by precedents created by an extreme, and therefore unjustifiable application of an old principle. The court below properly said that: 'While it may be true that the fact that no precedent can be found to sustain an action in any given case is cogent evidence that a principle does not exist upon which the right may be based, it is not the rule that the want of a precedent is a sufficient reason for turning the plaintiff out of court,' provided (I think should be added)," Mr. Justice Parker continues, "there can be found a clear and unequivocal principle of the common law, which either directly or mediately governs it, or which, by analogy or parity of reasoning, ought to govern it." Relief was denied the young lady. The following session of the legislature corrected the evil by passing a law making it a criminal offense to use another's photograph without that person's consent. This has been a long illustration. It has served its purpose best if it has left the very distinct impression that the law is a vital, living, growing thing. True, its roots are in the dim past, but it lives, and moves, and has its being in the problems of today. In no field of law is this more true than in our subject, Commercial Law.

WHO KNOWS THE LAW.—The layman is frequently of the opinion that a lawyer ought to be able to give him a definite answer as to just what the law is in a given set of facts. Why is it not possible to go to the sources which we have been discussing and from them ascertain definitely what the law is in a given case? Frequently the lawyer can do this, but one should not lose respect for the lawyer because he is not, in many cases, willing to give a definite answer, but may frame his reply in an opinion beginning "It would seem that the law in this case would be, etc.—" We have already suggested some of the difficulties that in part answer the question we now ask. Let us take one more illustration, a striking example from the United States Supreme Court. Few would question the statement that that Court is the highest type of judicial body in the world today. We are familiar with the rent profiteering legislation enacted in the District of Columbia, New York and at least five other States, as a result of the house shortage created by the world war. The United States Supreme Court, in the cases of Block v. Hirsh, 254 U.S. 531 and Marcus Brown Holding Co. v. Feldman et al., 254 U.S. 539, held the New York and the District of Columbia rent profiteering laws to be constitutional, but this decision is by a vote of five to four, and the arguments advanced in the two opinions, one by Mr. Justice Holmes, representing the majority of the court, and the other by Mr. Justice McKenna, are striking examples of how strongly the ablest body of jurists in the United States can differ on a legal question. Speaking for the majority in Block v. Hirsh, Mr. Justice Holmes says: "The main point against the law is that tenants are allowed to remain in possession at the same rent that they have been paying, unless modified by the commission established by the act, and that thus the use of the land and the right of the owner to do what he will with his own and to make what contracts he pleases are cut down. But if the public interest be established, the regulation of rates is one of the first forms in which it is asserted, and the validity of such regulation has been settled since Munn v. Illinois, 94 U.S. 113. It is said that a grain elevator may go out of business, whereas here the use is fastened upon the land. The power to go out of business, when it exists, is an illusory answer to gas companies and waterworks, but we need not stop at that. The regulation is put and justified only as a temporary measure. * * * A limit in time, to tide over a passing trouble, well may justify a law that could not be upheld as a permanent change." In the case of Marcus Brown Holding Co. v. Feldman, involving a similar New York law, Mr. Justice Holmes says: "The chief objections to these acts have been dealt with in Block v. Hirsh, supra. In the present case more emphasis is laid upon the impairment of the obligation of the contract of the lessees to surrender possession, and of the new lease, which was to have gone into effect upon October 1, last year. But contracts are made subject to this exercise of the power of the State when otherwise justified, as we have held this to be." Mr. Justice McKenna, in writing the dissenting opinion in Block v. Hirsh, supra, and with whom the late Chief Justice White, and Justices Van Devanter and McReynolds concurred, says: "If such exercise of government be legal, what exercise of government is illegal? Houses are a necessary of life, but other things are as necessary. May they, too, be taken from the direction of their owners and disposed of by the Government? * * * An affirmative answer seems to be the requirement of the decision. If the public interest may be concerned, as in the statute under review, with the control of any form of property, it can be concerned with the control of all forms of property. And, certainly, in the first instance, the necessity or expediency of control must be a matter of legislative judgment. * * * The facts are significant and suggest this inquiry: Have conditions come not only to the District of Columbia, embarrassing the Federal government, but to the world as well, that are not amenable to passing palliatives, and that socialism, or some form of socialism, is the only permanent corrective or accommodation? It is indeed strange that this court, in effect, is called upon to make way for it, and through an instrument of a constitution based on personal rights and the purposeful encouragement of individual incentive and energy, to declare legal a power exerted for their destruction. The inquiry occurs, have we come to the realization of the observation that 'War, unless it be fought for liberty, is the most deadly enemy of liberty.'"

In the Marcus Brown Holding Co. case, he again says for the same justices: "We are not disposed to further enlarge upon the case, or attempt to reconcile the explicit declaration of the Constitution against the power of the state to impair the obligations of a contract, or, under any pretense, to disregard the declaration. It is safer, saner, and more consonant with constitutional pre-eminence and its purposes, to regard the declaration of the Constitution as paramount, and not to weaken it by refined dialectics, or bend it to some impulse of emergency because of some accident of immediate overwhelming interest which appeals to the feelings and distorts the judgment." No more striking illustration of the most decided differences of opinion among nine of the ablest jurists in the world can be found. It is no wonder then that a lawyer at times hesitates in giving an opinion as to what the law may be.

THE FUNCTION OF THE COURT.—An infant bought a motorcycle on an installment contract at the agreed price of $325. He made an initial payment of $125, used the machine a month, damaged it to the amount of $156.25, and then returned it in this condition and demanded the return of his $125. These are the facts in the case of Petit v. Liston, 97 Oregon 464, a case decided in the Supreme Court of Oregon. The case involves the right of an infant to disaffirm a contract made by him, when purchasing an article which is not a necessity. The Oregon court had never before been called on to determine what the law in Oregon was as applied to such a situation. According to the rule in New York, as laid down in Rice v. Butler, 160 N. Y. 578, the infant could not recover the $125, but according to the rule in Pyne v. Wood, 145 Mass. 558, the infant would be entitled to his money. It thus became the problem of the Oregon court to refer to the theories back of these two decisions. After doing so, it approved of the New York view, rather than the Massachusetts view. This case indicates the function of a court. If a court, from the various sources of law which we have enumerated, can find an exact precedent for the case before it, or can find a general principle of law which can be applied, it renders a decision as to the law, as the Oregon court did. If no law can be found nor any principles which can be applied, the court is forced to deny the relief, as in the Roberson case, 171 N. Y. 538, adding, perhaps, to its opinion, as it did in that case, the suggestion that it is a matter Congress or a State legislature might properly remedy.

THE COURT SYSTEM.—Knowing the function of a court, the student should then have an outline of the court system of his own jurisdiction. We can only sketch, in a book to be used generally throughout the United States, the court systems. Each State has two sets of courts: the Federal and the State courts. We have a Federal and a State Government; it follows that there should be courts to interpret the laws of each of these two Governments. Matters pertaining to the United States Constitution, or matters affecting citizens of different States, are tried in the Federal courts. The same is true of admiralty and bankruptcy. There is at least one United States District Court in each State in the country, and Federal cases are begun in these courts. If either party is dissatisfied with the decision, he may appeal to the next higher court. The entire country is divided into nine Circuit Courts of Appeal, to which appeals from United States District Courts are taken. In case either party is dissatisfied with the decision in that court, he may, in certain cases, appeal to the court of last resort, the United States Supreme Court, presided over by a Chief Justice and eight Associate Justices at Washington. Each State has its own system of courts. Usually that system is more elaborate than that in the Federal Government. There is in each State a court of last resort, which we would expect to find designated the Supreme Court of New York, or whatever State it might be. Frequently there is a misuse of terms, as, for example, the court of last resort in New York is the Court of Appeals, and the Supreme Court is a lower court. This is true in a number of States. In addition to the court of last resort, there will be a court of general jurisdiction, frequently one of these courts for each county of the State, and then courts for the trial of smaller cases in the various cities and towns. The system of appeals is the same as in the Federal courts, either party who is dissatisfied having a right to appeal his case to the higher court. The question as to whether a particular case must be brought in a Federal court or a State court is too complicated to be taken up in detail. Sometimes the suit must be brought in the Federal court, as, for example, a bankruptcy matter, or a matter involving the United States Constitution, while in other cases, perhaps the majority, the suit must be brought in a State court. In other cases a person may have his option of either jurisdiction, as where a citizen of Texas wishes to sue a citizen of Rhode Island, and the amount involved is over $3000, then either the Federal or State courts of either State are open to the parties.

CHAPTER I

CONTRACTS—MUTUAL ASSENT

COMMERCIAL LAW is a general term used to cover the legal rules which relate most directly to everyday commercial transactions. It is a term of no exact boundary, but most commercial law is based in one way or another on the law of contracts, which is one of the largest subjects in the law. Bills and notes, for instance, are special forms of contracts. In order to understand business law at all, therefore, it is necessary at the outset to have some knowledge of the fundamental principles of the law of contracts.

DEFINITION OF CONTRACTS.—What is a contract? Simply a promise or set of promises which the law enforces as binding. Any promise, if it is binding, is a contract or part of a contract. So the law of contracts in their formation resolves itself into this: What promises are binding? A man may make all sorts of promises, but when has he a right legally to say "I have changed my mind, I am not going to do what I said I would," and when will he be liable in damages if he fails to do as he agreed?

CONTRACT TERMS EXPLAINED.—There are certain terms in contracts which the student will find repeatedly mentioned and with which he should be familiar at the outset. For example, contracts are spoken of as express contracts, and implied contracts. By an express contract we mean a contract the terms of which are fully set forth. Implied contracts are contracts the terms of which are not fully stated by the parties. There is a mutual agreement and promise, but the agreement and promise have not been expressly put in words. If I say to a man, "I will buy your horse, Dobbin, for $100" and he replies, "I will sell you the horse at that price," there is an express contract. I step into a taxi and simply say to the driver, "Take me to the Union Station." The driver says nothing, but takes me there. Here is an implied contract. By my conduct I impliedly agree to pay him the legal rate for the distance carried.

FORMAL AND INFORMAL CONTRACTS.—Contracts are sometimes also divided into formal contracts, and simple or parol contracts. There are three kinds of formal contracts recognized in our system of law: (1) Promises under seal. (2) Contracts of record, such as judgments and recognizances. (3) Negotiable instruments. Of the three, it may be most difficult to understand why a judgment is included as a form of contract, because a judgment is simply a judicial termination of a fact entered in the office of the county clerk, and generally a lien on the real property owned by the judgment debtor. The sole reason, apparently, for calling a judgment a contract, is that an action of debt may be brought in a court of law upon such a judgment. Sealed contracts and negotiable paper will be taken up in a later chapter. Simple, or parol contracts, are those not embraced in the three previous classifications which constitute the formal contracts. The term parol is a little ambiguous, as it is sometimes used as opposed to a written contract, meaning simply an oral one, and at other times it is used as opposed to the three previous formal contracts.

UNILATERAL AND BILATERAL CONTRACTS.—Contracts are also divided into unilateral and bilateral contracts. In a unilateral contract, the contract imposes obligations on one party only. A promissory note is an example of a unilateral contract. In a bilateral contract, obligation is imposed on both parties. John and Mary become engaged to each other. This is a bilateral contract, and either may sue the other for a breach. Most important results flow from the distinction between unilateral and bilateral contracts. This we shall consider later.

VOID, VOIDABLE AND UNENFORCEABLE CONTRACTS.—Contracts are also divided into void, voidable and unenforceable contracts. Strictly speaking, a void contract is no contract at all. Some statutes provide that no action shall be brought on certain contracts, and declare them absolutely void. A voidable contract is one which is good until the option of avoiding it is availed of by the party who has the option. For example, an infant with an income of $2000 a year contracts for the delivery of a Packard automobile on June 1. The car, being a luxury, makes the contract with the infant voidable on his part, and he may, before June 1, repudiate the contract and not be liable in a suit for breach of contract, or he may, if he choses, abide by the contract, take the car, and pay the purchase price when it is delivered. An unenforceable contract is one which in itself is perfectly good as a contract, but because of some rule of law cannot be enforced. For example, A agrees, orally, with the owner of 1 Broadway, to buy that property for $1,000,000. The terms of the contract are understood by both parties. This contract is not enforceable, because, as we shall see later, the Statute of Frauds requires every contract for the sale of real property to be in writing.

CONTRACTS UNDER SEAL.—There are two ways of making promises binding, and unless the promisor fulfils the requisites of one or the other of these two ways his promise will not be binding. The first of these ways relates to the form in which the promise is made; the second relates to the substance of the transaction, irrespective of the form. The way to make a promise binding by virtue of its form is to put it in writing and attach a seal to the writing. It is often thought that written promises are binding in any event, or that a promise that is not written is not binding in any event. Neither of these propositions, however, is true. A promise is not binding merely because it is in writing; it is necessary that something more shall be done. Not only must it be written, but a seal must be attached in order to make the promise binding by virtue of its form. Everyone is familiar with the common ending in written contracts—"witness my hand and seal," that is, my signature and seal.

WHAT IS A SEAL?—A seal may be—and was originally—made with sealing wax stamped with a crest, initial or what not. This is still a sufficient seal, but the common kind of seal is simply a wafer attached by mucilage to the writing. Another kind of seal, in use by corporations and notaries especially, consists simply of an impression made on paper without attaching any foreign substance whatever. Any of these methods of sealing a promise is good. In most States a written or printed scroll with the letters "L. S." written or printed within, or the word "Seal" written or printed may also be a seal if so intended. It may seem a ridiculous formality for the law to attach importance to this lapping a wafer and attaching it to the end of a writing. In a way it is ridiculous, but it is desirable to have some method by which a promise may be made binding. One method, as an original question, may be as good as another so long as it is an easy method, and attaching a seal is an easy method, and one which makes it possible to make a promise binding whenever you wish.

CHANGE BY STATUTE OF THE LAW AS TO SEALED CONTRACTS.— There has been in this country a certain hostility to the law of sealed instruments. It has been thought, with reason, that some of the rules governing contracts under seal have by their technicality promoted injustice. This has certainly been true of an old rule that contracts under seal could not be altered or discharged by any agreement not itself under seal. The rule, however, that a seal avoids the necessity of consideration is a desirable rule, since it is important to have some means by which those who so intend may make gratuitous promises binding. It would be better then to abolish undesirable incidents of sealed contracts by statute rather than to destroy totally the legal effect of a seal. However, in many States the distinction between sealed and unsealed contracts is totally abolished. In a number of other States the common-law rule has been changed by the enactment of statutory provisions to the effect that sealed contracts shall be presumed to have been made for a sufficient consideration, but this presumption is only prima facie, and lack of consideration may be affirmatively proved, even in the case of a sealed instrument. And under such statutes unsealed contracts remain as at common law, i. e., the burden of proving consideration rests upon the plaintiff who seeks to enforce such a contract.

REQUISITES OF SIMPLE CONTRACTS.—Sealed contracts are comparatively easy to understand. Simple contracts, which are promises made binding by virtue of their substance rather than their form, though called simple, are more difficult to understand, and more complex. They are also much more common than sealed contracts. A simple contract is a promise, or promises, to which the parties have assented, and for which a price called consideration has been paid. One may promise as much as he wishes, orally or in writing so long as he does not attach a seal to his signature, and then say he does not care to keep his promise, unless he has both been paid for the promise and there has been an assent by the promisor and promisee to the terms of the transaction. Mutual assent and consideration are, then, the requisites of simple contracts.

INTENT TO CONTRACT.—In the law of contracts, intention, as we ordinarily understand that term, plays little part. In fact, the Supreme Court of Connecticut, in the case of Davidson vs. Holden, 55 Conn. 103, said: "It is of no legal significance that the defendants did not intend to be individually liable, or that they did not know or believe that as a matter of law they would be."

It is our overt acts that count in contracts. Or shall we put it this way: In the eyes of the law overt acts manifest legal intention. A says to B: "I will sell you my watch for $25, and you may have until 9 o'clock tomorrow morning to decide." A meets B the next noon and says to him: "I am sorry you did not take the watch. It was a bargain." B replies: "Here is the price, I will take it. I intended to call you this morning but have been so busy I did not have an opportunity to do so. I told my wife last night I was going to accept your offer and I can produce five witnesses who were in the room and heard me say so." It is, nevertheless, no contract, for, as has been said, quoting from an old English case, "It is trite learning, that the thought of man is not tryable, for the devil himself knows not the thought of man." Occasionally there may be the overt act and still no contract, although the mere formalities of contract may have taken place. The facts in the case of McClurg v. Terry, 21 New Jersey Equity 225, were as follows: The plaintiff was an infant nineteen years of age, and had returned late in the evening to Jersey City, from an excursion, with the defendant and a number of young friends, among whom was a justice of the peace, and all being in good spirits, excited by the excursion, the plaintiff in jest challenged the defendant to be married to her on the spot; he in the same spirit accepted the challenge, and the justice, at their request, performed the ceremony, they making the proper responses. The ceremony was in the usual and proper form, the justice doubting whether it was in earnest or not. The defendant escorted the plaintiff to her home, and left her there as usual on occasions of such excursions; both acted and treated the matter as if no ceremony had taken place. In deciding the case, the court said: "In this case the evidence is clear that no marriage was intended by either party; that it was a mere jest got up in the exuberance of spirits to amuse the company and themselves. If this is so, there was no marriage." The overt act of the parties manifested no legal intention to be married. Should we change the facts in the following way, the court undoubtedly would have held a valid marriage: If, after the parties had gone through the marriage ceremony, as recited, they went on a two weeks' honeymoon, and on their return lived together as man and wife for a month and then suddenly decided to call the marriage off, on the ground that it was a joke and they did not intend the ceremony to be binding, regardless of what they said as to the transaction, their overt acts would be taken by the court as showing their real legal intention at the time the ceremony was entered into. One more illustration: When leaving the class tonight, there is a sudden downpour of rain, and the instructor remarks: "I will give ten dollars for an umbrella." A student offers an umbrella and claims the money. Here is an overt act, but a reasonable person would not take the words used literally. Generally speaking, agreements made jokingly and social agreements confer no contractual rights.

OFFER AND ACCEPTANCE.—The usual way that mutual assent is manifested is by an offer and an acceptance of the offer. Two persons are not likely to express at the identical minute the same proposition. It is as a practical matter, then, essential that one should make a proposition, and if a contract is to be made, that the other should assent to it. An offer may be made to one or more specified persons, or to anyone whomsoever who will do what the offer requests, as in case of an offer of a reward. An offer is itself a promise, but is a promise conditional on the payment of a consideration or return for it either by some act or some promise from the other party. According as the offer asks for an act or a promise it will fall into one or the other of the two great divisions of simple contracts; one kind is called unilateral (meaning one-sided), that is, a promise only on one side; the other is bilateral, a promise on each side.

ILLUSTRATIONS.—Let us give illustrations of these contracts. We say to John: "We will promise to give you, John, $100 if you will do a specified piece of work." That is a proposal to make an exchange of the work for the money in a sense, but more exactly it is an offer to exchange an agreement to give the money in return for the work. We are not saying to John: "If you will agree or promise to do that work we will promise to give you the money." We are saying that we will give him the money if he actually does the work. That offer requires the actual doing of the work before it is binding. Until then the price requested for the promise has not been paid. It is an offer of a unilateral contract. Again, when we say to a man: "If you will spade up our garden we will pay you $2 a day," we are making an offer for a unilateral contract. We are asking him to spade up the garden; not to promise to spade it up, but to do it, and when he does it he can hold us liable on our promise to pay him $2 a day. The promise will have become binding because we have been given the payment that we asked for in our promise. But if we say to a man: "If you will agree to work for us the next month we will pay you $100," and the man says, "All right," then we have a bilateral contract. We are asking him, as the price of our promise, not to work but to agree to work, and he has promised to do so. To say "I accept" is always sufficient acceptance in the case of a bilateral contract where a promise is requested, but if I said to you, "I will give you $5 if you will bring me a book here," it would not make a contract to say "I accept." I said I would give you $5 if you brought the book here, and nothing but bringing it here will form a contract. The offeree must always do what the offerer asks him. If an of-ferer asks for a promise, any form of words indicating assent would be sufficient, because they would mean, in effect: "I consent to make the promise you specify in your offer." The form of wording in simple contracts is immaterial. Any plain language is sufficient for an offer, and as for acceptance, it does not matter whether the acceptor says "all right," or "I accept your offer," or in what form he expresses his assent. The question is, does he express assent? Now, the offerer is at liberty to name any consideration in his offer that he sees fit. He can name, in other words, whatever price for his promise he chooses to ask. If the person addressed does not choose to pay that price, all he has to do is to reject the offer, but he can bind the of-ferer only on the terms proposed. Therefore, if the offerer asks for an act in return for his promise, that is, asks for an immediate payment, or work, or the giving of property for his promise, no contract can be made by the person addressed saying, "All right, I will do it;" that is not giving the price the offerer asked. On the other hand, should the offerer ask for a promise and not for an act, the acceptor must give the promise asked for.

OPTION WITHOUT CONSIDERATION.—A common business transaction

that presents very well the principles governing the formation of simple contracts is what is called an option. Suppose the owner of a mine says: "I will sell you this mine for $50,000, and you may have thirty days to decide whether you choose to accept the offer or not." Now, it does not matter whether that statement is oral or in writing; it is merely an offer, and not binding as the matter stands as far as we have stated. However, if it were in writing and a seal attached (in a State where seals still have the force which the common law gave them) it would be a binding promise to sell the mine at that price at any time within thirty days. If there is no seal attached, as long as the offer is unaccepted and unpaid for, it is not binding. The man who makes it may say: "I withdraw my offer. It is true that I promised to keep the offer open thirty days, but you did not pay me for that promise and I am going to break the promise. I withdraw my offer." Any offer for the formation of a simple contract, while unaccepted, may be withdrawn. But, if before it was withdrawn and within the thirty days' limit, the person to whom the option was given says, "Here is the $50,000 which you said you would take for your mine," the offerer would then be bound, and would have to perform his part of the contract.

OPTION WITH CONSIDERATION.—Let us change the character of the option a little. Suppose in consideration of $1000 paid down the owner of a mine promises to sell the mine for $50,000 at any time within thirty days. Here the offer, or the contract—for it is now more than an offer—has been paid for, and it is therefore binding. The person to whom the offer was made paid $1000 for the promise, therefore the promisor is bound to keep it. It was not an absolute promise to give the mine to the buyer, but it was a promise to sell it to him for $50,000 if he chose to take it within thirty days; that is a conditional promise. A conditional promise may be binding and paid for just as well as an absolute promise.

INSURANCE POLICY.—Take the case of a fire insurance policy. That is a conditional promise, a promise to pay indemnity for the destruction of a house by fire. Therefore, the performance of the insurance company's promise is conditional on the suffering by the insured of loss by fire. An insurance policy is ordinarily a unilateral contract; the premium is the consideration or price paid for the promise, and the promise is binding on the insurance company from the time when the premium is thus paid. Of course, the promise is only binding according to its terms. The insured has bought a conditional promise, a promise to pay if the house burns down. He gets that promise, but he will not become entitled to any money or any damages unless the house burns down nor unless he complies with the other conditions of his policy.

GUARANTEE.—Another kind of a promise worth referring to is a guarantee. A question arises whether a business house will sell something to a buyer on credit, and it decides it will not without a guarantee. Accordingly, John agrees, in writing, that if the business house in question will sell James a bill of goods, John will guarantee the payment of the price. That means, if James does not pay for the goods, John will. That is a unilateral contract in which the promise is conditional, and the consideration for that promise is the selling of goods to James.

PRELIMINARY NEGOTIATIONS—ADVERTISEMENTS.—An offer is sometimes difficult to distinguish from other things. Suppose the case of an advertisement. A business house advertises that it will sell goods for a certain price. Take the case of a bond list issued by a banking house. The list states that the banking house will sell specified kinds of bonds at quoted prices. John receives one of those lists, looks it over, sees something that looks good to him, and goes into the banking house and says: "I will take five of those bonds at the price named here." The banking house says: "We have sold all the bonds of that kind that we had;" or it says, "The market has changed on those bonds and there has been some advance in the price." Has John a cause of action against the banking house? He has if that bond list amounts to an offer—that is, if the list means that the banking house offers to enter into a contract with anyone receiving the list. But it has been held that that sort of advertisement does not prima facie amount to an offer, although it might be put in such clear words of agreement to sell on the part of the banking house that it would amount to an offer. Generally an advertisement of this sort, or anything that can fairly be called an advertisement of goods for sale, is held to mean simply that the advertiser has these goods for sale and names a price he is putting upon them; he invites customers to come in and deal with him in regard to them. It is an invitation to come and make a trade rather than a direct offer of a trade.

ILLUSTRATION.—Again to illustrate: You are looking at a new model of an automobile in a show-room window. You like it, enter the salesroom, and say you will take the car, tendering the price. The manager tells you that it is simply their demonstration car, that he will be glad to book your order for a car of the same model, and can make delivery in a month. You are not satisfied, and wish to sue, claiming that your tender of the price constituted an acceptance of the dealer's offer. Your position would be unsound and there would be no recovery in such a case. The placing of the demonstration car in the window is simply an invitation to the public to come in and deal with the seller. On the other hand, suppose you go into a second-hand automobile salesroom. There are fifty cars of various makes and models on the floor and each one is labeled with a different price. You pick out a 1918 Packard which is marked $1500. You tender the price to the salesman and say you will take the car. He refuses to sell. In this case your tender is an acceptance of his offer to sell. In the former instance, placing a price on the demonstration car was not a statement to the public generally that that particular car was for sale at that price, but in this case, where the cars are all second-hand cars, the reasonable interpretation of placing the price on the 1918 Packard is that that particular car is for sale. Quite likely, the dealer did not have any other Packard car in stock and would have no way of securing any of that model at that price.

ORAL AGREEMENT PRELIMINARY TO WRITTEN CONTRACT.—Another case of the same nature that comes up not infrequently is this: Parties talk over a business arrangement and then they say, "As this is an important matter let us put it down in writing; let us have a written contract containing what has been agreed upon." When it comes to drawing up the contract, however, they cannot agree. One party then says, "Well, we made a definite oral agreement any way; let us carry that out." The other replies, "Why, no, all that was dependent on our making a written agreement." The settlement of their dispute depends on how definite and absolute the oral agreement was. It is possible to make an oral agreement binding, although the parties do agree and do contemplate that it shall subsequently be reduced to writing, but generally the inference is that the oral agreement was merely a preliminary chaffering to fix the terms of the writing, and that everything is tentative until the writing is made and signed.

AUCTION SALES.—Another state of affairs involving preliminary invitations is presented by auction sales. The auctioneer puts goods up for sale, a bid is made, the auctioneer gets no other bid, and then says, "I will withdraw this from sale." Is the auctioneer liable? Has he made a contract to sell that article to the highest bidder? When the transaction is analyzed, is this what the auctioneer says in effect: "I offer to sell these goods to the highest bidder?" If this is the correct interpretation, then when the highest bidder says, in effect, "I agree to buy them," there would be a contract. On the other hand, if what the auctioneer says is in effect like what the advertiser says: "Here are some goods for sale, what do you bid, gentlemen," then the auctioneer is not making an offer himself. He is inviting offers from the people before him, and until he accepts one of those offers from the bidders before him there would be no contract; and until then the auctioneer could withdraw the goods. And that is the construction put upon the auction sale—that the auctioneer is not making an offer, but is simply inviting offers. Even if the auctioneer promises that he will accept the highest offer, that is, that he will sell to the highest bidder, his promise to accept the highest bid, not being paid for, would not be binding upon him were it not for a statute in some States which, in the sale of goods, would make an auctioneer bound to keep a promise to sell without reserve, that is, to the highest bidder, if he made such a promise.

BIDS OR TENDERS.—Somewhat similar to the case of the auctioneer is the case of tenders or bids for the construction of buildings, or for the sale of goods to a city or to a corporation. There, too, the corporation or the city is simply inviting offers. They do not say, "We offer to enter into a contract with anyone who makes the lowest bid," but rather, "We are thinking of entering into a contract, and we want to receive offers in regard to it." When the offers are made by the bids or tenders, any or none of them may be accepted, according as the receiver thinks best. It is sometimes required by law that public corporations, like cities or counties, shall accept the bid of the lowest responsible bidder, but, aside from such statutes, any or none of the bids may be accepted.

IMPLIED CONTRACTS.—An offer and acceptance are ordinarily made by words either spoken or written; but any method of communication which would convey to a reasonable man a clear meaning will serve as well as words. If A goes to his grocer and says "Send me a barrel of flour," he has in terms made no promise to pay for the flour, but the natural meaning of his words is that he agrees to pay. In this case A used words, though not words of promise; but the same result might follow where no words at all were used. Suppose A went into a shop where he was known, picked up an article from the counter, held it up so the proprietor could see what he was taking, and went out; this would be in legal effect a promise by A to pay for the article. A contract, where the promises of the parties are to be inferred not from express words of promise but from conduct or from language not in terms promissory, is called an implied promise or contract, as distinct from an express promise or contract, which is one where the undertaking is in express language. This difference between express and implied contracts relates merely to the mode of proving them. There is the same element of mutual assent in both cases, and the legal effect of the two kinds of obligations is identical. There is, however, another kind of obligation which is frequently called an implied contract, but sometimes called a quasi-contract, because it is not really a contract at all, though the obligation imposed is similar. If a husband fails to support his wife, for instance, she may bind him by purchases of goods necessary for her support. She may do this even though he directly forbids the sales to her. There is obviously no mutual assent in this case; the husband emphatically dissents and expresses his dissent, but he is bound just as if he had contracted.

TERMINATION OF OFFER BY REVOCATION OR REJECTION.—Since offers do not become binding until accepted according to their terms, up to that time they may be terminated without liability. This may happen in several ways. In the first place an offer may be revoked by the offerer. To effect a revocation he must actually notify the other party of his change of mind, before the latter has accepted. We have already stated that offers may be rejected by the person to whom they are made. For instance, we say, "We offer you one hundred shares of stock at a certain price, and you may have a week to think it over." You say, "I do not care for that offer, I reject it." You come around the next day and say, "On reflection I have concluded to accept that offer." The acceptance is within the seven days which we originally said might be used for reflection, but the offer has been terminated by the rejection. There is no longer any offer open, and consequently the acceptance amounts to nothing. A troublesome question in regard to the revocation of an offer for a unilateral contract is this: Suppose A offers B $5 for a book and B starts to get it but when he reaches the door, then A refuses to take the book. The general disposition is to try to hold that promise binding, and yet the difficulty is that the offeree has not fully done what he was asked to do, and if he chose to turn back and take the book away he could do so without liability. He could say, "I did not promise to bring the book. I brought it part way, the walk was long and I am going to take it back." If he is thus free to withdraw it seems impossible to deny that the other party is equally free. Bilateral contracts are more desirable than unilateral because in bilateral contracts the mutual promises bind the parties before they begin to perform and both parties are therefore protected while they are performing. In unilateral contracts, the contract is not completed until the act requested is fully done. Until then, therefore, either party may withdraw.

A COUNTER OFFER IS A REJECTION.—Another way in which offers may be terminated is by a counter offer on the part of the person to whom the offer was made. We say, "We will sell you stock for $100 a share, and you may have a week to think it over." You say, "I will give you $99 a share." We say, "No, we will not take it." You say, "Well, I will give you $100." You are too late; you rejected our offer of sale at $100 by saying you would give us $99. The minute you say you will give us $99, our offer is rejected. Of course, when you make the counter offer of $99, if we say we will accept your offer to buy, that would make a contract. Offers are constantly rejected by counter offers by people who really intend to enter into a contract. Suppose A says, "I will lease you my house a year for $800." You say, "All right, I will take it if you paper the dining-room." That rejects the offer. A new offer has been made by the person addressed, who offers, if the dining-room is papered, to take the house at $800.

TERMINATION OF OFFER BY DEATH OR INSANITY.—An offer is also terminated by the death or insanity of either party before acceptance. After a contract has once been formed neither subsequent death nor insanity terminates liability upon it unless the contract is of such a personal character that only performance by the contractor in person will fulfil it.

ILLUSTRATION.—In Beach v. First Methodist Episcopal Church, 96 Ill. 177, a fund was being raised to build a new church, and a subscription paper, as follows, was signed by Lorenzo Beach:

> "Fairbury, Feb. 14, 1874.
>
> "We, the undersigned, agree to pay the sum set opposite our respective names, for the purpose of erecting a new M. E. church in this place, said sums to be paid as follows: One-third to be paid when contract is let, one-third when building is enclosed, one-third when building is completed. Probable cost of said church from ten thousand dollars ($10,000) to twelve thousand dollars ($12,000)."

Mr. Beach attached and subscribed to that paper the following:

> "Fairbury, 1874.
>
> "Dr. Beach gives this subscription on the condition that the remainder of eight thousand dollars is subscribed.
>
> "Lorenzo Beach, $2000."

In April, 1875, Dr. Beach was adjudged insane by the county court. The court held that the "subscription made by Dr. Beach was, in its nature, a mere offer to pay that amount of money to the church upon the condition therein expressed. There is nothing in the record tending to show that the church, in this case, took any action upon the faith of this subscription, until after Dr. Beach was adjudged insane, or that the church paid money or incurred any liability. His insanity, by operation of law, was a revocation of the offer." Suppose a letter for a winter's supply of coal is sent to your coal dealer and is acknowledged by him, delivery to be made before October 1. On September 15, the coal dealer dies, and his estate refuses to fulfill the contract. In such a case, if you were compelled to buy coal at a higher price from another dealer, you would have a cause of action against the estate for the damage you suffer. The coal dealer's executor or administrator could very easily carry out a contract of this character. On the other hand, suppose you are running a series of lectures during the winter, and you have engaged a noted lecturer to deliver six lectures. After he has delivered three, he dies. In this case, death would terminate the contract, as this is clearly a contract for personal services and the executor or administrator of the deceased lecturer could not perform the contract for him, as could be done in the case of the coal dealer.

TERMINATION OF OFFER BY LAPSE OF TIME.—An offer may be terminated by delay on the part of the person addressed. An answer to an offer must be sent in time, whether mail or telegraph is used, or whether the parties are dealing face to face. An offer lapses if it is not accepted within the time the offer specifies if any time is specified. If no time is specified, then within a reasonable time. One may specify any length of time in his offer, and it will remain open for that time provided it is not rejected or revoked, and neither party dies or becomes insane, in the meantime. But frequently offers contain no express limit of time; then it is a question of what is a reasonable time, and reasonableness depends upon business customs, the character of the transaction, the way the offer is communicated, and similar circumstances. An offer on the floor of a stock exchange will not last very long. A reasonable time for acceptance of such an offer is immediately, and an offer sent by telegraph will not remain in force long. The use of the telegraph indicates that the offerer deems haste of importance. An offer sent by mail will last longer. An offer relating to things which change in value rapidly will not remain open for so long a time as an offer which relates to land, or something that does not change in value rapidly.

ILLUSTRATION.—In the case of Loring v. the City of Boston, 7 Met. (Mass.) 409, the facts were that on May 26, 1837, this advertisement was published in the daily papers of Boston: "$500 reward. The above reward is offered for the apprehension and conviction of any person who shall set fire to any building within the limits of the city. May 26th, 1837. Samuel A. Eliot, Mayor." In January, 1841, there was an extensive fire on Washington Street, and Loring, after considerable effort, was able to secure the apprehension and conviction of the criminal. He then sued to recover the reward, which the city of Boston refused to pay. The ground of defense was that the advertisement "offering the reward of $500 for the apprehension and conviction of persons setting fire to buildings in the city, was issued almost four years before the time at which the plaintiff arrested Marriott and prosecuted him to conviction." The opinion of the court reads: "three years and eight months is not a reasonable time within which, or rather to the extent of which, the offer in question can be considered as a continuing offer on the part of the city. In that length of time, the exigency under which it was made having passed, it must be presumed to have been forgotten by most of the officers and citizens of the community, and cannot be presumed to have been before the public as an actuating motive to vigilance and exertion on this subject; nor could it justly and reasonably have been so understood by the plaintiff. We are, therefore, of the opinion that the offer of the city had ceased before the plaintiff accepted and acted upon it as such, and that consequently no contract existed upon which this action, founded on an alleged express promise, can be maintained."

BOTH PARTIES MUST BE BOUND OR NEITHER.—Both parties to a simple contract must in effect be bound, and until they are, there is no contract. In a unilateral contract, before the promise becomes binding, the promisee must have actually performed what he was requested to do, that is, he must bind himself by actual performance before the offerer's promise is binding on him. In a bilateral contract, where each party makes a promise, neither promise can be binding unless and until the other one is. So that in the case of the proposed agreement to lease, as the proposed tenant might refuse to take the house if the dining-room was not papered, the proposed landlord has a similar right; that is, since one is not bound, the other is not.

CONTRACTS BY CORRESPONDENCE.—Contracts are often made by correspondence, simple contracts especially. That raises rather an important question as to how and when the contract is formed. Suppose a letter containing an offer is addressed from Boston to a man in New York. A reply is sent by him from New York accepting the offer. That reply goes astray. Is there a contract? Yes. It creates a contract by correspondence for a letter to be mailed by the acceptor provided the offerer imposes no conditions to the contrary, and impliedly authorizes the use of the mails, as he does by himself making an offer by mail. But suppose the offerer in his letter says, "If I hear from you by next Wednesday I shall consider this a contract." Then, unless the offerer receives an answer by the next Wednesday, there will be no contract. It will make no difference that an answer has been mailed, it must have been received; that is a condition of the offer. Suppose an offer is made by word of mouth, and it is accepted by sending a letter. Does the contract then become binding, irrespective of receipt of the letter? No, unless in some way the offerer has authorized the use of the mails in sending such an answer, and if the circumstances were such that the use of the mails would be customary, that would amount to an implied authorization. The use of the telegraph depends upon similar principles. If an offer is sent by telegraph, an answer may be sent by telegraph, and an acceptance started on its way will become binding although it is never received. Similarly, one may authorize a telegraphic answer to a letter containing an offer sent by mail, and if the use of the telegraph is authorized, a contract will arise at the moment that the telegram is sent.

ILLUSTRATIONS.—In the case of an option, if the acceptance was made by mail and lost in the mails, a binding contract would be formed if the use of the mail was expressly or impliedly authorized, and similarly if the option called for payment and a letter was mailed containing a draft or cash. There is a right to send a check or draft by mail if the parties had been dealing by mail. That authority would be implied. When parties are dealing by mail and there is a bargain that a check shall be sent, the check becomes the property of the person to whom it is sent as soon as it is mailed, and, therefore, when the letter with the check is put in the mail it operates as a payment on the option, and the loss of the draft is not the sender's loss, but the other man's. A lost draft, however, can be replaced and must be replaced. Authority to send actual cash by mail would not be so easily implied, especially if the amount were large, because it is contrary to good business custom; but if authority were given, the result would be the same as in the case of a check. It would, however, be a proper business precaution to register the letter if it contained cash. If the offerer, not having received the letter of acceptance and thinking none had been sent, sells the property to another person, though not morally blamable, he would get into trouble. The second purchaser would get title to the property, supposing that the property was actually transferred to him.

The lost letter created a contract, but it did not actually transfer title to the property, and, therefore, when the purchaser actually got possession of the property he would become the owner of it and could not be deprived of his title if he took it innocently. If, however, the person to whom the property was transferred had notice of the prior completion of a contract, he could not keep the property. In any event the seller would be liable in damages for breach of the contract completed by mailing the lost letter. Suppose an option is given by telephone to one who, just before the option expires, tries to get a connection by phone to accept and is unable to do so, and ten minutes after the time has expired a connection is secured? There is no contract and he has no action. It is no fault of the offerer that the acceptor was unable to accept in time, and, generally speaking, one who wishes to accept an offer must at his peril keep the means of acceptance open. It may be asked why does not the same principle apply in regard to mail as to the telephone; that is, why does not starting the acceptance by telephone complete the contract? Because there is no authority to send communication by telephone to the offerer when the acceptor has no telephone connection. When one sends an offer by mail the reason that he is bound by an acceptance sent by mail is because he, in effect, asks that an acceptance properly addressed to him be started on its course. He takes his chance as to the rest, but an offerer by telephone does not authorize a reply by talking into the telephone when there is no connection.

MISTAKES IN THE USE OF LANGUAGE IN OFFER AND ACCEPTANCE.— Another question which has to do with the express mutual assent of parties relates to the meaning of language used. Suppose an offerer says, "I will sell you a cargo of goods from the ship 'Peerless,' due to arrive from India, at a certain price." The buyer assents. There are two ships named "Peerless," and the buyer thinks one is meant, but the seller thinks the other is meant. Is there a contract for the sale of the cargo of "Peerless" No. 1, or a contract for the sale of the cargo of No. 2, or no contract at all? The answer is, that language bears the meaning which a reasonable person in the position of the person to whom the offer is made is justified in attaching to it. If a reasonable person in his position would think "Peerless" No. 1 was meant, then there is a contract for the cargo of No. 1. If he was not justified in thinking that, and ought to have thought No. 2 was meant, although in fact he did not think so, there was a contract for the cargo of "Peerless" No. 2. If either meaning were as reasonable as the other, then each party has a right to insist on his own meaning, and there would be no contract. This principle often comes up in contracts made by telegraph, where the words of the telegram are, by the mistake of the telegraph company, changed. For instance, a telegram purports to be an offer to sell a large quantity of laths at $1 a bundle. The terms as actually despatched by the seller in making his offer fixed the price at $1.20. The telegraph company dropped off the words "and twenty cents." A telegram is sent back by the buyer, "I accept your telegraphic offer." Then trouble arises when buyer and seller compare notes. Well, the offerer is bound. He selected the telegraph as the means of communication, and he must take the consequences of a misunderstanding, which arose from a mistake of the agency which the offerer himself selected. The question may be asked: Would there be any right of action against the telegraph company by the offerer, the sender of the telegram? The answer is yes. The company has broken the contract it impliedly made with the sender to use reasonable diligence in despatching and delivering the message. But the trouble with that action is that on telegraph blanks there is always this in substance: that on unrepeated telegrams this company is liable for mistakes only to an amount not exceeding twice the cost of the telegram; and it has been held in many States that that limit on unrepeated telegrams is not unreasonable. The sender of the telegram has agreed to the contract on the reverse side of the telegraph blank, and he ought to have his message repeated if he desires to hold the company liable in full damages if his message does not reach the party addressed in absolutely correct form. In other States, however, this limitation of liability is held to be against public policy and the company is liable for the full damage suffered.

CONDITION IN OFFER REQUIRING RECEIPT OF ACCEPTANCE.—An offerer, as has been said, may insert in his offer any condition he sees fit. He may therefore insert a condition that an acceptance shall reach him, not merely be despatched. The condition may specify the time within which the acceptance must arrive in order to be effectual. It is a wise precaution in all business offers of importance to insert such a condition in the offer. It will not be sufficient to add to the offer such words as "subject to prompt acceptance," for prompt acceptance would be given, within the meaning of the law, by despatching the acceptance, not by the receipt of it. The condition should be in such words as "subject to prompt receipt of your acceptance," or "subject to receipt of your acceptance," by a stated day or hour.

WHEN SILENCE GIVES CONSENT.—There is one way of manifesting mutual assent, namely, by silence, of which a word should be said. There is a proverb that "Silence gives consent." Is it so in law? Suppose a man goes into an insurance broker's and tosses some policies down and says, "Renew those policies, please." Nobody says anything and he leaves the policies there and goes out. The next night his buildings burn down. Are they insured? They are, in effect, if the insurance broker has contracted to renew the policies; otherwise the buildings are not insured. Now on the bare facts, as we have stated them, they are not insured; some other facts must always exist to make silence amount to assent. If, for instance, on previous occasions, the broker kept silence when such statements were made to him, and nevertheless carried out the proposal, it is a fair inference that he means by his silence this time what he meant the preceding time. Furthermore, silence, when the offer is unknown, can never amount to assent. In the case as we have put it, we did not say that the insurance broker even heard the offer; if he did, then the question would depend on whether he had ever done anything to justify the other person in believing that silence would mean assent in such a dealing, or whether business customs justified the assumption. The offerer cannot by his own act make the silence of the other person amount to an acceptance. Suppose an offer of this sort: "We offer to sell you 100 shares of stock at $50 a share, and unless we hear from you to the contrary by next Wednesday we shall conclude that you have accepted our offer." The offerer does not get any word before next Wednesday. Nevertheless, there is no contract. The person addressed has a right to say, "Confound his impudence, I am not going to waste a postage stamp on him, but I don't accept his offer. He has no business to suppose that if he doesn't hear from me to the contrary I assent." This sort of case is not infrequently referred to: A magazine is sent through the mails on a subscription for a year, the subscription runs out, the magazine is, nevertheless, still sent. Is the person who receives it bound to pay another year's subscription? Here you have a little more than silence; you have the receiver of the magazine continuing to receive it. If he refused to receive it, undoubtedly there would be no contract, but where a man takes property which is offered to him, he is bound by the proposal which was made to him in regard to the property. He ought to let the magazine alone if he doesn't want to pay for it. You may say that the receiver does not know that the subscription has run out, and if he did he would not take the magazine. But then he ought to know. He made the subscription originally. The difficulty is merely in his own forgetfulness, and he cannot rely on that.

ILLUSTRATION.—The leading case of Hobbs v. Massasoit Whip Co., 158 Mass. 194, is a good illustration. The plaintiff in this case had been in the habit of sending eel skins to the defendant and had received pay from him in due course. The skins in the shipment for payment of which suit was brought, were alleged by the defendant to be short of the required length, and in a condition unfit for use. They were kept by the defendant some months, and were then destroyed, without notification to the plaintiff. The latter sued for the price of the skins and the court held that the silence of the defendant and failure to notify the plaintiff that it did not wish to have this particular lot of skins, amounted to an acceptance. The court said: "In such a condition of things, the plaintiff was warranted in sending the defendant skins conforming to the requirements, and even if the offer was not such that the contract was made as soon as the skins corresponding to its terms were sent, sending them would impose on the defendant a duty to act at that time; and silence on its part, coupled with a retention of the skins for an unreasonable time, might be found by the jury to warrant the plaintiff in assuming that they were accepted, and thus to amount to an acceptance."

CHAPTER II
CONTRACTS—CONSIDERATION AND ENFORCEABILITY

CONSIDERATION MAY BE ANOTHER PROMISE OR AN ACT.—The second great requisite in the formation of simple contracts is consideration. A price must be paid for a promise in order to make it binding. The price paid may be another promise, in which case the contract is bilateral, or the price paid may be some act actually done or performed, in which case the contract is unilateral.

ADEQUACY OF CONSIDERATION IMMATERIAL.—Not any act, or the promise of any act, is sufficient consideration, as will be seen. Nevertheless, in general the law does not attempt to gauge the adequacy of the consideration; that is, parties may make such bargains as they wish as far as the price is concerned. A may say that he will sell his horse, which is worth $300, for $100, or for a promise to pay $100. That will be a perfectly good contract, if accepted, in spite of the fact that the promised horse is worth more than the promised price. Such difference in the value of the promise and the value of the price may go to a great extreme. The horse may be a thousand-dollar animal, and the price promised only $100, but when you wish to push the case to an extreme you are likely to get into this difficulty: Did the parties really mean to make a bargain? If what they were doing was arranging for a gift of the horse and putting up some little alleged consideration as a blind, that will not do; but any exchange the parties really in good faith bargain for, with certain exceptions hereafter stated, is sufficient.

A SMALLER SUM OF MONEY IS NOT SUFFICIENT CONSIDERATION FOR THE PROMISE SIMULTANEOUSLY TO PAY OR DISCHARGE A LARGER LIQUIDATED SUM.—This is the principal exception, that in contracts or promises relating to a fixed sum of money, the consideration cannot be the simultaneous payment or discharge of a smaller sum of money on the other side. If A promises B $100, it will not be good consideration for B to promise in exchange $50, or even $99.99, payable at the same time and place. In other words, the law does require adequacy in exchanges or agreements to exchange money. A owes B $100 and says to him, "I can't pay it all," or "I don't want to pay it all. Will you let me off for $50?" B replies, "Yes, I will take $50." That agreement is not binding, and even if the $50 is actually paid, B may afterwards come and say, "You paid me only part of the debt you owed me. It is true I said I would call the whole thing square, but there was no consideration sufficient in law for my promise, since you paid me only part of what you were bound to." This rule of common law, though generally well established, does not exist or is much qualified in a few States, such as: Georgia, Maine, Mississippi, New Hampshire, North Carolina, Virginia.

UNLIQUIDATED CLAIMS MAY BE DISCHARGED BY ANY AGREED SUM.—The case cited in the preceding paragraph must be distinguished from another. Suppose A owes B some money for services, the price of which was never exactly fixed, but which B says are of the value of $100. Then if B agrees to take $50 in satisfaction of his claim against A, B is bound; the transaction is effectual. The difference is between what is called a liquidated and an unliquidated claim.

DEFINITION OF LIQUIDATED CLAIM.—A liquidated claim is one of an exact amount definitely fixed. Such a claim, as has been said, cannot be satisfied by partial payment or promise of partial payment. But an unliquidated or a disputed claim—a claim subject to a real bona fide dispute, not merely a dispute trumped up for the purpose of disputing a good claim—may be discharged by any payment on which the parties agree. The law does not know how much the unliquidated claim is worth, and will allow parties to bargain for the sale of the unliquidated claim, just as it will let them bargain for the sale of a horse for which they may fix such a price as they choose, and that price will not be revised.

EFFECT OF RELEASES AND RECEIPTS.—If, however, the original claim were liquidated and undisputed, is there any sort of paper the debtor could get from the creditor that would release him absolutely? A receipt in full would not do it; a receipt in full is something to which business men attach more virtue than it possesses. It is merely evidence of an agreement to accept what has been received in full payment and proof may be given as to just what consideration passed for the receipt in full. As we have seen, such an agreement is not valid without consideration, and payment of part of a debt admittedly due is not sufficient consideration. The really effective instrument at common law is the release under seal. That will do the work whether the debtor paid part of the debt or not, since a sealed instrument needs no consideration. In jurisdictions where seals have been deprived of their efficacy at common law an insuperable difficulty, however, exists. In a few States—Alabama, Arkansas, Connecticut, Michigan, Mississippi, New Hampshire, New York, North Dakota, South Dakota, Tennessee—a receipt in full has been given the effect which the common law gave to a sealed instrument.

OTHER ILLUSTRATIONS.—Suppose the agreement to settle a liquidated claim were oral and suppose a witness heard the words. Such circumstances would not make any difference. It is assumed in all that has been said that the facts are proved. Suppose that neither party denied the facts. Let the creditor admit that he did receive this $50 as a full payment and did give the debtor a receipt in full. Still, he can say, "I propose to break my agreement since it was not supported by sufficient consideration, and I shall collect the balance." Another question is this: Suppose a man had a $100 bill and he wanted some change very badly, and another man had $99. Could the former take that for the $100 bill? He could. If a man wants a particular kind of money, as gold, or silver, or quarters, the principles stated do not apply; they apply only to dollars and cents as such.

PAST CONSIDERATION.—Strictly speaking, the term past consideration is a misnomer; something which is given before a promise is made cannot constitute a legal consideration. The courts have held that a warranty made after a sale has been completed is invalid. It has also been held that a guaranty after the obligation guaranteed has been entered into also is invalid unless there be new consideration. Although this is the general rule, there are several exceptions where a past consideration is recognized. Williston gives these exceptions as follows, although the boundaries between the groups are sometimes indefinite: "(1) Promises to pay a precedent debt; (2) Promises in consideration of some act previously done by the promisee at the request of the promisor; (3) Promises where past circumstances create a moral obligation on the part of the promisor to perform his promise. Under this head may be included cases of ratification and adoption of promises previously made for sufficient consideration but invalid when made for lack of authority or capacity."

PAYMENT OF PART OF A DEBT BY ONE WHO IS NOT THE DEBTOR.—Suppose a little different case: A owes B $100 for a liquidated claim. A's father says to B, "If you will let my son off, discharge him from this claim, I will pay $60, not a cent more." B agrees, and the $60 is paid. Now B never can get any more; the bargain is binding, and the reason is, that although A was bound to pay the whole $100, and could not, by paying B a part of the claim, give good consideration to B for his promise to cancel the balance. A's father was not bound to pay a cent and he may bargain for any exchange in return for a payment which he was not bound to make at all. Therefore, he may bargain that the debt shall be discharged.

PERFORMANCE OR PROMISE OF PERFORMANCE OF A LEGAL DUTY IS NOT SUFFICIENT CONSIDERATION.—In other words, the thing which will not be good consideration, whether done or promised, is the performance or partial performance of something which the man who performs or promises is under a legal duty to do anyway. If he ought to do it anyway, then it will not serve as a price for a new promise or agreement to discharge it. Another illustration of that may be given: Suppose a contractor agrees to build a house for $10,000; he gets sick of his job when he is about half through, says that it is not possible for him to make any money at that price and he is going to quit. "Well," the employer says, "if you will keep on I will give you a couple of thousand dollars more." Accordingly the builder keeps on. That won't do. The builder in keeping on building is doing no more than he was previously bound to do. If he wants to have a binding agreement for the extra $2,000 with his employer, he must secure a promise under seal, for his own promise of performance will not support the promise to pay.

FORBEARANCE AS CONSIDERATION.—Another kind of consideration that is worth calling attention to is forbearance. A has a valid claim against B. He says he is going to sue. B says if he won't sue, or won't sue for the present, B will pay him an agreed sum. That is a good contract so long as it is not open to the objection referred to a moment ago; that is, so long as A's claim is not for a liquidated sum of money and B's promise is not merely a promise to pay part of that liquidated sum. A may promise what B requests, either to forbear temporarily or to forbear perpetually. Either will be good. But suppose A has no valid claim against B, but B is reputed to be rather an easy mark in the community and A is a person of little scruple; he accordingly trumps up a claim against B with the hope of getting a compromise. Is forbearance of that claim by A good consideration for B's promise? It is not. A's claim must be a bona fide one in order to make surrender of it or the forbearance to press it, either temporarily or permanently, a good consideration for a promise of payment.

STATUTE OF LIMITATIONS.—Another case of a promise relating to a subject of very frequent importance in commercial law, and law generally, is a promise to pay a debt barred by the statute of limitations, and this occasion requires a preliminary word in regard to that statute. This statute prohibits the bringing of an action or a claim after the expiration of a certain period. It is a different period for different sorts of claims. Action on a judgment in most States may be begun within twenty years after such judgment is rendered; so in some States may an action on a contract under seal. On the other hand, ordinary contractual claims generally expire in six years. Claims in tort, that is, for injury to person or property, last even a shorter time, but the ordinary contractual statute of limitations is six years. The statute begins to run against a promissory note, or other contract, not from the time when it is made, but from the time when it is by its terms to be performed. A note made now, payable the first of January next, will not be barred until six years from the first of January, not six years from now; and if it was made payable in ten years, as a mortgage note might well be, the statute would not bar it for sixteen years.

PROMISE TO PAY BARRED DEBT.—It has been held, though the reasons are not very easy to explain, that a new promise will revive a debt so far as the statute of limitations is concerned. There need be no consideration for such a promise other than the existence of the old indebtedness; that is said to be a sufficient consideration, although, of course, it can hardly be said to be given as a price for the new promise. Take a promissory note payable January 1, 1905. If nothing happens, that is barred on January 1, 1911, but if in 1911 or 1912 the maker says, in effect, "I know I owe that old note. I have not paid is, but I will pay it," he will be liable on that new promise, and the statute will begin to run again and run for six years from the making of that new promise. It is not enough that the debtor should admit that there was a liability; he must promise to pay it in order to make himself liable. Suppose, instead of a new promise made after the statute had run in 1911 or 1912, the maker had said before the maturity of the note, we will say in the course of 1910, "Don't worry about that note, I shall pay it," that also will start the statute running afresh. In other words, the new promise may be made before the maturity of the note, or before the statute has completely run as well as after the statute has completely run. In either case the new promise will start a fresh liability and keep the note alive for six years from the time the new promise was made. Of course, if the new promise is made the day after maturity of the old obligation, the total effect will be simply to extend the time of the statute one day, because only one day of the six years had run at the time the new promise was made, and counting six years from the date of the new promise gives only one day more.

PART PAYMENT OF BARRED DEBTS.—Not only will a new promise in express terms keep the statute of limitations from barring a claim, but any part payment will have the same effect, unless at the time the part payment is made some qualification is expressly stated. A debtor may say, "I will pay you this part of my debt, but this is all," and incur no further liability; but a part payment without such a qualification starts the statute running afresh as to the balance of the debt. It is by these part payments that notes are frequently kept alive for a long series of years. Interest payments are as effectual for the purpose as payments on account of part of the principal. A new six years begins to run from each payment of interest. The debtor may, however, say, "I will pay you half this debt," or "I will pay you the debt in installments of $10 a month." Such promises are binding according to their terms, and do away with the statute of limitations to that extent, but they do not enable the creditor to recover anything more than the debtor promises. A question may be asked here which is frequently of importance regarding an outlawed note with a payment of interest thereon by the maker. Would an endorser who had waived demand and notice be liable for six years more? Yes, if the payment was made before the statute had completely run in favor of the endorser. Otherwise, no. And if the endorser had not waived demand and notice, the statute could in no case be prolonged against him by any act of the maker.

REVIVAL OF DEBTS DISCHARGED BY BANKRUPTCY OR VOIDABLE FOR INFANCY.—A somewhat similar sort of revival of an old obligation may occur where a debt is discharged in bankruptcy. If a discharged bankrupt promises to pay his indebtedness or makes a payment on account of it, it will revive his old obligation and he will be liable again. And, similarly, though one whom the law calls an infant (that is, a minor under the age of twenty-one) who incurs indebtedness prior to his majority, can avoid liability (unless the indebtedness was incurred for what are called necessaries, that is, food, clothing, shelter and things of that sort); yet if he promises after he has become of age that he will pay these debts, from which he might escape, thereafter he is liable.

CONTRACTS WHICH MUST BE IN WRITING.—There is, in some contracts, one other requisite, besides those already mentioned, necessary to make them enforceable, and that is a writing. It has already been said that writing is not, as such, essential to the validity of contracts, but there are exceptional kinds of contracts which the law has required to be in writing for many years. This is by virtue of what is known as the "Statute of Frauds." This was passed in England in the year 1676, and is known as "Chapter 3, of the Statute of 29, Charles II." This statute was passed for the purpose of preventing frauds and perjuries which were particularly prevalent at the time it was enacted. It is doubtful as to how much good the statute has accomplished. There is no question that in many cases it has caused fraud and perjury rather than prevented it. The statute, however, as passed in England, has been reenacted in practically every State in this country with slight modifications, and it is, therefore, a part of contract law to which attention must be given. Originally, the statute read as follows: "No action shall be brought (1) whereby to charge any executor or administrator upon any special promise to answer damages out of his own estate; (2) or whereby to charge the defendant upon any special promise to answer for the debt, default, or miscarriage of another person; (3) or to charge any person upon any agreement made in consideration of marriage; (4) or upon any contract or sale of lands, tenements, or hereditaments, or any interest in or concerning them; (5) or upon any agreement that is not to be performed within the space of one year from the making thereof; unless the agreement upon which such action shall be brought, or some memorandum or note thereof shall be in writing, and signed by the party to be charged therewith or some person thereunto by him lawfully authorized." A word of comment is necessary to explain the general import of these various sections.

Section 1: An executor or administrator is appointed to settle a deceased person's estate. He is not obliged to personally pay the debts of the deceased person out of his own pocket, if the estate is not sufficient. His liability is limited by the assets of the deceased, but if, in order to save the credit of the deceased or for any other reason, he chooses to promise "to answer damages out of his own estate" that promise must be in writing. This is the situation referred to by this section.

Section 2: This is a very important class and leads us to call attention to the distinction between a guaranty and a contract somewhat similar. Suppose A writes to Jordan, Marsh Company: "Please sell B six good shirts and charge the same to my account." That is not a guaranty. A is in that case a purchaser just as much as if he ordered the shirts sent to himself. Nor is it any more a guaranty if it was further agreed between A and B that B should pay A for the shirts. On the other hand, if A should write to Jordan, Marsh Company, "Let B have six shirts and if he doesn't pay, I will," then you would have a guaranty. It is of the essence of a guaranty that there should be a principal debtor and that the guarantor's liability should be only secondary. A guaranty must be in writing. To put the matter in another way, when there are three parties to a transaction like the above, the writing is necessary. Where there are two parties, no writing is necessary. Where A says to Jordan, Marsh Company, "Let B have six shirts, and if he doesn't pay, I will," we have three parties: A, the guarantor; B, the principal debtor, and Jordan, Marsh Company, the creditor. This must be in writing. Where A says to Jordan, Marsh Company orally, "Give B six shirts and charge to my account," we have simply two parties, A, the principal debtor, and Jordan, Marsh Company, the creditor. Hence no writing is necessary. In connection with this section, it must be kept in mind that some oral contracts which would be good under this section may not be enforceable under another section which we shall refer to later, because the amount involved is over a specified sum.

Section 3: The agreement referred to by this section is not the contract or promise to marry, but is for a marriage settlement such as a promise to make a payment of money or a settlement of property in consideration of a marriage actually taking place.

Section 4: Any contract for the sale of land, or any interest in or concerning land, requires a writing in order to make it binding. The commonest kind of contracts in regard to land are leases or contracts for leases. An oral lease creates what is called a "tenancy at will," that is, the agreement, in so far as it specifies a fixed term, is wholly invalid, but while the tenant occupies he must pay at the agreed rate; but he has no right to stay in; he may be turned out, even though he pays his rent promptly, on notice equal to the time between rent days; and, similarly, he has a right to go out on giving the same short notice.

Section 5: An agreement not to be performed within a year must be in writing, and this provision of the statute has been the subject of rather an odd construction by the courts. The words "not to be performed within a year" have been construed to mean "which cannot possibly be performed within a year." Suppose A hires B for a year from to-morrow and contrast with that case a promise to hire B for B's life, or for the promisor's life. Now the first of those bargains is within the statute and must be in writing, but the second, although it seems for a much longer period, being for the whole life of the promisor or promisee, is not within the statute. The man on whose death the promise depends may die within a year, so there is a possibility of performance within a year. A promise to employ B for all his life, since that may possibly be done within a year, need not be put in writing. But a promise to hire a man for a year from to-morrow cannot be performed in a year. True, he may die within a year, and then the contract cannot be enforced, but there will be no performance. What was agreed, by the parties, was service for a year from to-morrow and that cannot possibly be done earlier than a year from to-morrow.

SALE OF GOODS.—A contract for the sale of goods exceeding in value a certain amount must also be in writing unless part or all of the goods have been delivered or part or all of the price paid. The value of the goods which brings a sale within this section of the Statute of Frauds varies in different States, and local statutes, therefore, should be consulted to ascertain the law in this connection.

Besides the kinds of contracts enumerated in the English statute and which have generally been adopted in this country there are two or three other classes of contracts which in a number of States are required by statute to be in writing. Of this sort is a contract to make a will. That is not a very common sort of contract, but sometimes a man promises in consideration of certain services to make a will in another's favor. The possibility of fraud in such cases is considerable. The testator is always dead before the question comes up, and then if the alleged promisee were allowed to prove by oral statements a contract to bequeath the testator's property on terms which the promisee says were agreed upon between them, it would afford a chance to produce the same effect as if oral wills were allowed. So a contract of a real estate agent for commissions is in some States required to be in writing. A contract with an agent empowering him to sell real estate, though not regarded at common law as within the prohibition of the section of the statute for the sale of an interest in land to be in writing, is by special enactment in many States required to be in writing. A contract for a loan of money reserving a rate of interest higher than that ordinarily allowed by law is sometimes required to be in writing.

WHAT CONSTITUTES WRITING.—The writing being a matter of proof, it is not essential that it be made at the time the contract is entered into. If made at any time before an action upon the contract is begun, that is a sufficient compliance with the statute. The writing, in order to be sufficient, must show who the parties to the agreement are, if not by naming them, by such a description as points to a specific person. Thus a letter addressed simply "Sir," and signed by the party charged, but not containing the name of the person addressed, is not sufficient. It is also required that all the terms of the contract appear in the writing, such as the subject matter, price, terms of credit or any express warranty, but, as often happens, they need not all be expressed in one writing. Contracts are frequently made as the result of an extended correspondence, and in such a case the various letters can be put together and construed as one writing if they obviously refer to one another, and thus all the terms appear in writing. The statutes in some States require "subscription" of the signature, and in that case the signing must be at the end; but where there is not such requirement a signing in the body of the instrument is sufficient.

ALTERATION OF WRITTEN CONTRACT BY SPOKEN WORDS.—Failure to understand and observe the rule restricting parol evidence to vary written contracts leads to a great deal of trouble. The parol evidence rule is this: Where parties have executed a written contract purporting to state the terms of their agreement, the court will not receive evidence that they orally agreed to something less or more or different, at or before the time when the written agreement was executed. That written agreement is taken as conclusive evidence of the contract made at that time. In trying to ascertain what the writing means, however, the court will permit the surrounding circumstances to be shown, and the meaning of technical or trade terms or abbreviations may be proved. It may be shown also that the parties did not intend the written agreement to be effective until some particular event happened; but if the writing was executed as an expression of the intention of the parties at that time, the only endeavor of the court will be to ascertain the meaning of the written words and to enforce them as written. The question of oral agreements made subsequent to the writing is not so simple. We must here distinguish between (1) contracts of which the law requires written evidence because they are within the Statute of Frauds, and (2) contracts which the law does not require to be in writing, but which, nevertheless, are written. Contracts of the latter sort may be rescinded, added to or subtracted from by any subsequent agreement which conforms to the requirements of the law governing mutual consent and consideration, though of course it is very desirable, to avoid dispute, that any variation or rescission of a written contract should itself be in writing. If, however, the Statute of Frauds required the original contract to be in writing, though it may orally be rescinded, it cannot be varied by oral agreement. To permit such an oral agreement would in effect violate the Statute of Frauds by permitting an agreement partly in writing but partly oral to be enforced. Thus, if a written contract for the sale of goods (exceeding in value the amount permitted to be contracted for orally) was made, and the parties afterwards orally agreed to change the price, the time of delivery, or any other terms of the contract, the subsequent oral agreement would be invalid.

THE LIMITS OF CONTRACTUAL RELATIONS.—As a general rule a contract does not impose liabilities or confer rights on a person who is not a party to it. It follows from the very nature of a contract that a person who is not a party to it cannot be included in the rights or liabilities which it creates, so that he will be entitled to sue or render himself liable to be sued upon it. A contract is the result of a voluntary agreement entered into by the parties. Therefore, any contractual rights or liabilities existing by virtue of such voluntary agreement between Smith and Jones are no concern of White and Black. They cannot be bound by any of the provisions of the contract between Smith and Jones, nor can a breach of that contract give them any rights. There are apparent exceptions to the rule we have just mentioned. One is in the case of agency. Here one person represents another in entering into a contract. A contract, however, made by an agent can bind a principal only by force of a previous authority or a subsequent ratification, so that really the contract which binds the principal is his own contract. The other exception is where the rights and liabilities created by a contract may pass to a person other than the original party to it, either by act of the parties themselves or by operation of law. Such would be the case where Smith and Jones have performed the terms of their contract except that Smith has not paid the agreed amount to Jones. Jones assigns his right to collect this amount to White. Such an assignment is permissible, as we will learn when we consider that subject later on. Such is an assignment by act of the parties themselves. Even this exception is limited, as the obligations incurred in purely personal service contracts are not subject to assignment. Thus, if I employ artist Greene to paint my portrait, he could not assign this contract and compel me to accept a portrait painted by artist Brown.

THE RULE OF LAWRENCE v. FOX.—We shall now take up a very generally recognized exception to the principle we have just discussed. The question in its simplest form is this: If Smith and Jones make a contract for the benefit of Greene, may Greene sue on that contract? From what we have said in the preceding paragraph a negative answer might seem to be correct. However, to-day, stated in general terms, and leaving out of the question the limitations recognized in various jurisdictions, the very general rule is that a third party (Greene in our illustration) may enforce a promise made for his benefit, even though he is a stranger both to the contract and to the consideration. In other words, it is held not to be necessary that any consideration move from the third party. It is enough if there is a sufficient consideration between the parties who make the agreement for the benefit of the third party. So in the leading case of Lawrence v. Fox, 20 New York 268, where a debtor of the plaintiff had loaned money to the defendant and the defendant had promised him to pay the plaintiff, although the plaintiff was not a party to the contract, it was held that where a promise is "made to one for the benefit of another, he for whose benefit it is made may bring an action for its breach."

QUALIFICATION OF RULE.—We must call attention to one qualification quite generally recognized. Under this rule, that a beneficiary may enforce a contract, it is necessary that the contract must have been intended for the benefit of a third person. It is not sufficient that the performance may just happen to benefit a third person; it must have been intended for the benefit of a more or less definite person. Thus, where a county board had entered into a contract with a construction company which was building a bridge for it and maintaining a temporary foot bridge during the operation, by the terms of which contract the construction company assumed responsibility for all injuries suffered by pedestrians using the temporary foot bridge, it was held that a person who was injured because of the failure to light the foot bridge properly, was not such a third person as might sue under the rule of Lawrence v. Fox, on the contract made between the county board and the construction company.

APPLICATION OF RULE.—The rule in Lawrence v. Fox has been applied to contracts under seal in many jurisdictions, although there are some decisions to the contrary. A common application of this doctrine is found in the sale of real property with a mortgage upon it. The new purchaser as a part of the purchase price makes an agreement whereby he assumes the payment of the mortgagee. The question of whether the mortgagee, who is really the third party for whose benefit the contract is made, may sue the new owner, is generally answered in the affirmative.

CAPACITY OF PARTIES.—All persons are ordinarily presumed to be capable of contracting, but the law imposes upon some—in varying amounts and for their own protection—disabilities to make contracts which may be enforced against them; and, upon some, for considerations of public policy, disabilities to make enforceable contracts. These persons are (1) Infants; (2) Insane persons; (3) Drunkards; (4) Married women—to a limited extent; (5) Aliens; (6) Artificial persons or corporations.

WHO ARE INFANTS.—All persons under the age of twenty-one are considered infants, except that in some States, by statute, women attain their majority at eighteen. The law endeavors to protect those who have no experience and judgment against the loss of their property because of their inability to deal safely with others who might take an advantage of that fact. It may well be that one who has nearly attained his majority is as able in fact to protect his interests as one of full age, but the essence of the law is that it is a rule of universal application, and the law cannot measure the ability in each particular case. To do the greatest good for the greatest number, therefore, it conclusively presumes that those under twenty-one have not yet gained the ability to cope with others in the preservation of their property.

CONTRACTS OF AN INFANT.—An infant's contracts are voidable; that is, though they bind the other party to the bargain the infant himself may avoid them. If he avoids them the adult with whom he contracted is entitled to recover whatever he may have given the infant which still remains in the latter's possession; but if the infant has spent or used, or for any reason no longer has the consideration which the adult gave him, the infant may avoid his own obligation if he has not already performed it, and if he has already performed it he may reclaim what he has given. After he comes of age, but not before, the infant may ratify his contracts and they then become binding upon him. The retention after coming of age of property received by the infant during his minority amounts to a ratification. There are a few obligations of an infant which on grounds of public policy are binding upon him. This is true of a contract to perform military service. The marriage of an infant is binding though his engagement is not. It is frequently said that his contract for necessaries is binding; strictly this is not true. The infant is liable for necessaries, but his obligation does not depend upon his contract; it is an obligation imposed by law—what has been called a quasi-contract. The importance of this distinction is shown if the price agreed upon exceeded the real value of the necessaries. If the contract were binding, the infant would be bound to pay the agreed price, but in fact he is liable only for the fair value. What is necessary for an infant depends upon his station in life, upon whether he already has a sufficient supply of the necessary article in question, and upon whether he is receiving proper support from a parent or guardian. The privilege of an infant is generally held to exist even though the party dealing with him not only reasonably believed the infant of age, but had received actual representations from the infant to that effect.

INSANE PERSONS AND DRUNKARDS—The law affords protection to insane persons and, to a less extent, to drunkards, for the same reason as in the case of infants, namely, that those who are incapable of understanding what they are doing and of comprehending the effect of their contracts upon their property should be safeguarded against the designs of the more capable. This protection is given them by declaring some of their contracts void, and allowing them, or those legally representing them, to avoid all others with the exception of a few. Also, as in the case of infants, this privilege as to such contracts is for the insane person's protection only, and the other party to the contract may not avoid it by pleading that it was made with an incompetent person.

WHOM DOES THE LAW CONSIDER INSANE?—Modern science has clearly established that a person may be insane on one subject, and yet possess a clear understanding and be perfectly sound on another. If the contract deals with a subject of which the person has a clear understanding, he is not in need of protection and is given none. Those only are given the protection who do not possess the mind to understand in a reasonable manner the nature and effect of the act in which they engage.

BINDING OBLIGATIONS FOR NECESSARIES.—The insane must live as well as the sane; consequently they are bound to pay for necessaries furnished them but only the reasonable value, as has been explained in the case of infants. The rules for determining what these necessaries may be are the same as in the case of infants.

OTHER CONTRACTS.—It is often a difficult matter to know when a person is insane, much more difficult than it is to determine a person's age. One of the contracting parties may have acted in perfect good faith, being ignorant of the other's unsoundness of mind and having no judicial determination of insanity or other warning to put him on his guard. The contract even may be reasonable in its terms, and it may have been so acted upon that the parties to it cannot be restored to their original position. In such a case, while the law should protect the incompetent, it would be clear injustice to protect him to such an extent as to make the other party suffer through no fault of his own. It has been quite generally determined in this country, therefore, that where a person does not know of the other's insanity and there has been no judicial determination of such insanity to notify the world of it, and the contract is a fair one, and has been so acted upon that the parties cannot be restored to their original position, it is binding upon the lunatic as well as upon the other party.

VOID CONTRACTS.—In some States it is held, however, that all contracts of an insane person are void. In such States the rule above stated would not hold. The law of each State must be consulted to determine the law in the particular State. In some States, notably New York and Massachusetts, an insane person's deed of lands has been held to be void, without reference to whether or not the other party entered into the contract in good faith without notice, or that it has been so far acted upon that the parties cannot be restored to their original position. As in the case of infants, an insane person's power of attorney has been declared by high authority to be absolutely void.

VOIDABLE CONTRACTS.—In most jurisdictions an insane person's contracts are voidable by him or by his guardian, provided (1) that the other person knew of his insanity at the time of making the contract, or (2) he had been declared insane by some court, or (3) the parties can be restored to their original position.

RATIFICATION AND AVOIDANCE.—When the insane person's reason has been restored, if the contract is a voidable one, as explained in the foregoing rules, though he may by acts or words avoid the contract he made during his insanity, he may in like manner ratify it, or he may ratify it by not avoiding it within a reasonable time after recovering his reason while continuing to keep something capable of being returned, which he obtained under the contract.

WHAT CONSTITUTES DRUNKENNESS.—It is not ordinary drunkenness which excuses a man from his contracts, and enables him to claim the protection given generally to incapable persons. The person must have been utterly deprived of his reason and understanding, so that he could not comprehend the nature or effect of the act in which he was engaged. That he was so much under the influence of liquor that his judgment was not as good as in his normal state does not excuse him.

MARRIED WOMEN.—It is practically impossible to state in brief form the law upon the subject of married women's contracts. The difficulty arises from the diverse changes made in the plain and clear rules of the common law by statutes in the different States. The old law is wholly incompatible with the enlightened view now held in regard to women, their family, social and business standing, and the changes have been made to give them the rights to which they are justly entitled. But, inasmuch as the statutes have not been uniform in the different States, the law to-day is not wholly uniform. The statutes and decisions in each State must be consulted to determine the law on the subject as it is to-day. Through these changes the law has become very complicated, and business men should obtain legal advice before entering into important business dealings with married women.

THE OLD RULE.—Upon her marriage a woman's existence became merged in that of her husband, and the husband and wife were regarded for many purposes as one person. What tangible personal property she had became his immediately upon marriage, and he had the right to reduce her bills, notes, bonds and other debts to his possession. Her real property she retained the title to, subject to the right of the husband to have the use of it during his life, if children were born of the marriage. He was bound to supply her with necessaries, and so long as he did this her contracts for things of even ordinary use were void; but if he failed to supply the necessaries her contract for them would be valid. All her other contracts were absolutely void—not voidable. Her position, then, was worse than an infant's. She could have personal property of her own only if it was given to someone else to hold the title and pay over the income to her, and even this "separate estate," as it was called, could not be bound by her contracts.

CHANGES MADE BY STATUTE.—The law of married women's contracts has been greatly changed by legislative enactments, to give married women the rights which the more enlightened view of the present time accords to them. The first changes aimed quite generally to give her greater rights over her "separate estate," giving her power to make binding contracts with reference to it, or to make binding contracts if she were carrying on a trade or business of her own. But the earlier statutes frequently did not give her power to contract with her husband, or to make binding contracts if she had no separate estate, or was not carrying on a separate business. Later enactments have largely corrected these defects, but the old rule still stands except as it has been changed by statute, and, therefore, the statutes of each State and the decisions interpreting them must be consulted to determine accurately the law in each State. It may, however, be said that generally a married woman may now contract except with her husband, and except as surety for him. In many States she can even make contracts of these excepted classes.

ALIENS.—An alien is one born out of the jurisdiction of the United States, of a father not a citizen of this country, and who has not been naturalized. In times of peace, aliens may hold property and make contracts and seek the protection of our courts as freely as citizens. When war breaks out between this country and another the making of contracts between citizens of the two countries is prohibited. If such contracts are made during a state of war, they are illegal and void, and the courts of this country will not lend their aid to enforce them, either during the war or after its termination. Contracts made before the war breaks out are good, but cannot be enforced, nor can remedies for their breach be obtained, while the war is in progress. When the war ceases, however, the courts will lend their aid to the enforcement of such contracts.

CORPORATIONS.—A corporation may contract as freely as an individual so long as its contracts are within the business powers and scope of the business which its charter authorizes it to conduct. And even if a corporation has made a contract outside of the scope of its business, and the contract has been acted upon so that either party has had the benefit of the contract, an action will lie in favor of the other for the benefits so conferred. But a contract outside of the business which its charter permits the corporation to engage in, and which is wholly executory, the courts will not enforce. Such contracts are said to be ultra vires. Contracts with a corporation may be in the same form as contracts between individuals, and the corporation need use its seal only where an ordinary person is required to use one. The officer or officers making the contract on behalf of a corporation must, however, be authorized so to do either by the directors or by the general powers attached to such officers. In law corporations are deemed to be artificial persons subject in a general way to provisions governing natural persons.

CHAPTER III
CONTRACTS—PERFORMANCE
AND TERMINATION

PRIMARY RULE.-After a contract has been formed, it does not make much difference whether it is under seal or whether it is a simple contract; the rules governing the contract, subsequent to its formation, are very much the same though there are a few distinctions. The primary rule running through the law, governing obligations to perform contracts, is that if a man has once formed a good contract he must do as he agreed, and if he fails substantially (not merely slightly) to do so the other party may refuse to perform on his part. If you remember that fundamental principle you cannot generally go far wrong.

CONDITIONAL CONTRACTS—INSURANCE.-What one agrees to often depends on the conditions which he includes as part of his promise. Take the insurance policy previously alluded to. An insurance company promises to pay $5,000, but it does not promise to pay in any event; the condition "if the house burns down" is obviously a qualification of the promise. But there are other conditions in the insurance policy. The insurance company says that it will not be liable if gasoline is kept in the house beyond a small quantity necessary for cleaning. That, too, is a condition of its promise to pay $5,000; so that "if the house burns down," "if gasoline is not kept in the house," "if the house is not unoccupied more than three months," and "if mechanics are not allowed in possession of the property for more than a certain length of time," are all conditions, and the company's main promise need only be kept if the conditions are complied with. That is why an insurance policy is not always quite as good as it seems—because there is a large promise in large print; but there are a good many qualifications in smaller print which are really part of the promise and must be taken into account.

CONDITIONS IN BUILDING CONTRACTS.—Another kind of conditional promise often occurs in building contracts. The employer agrees to pay the builder or contractor on the production of an architect's certificate. Now it doesn't do the builder any good to build that house unless he gets the architect's certificate, for he has been promised pay only on condition that he produce it. That is the promise between the parties. That is the only promise.

WHEN PERFORMANCE OF CONDITIONS IS EXCUSED.—It is obvious that these conditions in promises may be sometimes used to defeat the ends of justice, and undoubtedly at times they are so used. A person who draws a contract cleverly will put in a great many conditions qualifying his own liability, and will try to make the promise on the other side as unconditional as possible. The law cannot wholly do away with these conditions, because in general, so long as parties do not make illegal bargains, they have a right to make such bargains as suit themselves. The court cannot make their agreement for them, but it is held that if a condition will lead to a real forfeiture by an innocent promisee, the law will relieve the promisee. Thus, in the architect's certificate case, if the house was properly built and it was merely ill temper on the part of the architect that caused him to withhold giving the certificate, the court would allow the builder to recover, and even if the architect had some good reason for refusing the certificate, the court would not allow the builder to be permanently prevented from recovering anything on the contract, providing the builder had substantially though not entirely performed his contract and had acted in good faith. If, however, his default was wilful, if he had tried to beat the specifications, and the architect had found him out and therefore refused the certificate, the only thing the builder could do would be to go at it again, tear out his faulty construction and build as he had agreed.

IN CONTRACTS OF EMPLOYMENT, WORK MUST BE PERFORMED BEFORE PAYMENT IS DUE.—There are other matters which qualify the obligation of a promisor to perform besides express conditions such as those we have alluded to. Take this case: John promises to work for the A. B. Company; the A. B. Company promises to employ him and to pay him a salary of $1,000 a year. John comes to work the first day and works a while, and then he says he would like his thousand dollars. The A. B. Company says, "Well, you have got to do your work first." John says, "Why should I work first and trust you for pay, rather than you pay first and trust me for the work? I will keep on working, but I want the pay now." Of course, the employer is right in refusing to pay until the work has been done, even though the promise of the employer is not expressly qualified by the statement that after the work has been done he will pay $1,000. It has been dictated by custom, rather than by anything else, that where work is to be performed on one side and money to be paid on the other, in the absence of any statement in the contract to the contrary, the work must be done before the pay is given. The result is this: that John must work anyway, his promise to work being absolute; but the employer's promise to pay the money is, in effect, conditional. It is subject to an implied condition, as it is called, that John shall have done the work he agreed to do. The promise of the employer is, in effect, "I will pay if you previously have done the work." But John's promise is absolute: "I will work." He has to trust for the pay.

PERFORMANCE FIRST DUE UNDER A CONTRACT MUST BE GIVEN BEFORE PERFORMANCE SUBSEQUENTLY DUE FROM THE OTHER PARTY CAN BE DEMANDED.—And that case is an illustration of a broader principle which may be stated in this way: where the performance promised one party to a contract is to precede in time the performance by the other side, the party who is to perform first is bound absolutely to perform; whereas the party who is to perform subsequently may refuse to perform unless and until the other party performs. In the cases thus far alluded to, the promises of the two parties could not be performed at the same time. You cannot work for a year and pay $1,000 simultaneously. One performance takes a whole year and the other performance takes only a moment.

PERFORMANCES CONCURRENTLY DUE.—But frequently there arise cases where both promises can take place at the same time. The commonest illustration of that is a contract to buy and sell. You can pay the price and hand over the goods simultaneously, and when a contract is of this character, that is, where both performances can be rendered at the same time, the rule is that in the absence of agreement to the contrary, they must be performed simultaneously. John agrees to buy James' horse and pay $200 for it, and James agrees to sell the horse for $200; that is a bilateral contract of purchase and sale. Now suppose neither party does anything, has each party broken his promise? It might seem so, for John has not bought the horse or paid for it as he agreed, nor has James sold the horse. But where each party is bound to perform simultaneously with the other, if either wants to acquire any rights under the contract he must do what is called putting the other party in default, that is, he must offer to perform himself. John, therefore, must go to James, offer $200 and demand the horse if he wants to assert that James has broken his contract. And James, on the other hand, if he wishes to enforce the contract, must go with the horse to John and say, "Here is the horse which I will hand over to you on receiving simultaneously the $200 which you promised me for it." The obligation of the two promises when they can be performed simultaneously is called concurrently conditional, that is, each party has a concurrent right to performance by the other, and has a right to refuse performance until he receives, concurrently with his own performance, performance by the other party.

INSTALLMENT CONTRACTS.—Sometimes contracts are more complicated than those which we have stated, such as contracts of service and contracts to buy and sell. This, for instance, is a type of a very common sort of contract in business: a leather manufacturer uses large quantities of tanning extract in his tannery. He makes a contract for a regular supply, so many barrels each week for a year, for which he agrees to pay a specified price a barrel on delivery. For a time the extract promised him is sent just as agreed. We will suppose, then, that perhaps the extract manufacturer is slow in sending what he promised; there is a delay; perhaps the extract that is furnished is not as good as it was or as the contract called for. What can the leather manufacturer do about it? Of course, he can keep on with the contract, taking what the extract manufacturer sends him, getting as much performance as he can, and then sue for such damages as he may suffer because of the failure to give what was promised completely. But he does not always want to do that. Suppose it is necessary for his business that he should get tanning extract and get it regularly. He does not want to wait and take chances on the extract manufacturer's delays in delivery and inferiorities in quality. He wants to make a contract with somebody else and get out of his bargain with the first extract manufacturer altogether. May he do so? No question in contracts comes up in business more often than that. And the answer to the question is this: it depends on the materiality of the breach, taking into consideration the terms of the contract and the extent of the default. Is the breach so serious as to make it fair and just in a business sense to call the contract wholly off; or will justice be better obtained by making the injured party keep on with the contract and seek redress in damages for any minor default?

MATERIALITY OF BREACH IN CONTRACTS OF EMPLOYMENT.—The same thing comes up very often in contracts of employment. Suppose an employer hires an employee for a year, and in the course of the year the employee at some time or other fails to fulfill his contractual duty as an employee. He is negligent and in some respect fails to comply with his contract to render good and efficient service. Can the employer discharge him? We must ask how serious is the breach. A merely negligent breach of duty is not so serious as one which is wilful. Or the breach might be on the other side of the contract. Suppose the employer has promised to pay a certain sum each month as salary during the year, and does not pay promptly. Has the employee a right to say, "You pay my salary on the first day of the month as you agreed, or I leave"? No, he does not have a right to speak so positively as that. A single day's delay in the payment of one month's installment of salary would not justify throwing up a year's contract. On the other hand, if the delay ran along for any considerable time, it would justify the employee in refusing to continue. You will see that this principle of materiality of the breach on one side, as justifying a refusal to perform on the other, is rather an indefinite one. It involves questions of degree. That is so in the nature of the case. The indefiniteness of the rule, therefore, cannot very well be helped.

ILLUSTRATIONS AND DISTINCTIONS.—A few concrete illustrations may help to bring out the points under discussion. Suppose an agreement for the sale of real estate, and, for instance, the buyer is unable to be on hand the day the sale is to be completed, and the owner is present, and, finding the buyer absent, immediately sells the land to another. Now is there any action against the owner, or might he justly refuse to go on with the contract because of the momentary breach of contract? No, he cannot refuse to go on in the case of a contract of that sort to sell real estate, unless the contract very expressly provided that the transaction must be carried through at the specified time and place or not at all. The case would be governed otherwise by the principle of materiality of the breach, to which we have alluded. A brief delay would not be a sufficiently material breach to justify the seller in refusing to go on, but a long delay, of course, would be sufficient. In sales of personal property time is regarded by the law as more important than in sales of land. In contracts to sell stocks varying rapidly in value, time is a very important element. Suppose now that an option for a piece of land was given by the owner. May he dispose of the land to another a few minutes after the time specified in the option for the acceptance of the offer? That is different from the case previously put. The option is in effect an offer to make a sale, and the offer is by its terms to expire, we will say, at 12 o'clock, noon, October 23. It will expire at that time, and an acceptance a minute later will be too late. The difference is in the terms of the promise made by the different parties. In the case put first, there is an unqualified contract to buy and sell. In the case now put there is a promise to sell only if the price is tendered or if acceptance is made prior to 12 o'clock, noon, October 23. The terms of the option, assuming in its favor that it was given for consideration or was under seal and therefore not merely a revocable offer, were expressly conditional. The vital thing in contracts is to be sure of the terms of your promise. The term option indicates a right which exists up to a certain point; beyond that point there is no right.

PROSPECTIVE INABILITY OF ONE PARTY EXCUSES THE OTHER.—There is one other thing besides actual breach by his co-contractor, which justifies one party to a contract in refusing to go on with the contract, and that may be called prospective inability to perform on the part of the other side.

INSOLVENCY OR BANKRUPTCY.—Let us give one or two illustrations of that. You have entered into a contract to sell a merchant 100 barrels of flour on thirty days' credit. The time has come for the delivery of the flour, but the merchant is insolvent. He says to you, "I want you to deliver that flour; the agreed day has come." You say, "But you cannot pay for the flour." "Well," he replies, "it is not time to pay for it. You agreed to give me thirty days' credit: perhaps I shall be able to pay all right then. I have not broken my promise yet, and as long as I am not in default in my promise you have no right to break yours." You have a right to refuse to deliver the flour because, though the buyer has not yet broken his contract, the prospect of his being able to keep it, in view of his insolvency, is so slight that his prospective inability to perform in the future, when the time comes, excuses you from going on now. Insolvency or bankruptcy of one party to a contract will always excuse the other party from giving credit or going on with an executory contract, unless concurrent performance is made by the insolvent party or security given for future performance.

REPUDIATION.—Repudiation of a contract by one party is also a good excuse. Repudiation means a wrongful assertion by one party to a contract that he is not going to perform in the future what he agreed. After such repudiation the other party may say, "I am not going to perform now what I agreed to perform, since you have said you will not perform in the future what you agreed. I shall not go ahead and trust you, even though I did by the contract agree to give you credit, in view of the fact that you have now repudiated your agreement by saying that you are not going to do what you agreed." Repudiation may be indicated by acts as well as by words, and often is indicated partly by words and partly by acts.

TRANSFER OF PROPERTY TO WHICH THE CONTRACT RELATES.—Still another illustration of prospective inability arises where a contract relates to specific property, as a certain piece of land, and before the time for performance comes, the owner of the land, who had agreed to sell it we will suppose, transfers it to somebody else or mortgages it. The man who had agreed to buy that piece of land may withdraw from the contract. He may say, "You might get the land back at the time you agreed to perform, but I am not going to take any chances on that. I am off the bargain altogether."

IMPORTANCE OF EXACT PROVISIONS IN CONTRACTS.—So much for the rather difficult subject of the mutual duties of parties to a contract in the performance of it. The best way to avoid doubt or uncertainty in such matters is to provide very exactly in the contract what the rights of the parties shall be in certain contingencies. The law always respects the intention of the parties when it is manifested, and it is only when they have said nothing about their intention that the rules which we have considered become important.

FRAUD.—The next question in regard to contracts arises out of certain grounds of defense that may come up and the most important of these is fraud. Fraud is deception; it is inducing the other party to believe something which is not true, and, by inducing him to believe that, influencing his action. The ordinary way in which fraud is manifested is by misrepresentations. A purchase or sale of stock or of goods may be induced by fraud. A loan may be obtained from a bank by fraud, that is, by misrepresentation of material facts which influence the other side to act.

MISSTATEMENTS OF OPINION ARE NOT FRAUDULENT.—Now what kind of misrepresentation amounts to fraud? There must be misrepresentation of a fact. Merely misrepresentation of opinion is insufficient and what is opinion and what is fact has been the basis of a good many lawsuits. John offers his horse to James for sale at $300. He says that it is the best horse in town. Well, it is not the best horse in town by a good deal, but that sort of statement cannot be the basis of an allegation of fraud. That a thing is "good," or "the best in the market," or similar general statements, all of which ought to be known to the hearer to be simply expressions of opinion, are not statements of positive fact. Take these two statements in regard to the horse. "He can trot very fast." That is a mere statement of opinion. To some minds eight miles an hour is very fast; to more enterprising persons fifteen miles an hour is necessary in order to make travel seem fast. Those are matters of opinion. But a statement that the horse can trot twelve miles an hour, or has trotted one mile in three minutes on the track, are statements of fact, and if untrue are fraudulent. A statement of value is a statement of opinion and cannot be the basis of fraud. A statement that the horse is worth $300, or is worth twice as much as the owner is asking for him, cannot be relied upon; but a statement that $300 was paid for this horse, or was offered for him, is an assertion of fact, and if untrue would be the basis of an allegation of fraud.

PROMISES ARE NOT FRAUDULENT BECAUSE BROKEN.—A promise is not a statement of fact. A man may promise to do something and fail to carry out the promise, and in consequence the person he was dealing with may regret the bargain he entered into, but his only remedy is to sue for damages for breach of the promise if it was part of a contract. He cannot assert that merely because the promise was not kept the transaction was fraudulent. But if a man makes a promise knowing when he makes it that he cannot keep it, he is committing a fraud. The commonest illustration of this is where a man buys goods on credit, having at the time an intention not to pay for them, or well knowing that he cannot pay for them.

STATEMENTS MUST HAVE BEEN CALCULATED TO INDUCE ACTION.— Generally speaking, the statement relied on as fraudulent must have been made with the purpose of inducing action. For instance, suppose John likes to tell large stories. He tells James things about his neighbor's horse. John does not do this for any purpose except to brag about living near a man who has such a splendid horse, but James suddenly takes the notion he would like to have that horse and he goes and buys it. Now it was not legal fraud on John's part to tell those lies about the horse, even though they did induce James to go and buy it, unless John, as a reasonable man, ought to have known that James was likely to buy the horse, as might have been the case if James had been talking about buying him. Then it would be fraud, and it would not make any difference in regard to its being fraudulent that John had nothing to gain by telling these lies, that he was simply doing it for the fun of the thing.

REMEDIES FOR FRAUD.—What remedy has the defrauded person? The law gives him two remedies of which he may take his choice; he cannot have both, but he can have either. One is to sue the fraudulent person for such damages as have been suffered, and the other is to rescind the transaction, to get back what has been given, or to refuse to go on with the contract at all if it is still wholly executory.

DURESS AND UNDUE INFLUENCE.—There are certain defences similar to fraud; duress, or undue influence, is one of them. However, this is comparatively rare. It is compelling a person to do what he does not want to do, making him agree to a bargain that he would not agree to accept under compulsion, as by fear of personal violence or imprisonment; and a bargain made under these circumstances can be rescinded or set aside. Merely threatening to enforce your legal rights by suit against another is not duress, though it may in fact induce him to agree to what he would not otherwise have agreed; but to threaten criminal prosecution as a means of extorting money or inducing an agreement is illegal and in many jurisdictions is itself a crime.

MISTAKE OF FACT.—In certain cases, also, a mutual mistake of a vital fact is ground for setting aside a contract, but these cases are not very common. Mistakes generally do not prevent the enforcement of contracts. Usually where there is a mistake, it is of a character for which one party or the other is to blame. If the mistake arises out of deception it is fraud. If the mistake arises simply because the mistaken party has failed to inform himself of the facts, as he might have done, then it is no defence at all. But if both parties were acting under the mutual assumption that some vital fact was true in making a bargain, either one of them may avoid or rescind the bargain when it appears they were both mistaken.

IMPOSSIBILITY.—Impossibility is sometimes a defence to the performance of a contract. Perhaps the simplest illustration of this arises in a contract for personal services of any kind. Illness or death of the person who promises the services excuses performance. Death does not usually terminate a contract or serve as a defence to it. If a man contracts to sell 100 bushels of grain and dies the next day his estate is liable on the contract just as if he continued alive; but if he agreed to hire a man as an employee for a year, his death or the employee's death within the year would terminate the obligation of both. Unexpected difficulty is not impossibility. For instance, take a building contract: the builder agrees to put up a building within a certain time; he is prevented by strikes. Nevertheless, he is liable for not doing as he agreed. He should have put a condition in his promise, qualifying his agreement to build, that if strikes prevented, he would not be liable. So, if the foundation gave way and the building tumbled down before it was finished, the builder must put it up again. Also, if lightning struck it, he must put it up again.

ILLEGAL CONTRACTS.—One other matter to be considered in connection with contracts and defences to them is illegality. Some kinds of illegal contracts are so obviously illegal that it is not necessary to say anything about them. Anybody would know that they were illegal and that they could not be enforced for that reason. A contract to steal or murder or take part in any crime is a good example. But other kinds of illegal contracts are not so obviously wicked as to make it clear that they are unenforceable. It may be worth while to mention a few of these kinds of illegality.

CONTRACTS IN RESTRAINT OF TRADE.—One class of contracts which has become very important in late years in business is the contract in restraint of trade, so called. The original contracts in restraint of trade were contracts by which one man agreed that he would not thereafter exercise his trade or profession, the object generally being that the promisee should be freed from the competition of the man who had promised to refrain from exercising his trade; and the law became settled a good many years ago that if the promise was general not to exercise the trade or profession anywhere, or at any time, it was illegal, but that if it was only for a reasonably limited space of time it would not be illegal. That old law still exists, but there has grown up further a much more important class of cases where contracts are made to further an attempted monopoly, and one may say pretty broadly that all such attempts are illegal. It does not matter how much business reason there is for it; any attempt to combine in order to get a monopoly, or in order to put up prices, is bad. Moreover, if the attempted restraint of trade or monopoly concerns interstate commerce, the agreement is a Federal crime under the Sherman law.

GAMBLING CONTRACTS.—Another kind of illegal contract is a gambling contract. This seems obvious in agreements for the more extreme kinds of gambling, but in certain business transactions where the matter becomes important, the dividing line is not so clear; especially in dealings on stock exchanges and exchanges for sales of staple products, such as grain, cotton and coffee. The stock exchanges and other exchanges are made the means of a great deal of speculation, which is virtually gambling. Now, in what cases does the law regard these transactions as gambling and, therefore unenforceable, and in what cases are they legal? The answer is, if an actual delivery of the stock, or commodity bought, is contemplated, then the transaction is not gambling in the legal sense; but if a settlement merely of the differences in buying and selling prices is contemplated, as the only performance of the bargain, then the transaction is gambling. The difference is between a stock-exchange business and a bucket-shop business. If you give an order to a stock-exchange house to buy stock, even though you put up but a small margin and could put up but a small margin, and the stock-exchange house knows you could put up but a small margin, nevertheless, the stock-exchange house actually buys that stock, and it is delivered to it. The stock-exchange house would then have a right to demand of you that you pay for that stock in full and take delivery of it, and could sue you for the price if you failed to comply with the demand. However, as a matter of fact, it does not ordinarily do that. If it wants to get the price which you promised to pay, and you fail on demand to take up the stock, it sells the stock which it has been holding as security. The bucket-shop, on the other hand, though it takes your order to buy, does not actually buy the stock; it simply settles with you when you want to settle, or when it wants to settle, because the margin is not sufficiently kept good, by calculating the difference between the price at which the stock was supposedly bought and the price at which it is supposedly sold, those prices being fixed by the ruling market quotations at the time. It would be perfectly possible to make a gambling transaction out of the stock-exchange transaction by a very slight change. If a stock-exchange house should agree, for instance, that the customer should not be compelled to take delivery of the stock, then that added agreement would make the transaction between broker and customer a gambling transaction, even though the broker actually bought the stock on the exchange, and, as between himself and the other broker on the exchange with whom he dealt, there was a perfectly valid sale of the stock. In some jurisdictions, by statute, speculative contracts which are not gambling contracts at common law are made illegal.

BREACH OF FIDUCIARY DUTIES.—Another very important class of illegal transactions arises from breach of fiduciary duties. A fiduciary is rather hard to define. He is somebody that owes a duty higher than a mere contractual obligation, a duty involving something of trust and confidence. A trustee is a fiduciary, so is an agent. A director or officer of a corporation is a fiduciary, and any dealing in which a fiduciary violates his duty to the person for whom he is fiduciary is illegal, and any agreement for such a violation is an illegal contract. It is illegal for a trustee to bargain for any advantage from his trust other than his regular compensation. It would be illegal for a trustee to bargain with a bank to give the bank a trust account in return for some personal advantage, as a loan to be made to the trustee personally. It would be a breach of fiduciary duty for a corporation officer and director to bargain for any personal advantage by virtue of his official action.

KNOWLEDGE OF ANOTHER'S ILLEGAL PURPOSE.—The knowledge of another's illegal purpose will not make the person who knows of it himself guilty of illegality; but if one not only knows but in any way promotes the illegal purpose of another, he will be considered a party to the illegality. A may sell goods to B, knowing that B is going to use them illegally, and A's sale will not be illegal; but if A does anything to help B in using them illegally, or if the goods are of such a character that they can be used only illegally, then A would be guilty of illegality himself.

MEANING OF ASSIGNMENTS.—Much of the difficulty regarding assignment of contracts is due to different meanings which may be attached to the word assignment. When property is assigned the assignee becomes the owner in every sense, if the person from whom he took the assignment had a valid title. This is not true of the assignment of contracts. By the common law, contract rights or "choses in action," as they are termed in law, were not assignable, the reason being that one who contracted with A, cannot without his consent become bound to B.

POWER OF ATTORNEY TO COLLECT A CLAIM.—Though when a man had a contract right he could not by common law make B in a complete sense the owner of the claim, he could give B a power to collect the claim as his, A's, agent, and authorize him to keep the proceeds when the claim was collected. It long ago became established that when an owner of a claim purported to make an assignment of a claim he thereby gave the assignee the power to enforce the claim in his stead, and this power given the assignee is irrevocable.

EFFECT OF ASSIGNMENT OF RIGHTS.—It may be supposed that the effect of an assignment of a right, though the result may be worked out by treating the assignee as an agent or attorney of the assignor, is the same as if the assignee were fully substituted in the position of the assignor as owner of the claim, but this is not quite true. Assuming that the claim is not represented by negotiable paper, the legal owner of the claim is still the assignor. This is shown by the fact that if the debtor pays the assignor in ignorance of the assignment, the debt is discharged and the assignee can only go against his assignor for the latter's fraudulent conduct in collecting the claim after having assigned it. So, too, if the assignor makes a subsequent assignment, this subsequent assignee also has a power of attorney to collect the claim and keep the proceeds; so that if the second assignee in good faith collects the claim in ignorance of the prior assignment, he can keep what he has collected; nor is the debtor liable to the first assignee who must as before seek redress from his assignor. It is, therefore, always important for the assignee of a non-negotiable chose in action to give immediate notice of his assignment to the debtor. If after such notice the debtor should pay the assignor or a subsequent assignee, such payment would not discharge the debtor, and the first assignee could collect the claim from him.

NON-ASSIGNABLE RIGHTS.—Rights cannot be assigned which are personal in their nature. The one who has contracted to paint a picture cannot delegate the duty to another, no matter how skillful. One who has a right to the personal services of an employee cannot assign that right to another. A publisher who has a right to publish all books written by a certain author cannot assign his right to another publisher.

ASSIGNMENT OF DUTIES.—The duties under a contract are not assignable under any circumstances. That is, one who owes money or is bound to any performance can not by any act of his own or by any act in agreement with any other person except his creditor, divest himself of liability and substitute the liability of another. This is sufficiently obvious when attention is called to it; for otherwise debtors would find an easy practical way of escaping from their debts by assigning the duty to pay to irresponsible persons. But the principle is not always recognized. A person who is subject to a duty, though he cannot escape liability, may delegate the performance of his obligation provided the duty is of such a character that performance by an agent will be substantially the same thing as performance by the obligor himself. Thus if a contractor engages to build a house, he may delegate the actual building to another, but he cannot escape responsibility for the work. One who owes a mortgage may delegate the payment of the mortgage to a purchaser of the land who assumes and agrees to pay the debt. If the purchaser of the land actually pays, the debt is discharged; but if he fails to do so, the mortgagee may sue the original mortgagor and the latter will be obliged to bring another action against the purchaser who promised to pay the debt and failed to do so. So where a partnership is changed and a new firm formed, it is very common for the new firm to assume the obligations of the old firm.

ORIGINAL DEBTOR NOT DISCHARGED UNLESS THERE IS A NOVA-

TION.—Though a creditor cannot be deprived of his right against his original debtor without his consent, he may consent. If he does thus consent to take in lieu of the obligation of his original debtor that of the person who assumed the debt, what is called a novation is created. That frequently happens where a new firm succeeds an old one. The new firm goes on dealing with the old creditors, and they impliedly, if not expressly, assent to taking the new firm instead of the old firm as a debtor. But in order to make out a novation you have got to find as a fact that the creditor agreed to give up his right against the old debtor. If the creditor does not assent to a novation then the situation is that the creditor retains his claim against the old debtor, but the person who has assumed the debt has contracted to pay that debt. If he keeps his contract he will pay it and the debt will be cancelled. If he does not keep his contract the creditor will sue the original debtor and the original debtor will sue the man who assumed the debt.

ASSIGNMENT OF BILATERAL CONTRACTS.—In bilateral contracts each party is under a duty to perform his promise, and also has a right to the performance of the other party. If an attempt is made to assign such a contract the effect is this: the assignor delegates to the assignee the duty of performing the assignor's promise, but the assignor himself still remains liable if his agent, the assignee, fails to carry out the duty. Further, the assignor authorizes the assignee to receive the payment or performance due from the other party to the contract and to keep it for himself.

WHAT AMOUNTS TO AN ASSIGNMENT.—No particular words are necessary to constitute an assignment. Any words which show an intention that another shall be the owner of a right are sufficient to constitute the latter an assignee. Especially it should be observed that an order directed to a debtor of the drawer ordering him to pay the debt to a named payee, is an assignment of the debt when delivered to the payee. This case must be sharply distinguished from a bill of exchange or check. A bill of exchange or check is an order to pay a certain amount unconditionally, irrespective of the existence of any particular fund. It is only an order to pay from a particular fund, that is, an order which is conditional expressly or impliedly on the existence of that fund, which constitutes an assignment.

PARTIAL ASSIGNMENT.—A creditor may not only assign his whole claim to an assignee, but he may assign part of it. Such a partial assignment authorizes the assignee to collect the portion of the claim assigned and keep it for himself. But the debtor is not bound to pay the claim piecemeal; he may insist on making but a single payment unless his contract with his creditor provides otherwise. A bank in accepting a deposit contracts to pay that deposit in such amounts as the depositor may indicate on the checks drawn by him, but an ordinary debtor who owes $100 cannot be required to pay in such amounts as his creditor may see fit to demand. For this reason a few courts hold that even if the debtor has notice of a partial assignment, he may pay the whole debt to the original creditor though that results in defrauding the partial assignee. Most courts hold, however, that the debtor when notified of the facts cannot do this, and if he objects to paying fractional parts of his indebtedness he must pay the whole sum into court to be distributed by it among the parties entitled. So, on a question of this character, the local statute should be examined.

ASSIGNMENT OF FUTURE CLAIMS.—Assignments of future claims, as well as of existing claims, may be made, but there are in many States some special provisions of statute law in regard to assigning future wages. Such assignments must often be recorded, and there are certain other special statutory provisions in regard to them. The assignment of future debts is also subject to this qualification: The law does not allow the assignment of a future claim unless the contract or employment out of which the claim is expected to arise has already been made or is already in existence.

DISCHARGE OF CONTRACTS.—Contracts are discharged in much the same way as they are made. The simplest way of discharging a contract is by performing it. When both parties do exactly what they agreed to do the contract is discharged by performance. Where seals still retain their common law effect, it may be discharged without performance by agreement under seal that it shall be discharged, just as a contract may be made by an agreement under seal. The agreement under seal to discharge a contract is called a release. You may release any right that you have—a right for money, a right to have work done or any right. Just as contracts may be made either under seal or by an agreement with consideration, so they may be discharged not only by a release under seal but by an agreement for rescission of the contract. But this agreement must have consideration.

ILLUSTRATIONS.—Suppose A has promised to build a house and B has promised to pay $10,000 for it. Before anything has been done, A and B agree to call that contract off. This is a valid agreement for rescission, because each party agrees to give up something—one party to give up his right to have the house built, the other party to give up the right to get $10,000 pay. So an agreement between employer and employee that a contract shall be terminated before the time originally agreed has sufficient consideration—the employer gives up his right to the employee's services, the employee gives up his right for future pay. But compare with these this case: A owes B a thousand dollars; it is simply a debt. A and B agree to call that square. That agreement is of no validity, for here only one party agrees to give up anything. The creditor agrees to give up his thousand dollars, and he does not get any promised amount in return for it. But that obligation, that debt, could be satisfied if valid consideration were given for the surrender of the claim; and anything agreed upon, as a horse, or ten shares of stock, or anything else the parties agreed to, would be good consideration for the agreement to surrender the claim, so long as one did not get into the difficulty alluded to under the heading of consideration, of trying to surrender a right to a larger liquidated sum in consideration of the payment of a smaller sum of money.

SENDING A CHECK AS FULL PAYMENT.—It is very common for a debtor in making payment by check of his debt to seek to make the check operate as a receipt in full of all claims by the creditor against him. He may do this by writing on the check itself that it is "in full of all demands" or "in full payment" of a certain bill; or he may by a letter accompanying the check state that the check is sent as full satisfaction. The acceptance by the creditor of the check under either of these circumstances is an assent by him to the proposition stated on the check or in the accompanying letter, that the check is in full payment. Such an assent, however, does not necessarily prove that the debtor is discharged; consideration as well as mutual assent is essential to the validity of any agreement which is not under seal. Accordingly if the debt was a liquidated and undisputed one, and the check was for less than the amount due, the agreement of the creditor to take it in full satisfaction is not supported by sufficient consideration under principles previously considered. On the other hand, if the debt was an unliquidated one, or there was an honest dispute in regard to the amount due, the creditor's claim is fully satisfied.

RECEIPT IN FULL.—It may be said generally that though a receipt in full is often thought by business men to be a discharge irrespective of consideration, like a release, this is not true in most States. A receipt in full is good evidence, if payment has been made in full, that it has been so made; but where payment has not been made in full a receipt will not be effectual without consideration, as a release under seal would be.

RENUNCIATION OF OBLIGATION ON NEGOTIABLE INSTRUMENT.— There is one case where the law allows a party who has a right to surrender it without consideration. This is by virtue of the Negotiable Instruments Law, which provides that the holder of a note may discharge any party to it by a written renunciation of his claim. No particular form of words is necessary, but the renunciation must be in writing. No consideration is necessary.

ALTERATION OF WRITTEN CONTRACTS.—The alteration of a written contract in a material particular with fraudulent intent by a promisee in effect discharges the contract so far as he is concerned. He cannot enforce it either in its original form or its altered form, though the other party to the contract may enforce it against him. If the alteration is not material, the contract may be enforced even by the party who altered it whatever the motive of the alteration may have been. If the alteration is material but not fraudulently intended, that party is generally allowed to enforce the contract in its original form. No alteration by a third person affects the rights of a party to a contract. By material alteration is meant one which if given effect would alter the legal obligations of the parties to the contract. The rule of the Negotiable Instruments Law in regard to alteration of negotiable instruments, it should be observed, is somewhat more severe than that generally prevailing in regard to other contracts.

SUGGESTIONS FOR DRAFTING CONTRACTS.—While it is unwise to attempt the drafting of any contract at all complicated, without the services of an attorney, there are certain times when it may be necessary to act suddenly, and a few fundamental facts should be kept in mind. If you are called upon to draft a contract for two other people, the first requisite is to obtain as full information as possible from both parties as to the plans they have in mind. After obtaining this, the details should be arranged in writing, gone over carefully by the draftsman, and submitted to the parties for their approval. A most common mistake made by laymen is to fail to cover contingencies which are more or less likely to happen. For example, what effect would the death of either party have on the contract? This should be provided for. The careful draftsman, whether he be a layman or a lawyer, should draw contracts with the idea of making them so plain that litigation will not result. Contracts should always be drawn in duplicate, so that each party may have a copy, and it is well, if you are the draftsman, to keep a copy for yourself. It is not necessary to appear before a notary public unless you are dealing with a deed, or a similar formal document. If there is good consideration for the contract, no seal is necessary, but under some statutes, a sealed contract is good for a longer period of time, so that there is an added advantage in having the contract under seal.

QUASI CONTRACTS.—The term quasi contract is one which has appeared within the last thirty years. The law in this branch of contracts is still in the process of development and the field of quasi contracts is still not one of settled limits. For our purposes we confine ourselves to those obligations arising from "unjust enrichment," that is, the receipt by one person from another of a benefit, the retention of which is unjust. The term "enrichment" has recently been criticized by one of the ablest writers on this topic, as there are many cases where it is sufficient to show that the defendant has received something which he desired, although the question whether he is thereby enriched, is immaterial. In Vickery v. Ritchie, 202 Mass. 247, we find that where A renders services, and furnishes materials and supplies for the erection of a building for B under a supposed contract and the contract itself is invalid, B is under a supposed quasi contractual obligation to pay A for the services he has rendered and the material he has furnished, regardless of whether B's property is increased in value. We may state the point to be emphasized in quasi contract is the fact that the retention of the benefit received by the defendant would be unjust rather than "enrichment."

DISTINGUISHING CHARACTERISTICS.—There are four characteristics which distinguish quasi-contracts: 1. The obligations of quasi contracts are imposed by law without reference to the assent of the obligor. 2. They are imposed because of a special state of facts and in favor of a particular person and do not rest upon one at all times and in favor of all persons. 3. Although equitable in their origin they are enforced by a common law court. 4. They require that the obligee shall be compensated for the benefit which he has conferred upon the obligor and not for any loss suffered by the obligee.

APPLICATION OF THE PRINCIPLE.—The following are the more common illustrations of the application of the principles of quasi contracts. Where there has been a mistake, and hence the minds of the parties never really met, yet benefit has really been conferred; or, where the attempted contract cannot be enforced as a contract, because it did not comply with the statute, or was illegal, and yet one of the parties has received a benefit; or, where a benefit has been conferred under compulsion or duress.

MISTAKE.—Where parties have attempted to make a contract and a mistake of fact occurs, no contract results. The minds of the parties never really meet. Yet if benefits have been conferred, justice requires that the benefit should be returned, or compensation given, and this, in fact, is just what the law seeks to do when there has been such a mistake that upon the attempted contract itself no suit can be brought. The essentials of mistake, and the way in which a mistake usually arises, are:

(1) It would not be a mistake if a party had paid money when he had any reason to suppose it was not due. A recovery of money under such circumstances cannot be allowed.

(2) The payment must have been induced by mistake in order to allow the recovery. This rule prevents the recovery of money paid in settlement of a disputed matter; but it must be assumed that it was to the party's interest to make the payment. However, suppose that a compromise settlement has been made in the belief that certain facts were different from what they really were. Here the mistake would have induced the payment, and, hence, in such a situation a recovery will be allowed.

(3) The fact regarding which a mistake has been made must also be a material fact, and the fact must have been a part of the transaction itself, not collateral to it in any way. A mistake as to the value of an article purchased, for instance, is not a material fact.

(4) Ordinarily, money paid under mistake of law cannot be recovered, although it is against conscience for the defendant to retain it. A mistake as to the law of another State, however, is a mistake of fact, and money paid under such a mistake can be recovered.

(5) Where the party who mistakenly parted with the money did so because of his own negligence, and to allow a recovery would throw a loss on the other party, he cannot recover what he parted with. One party cannot make another suffer because of his own negligence. Where a party paid money under mistake, and the payee was negligent, the party paying may recover.

(6) When parties suppose they have made a contract, and money has been paid, or services rendered, under that supposed contract, but in fact there was no valid contract at all, or there was a mutual mistake as to a term, this money, or the value of the services, may be recovered.

(7) When money has been paid for the transfer of something by defendant, whether recovery will be allowed in case it should turn out that the defendant had no title, depends on the nature of transaction. If the defendant made a warranty that he had title, a recovery may be had. If, however, the defendant simply sold what he had, whether that was something or nothing, a recovery cannot be allowed unless, as is the law in some States, a vendor impliedly warrants his title by the fact of having possession.

(8) In the case of parties mistaking the existence of a subject matter of sale, if the understanding was that A was purchasing an existing thing, then he can recover the money paid if it should turn out that the thing was not in existence. But if he bought simply a chance, he cannot recover.

BENEFITS CONFERRED UNDER COLOR OF CONTRACT.—Aside from the cases of mistake, there are other grounds for allowing recovery under the principle of quasi contract. A group of these is made up of cases where there cannot be a recovery upon the contract itself, although the parties have come together and agreed without any mistake or misunderstanding, because of the absence of some essential necessary to create an enforceable contract obligation; yet a benefit has been conferred upon the one party who, but for the lack of that essential, would have been liable in an action upon the contract itself. Such cases arise largely where there has been a partial performance of an illegal contract, or of a contract unenforceable because of non-compliance with the statute of frauds, or where full performance is excused by impossibility. Some States also allow recovery on the theory of benefits conferred, where, after partial performance, a party defaults under circumstances not excusing default.

BENEFITS CONFERRED WITHOUT CONTRACT.—We next take up that class of relations where there has been an absence of distinct offer and acceptance, and yet a benefit has been conferred resulting in an unjust enrichment of the other party. If A confers benefit on B, though at B's request, it may be merely a gift. A cannot afterward change his mind and recover for that, as if there had been a contract. A may have paid B's debt in order to prevent a sale of his own property. He may then recover the amount so paid. For example, A left his property with B to have some repairs made. A third party recovered a judgment against B, and A's property was seized on an execution. A paid the judgment in order to release his own property. It was held that he might recover the money so paid from B, who should have paid the judgment. Or A may have paid B's debt because he was surety for B. He then may recover from B the amount so paid; or, if B had two sureties, A and C, and A paid the whole or more than his share, he could recover the share of such payment which C should have paid, on the principle of contribution that equality is equity. But A must have actually made the payment of more than his proportionate share.

CHAPTER IV

PRINCIPAL AND AGENT; MASTER AND SERVANT

THE IMPORTANCE OF AGENCY.—Now that we have finished our discussion of the general principles of contract law, it remains for us to apply these principles to the specific topics of commercial law. Of these, the law of agency is one of the most important. It is perfectly obvious that a man can be in only one locality at a given time. Under modern business conditions he may wish to perform acts in different places at the same time. When business men were first confronted with problems of this kind, the principles of the law of agency began to develop. They resorted to the simple expedient of having others represent them. If these representatives were properly instructed in their duties and faithful in discharging them, there was, of course, no reason why the will of the person who had appointed them was not as fully accomplished as if he had performed the act himself. The Latin maxim, "Qui facit per alium facit per se," that is, "He who acts through another, acts himself," is the basis of the law of agency. The growing importance of the law of agency is strikingly apparent in one branch of modern business. Fifty years ago, the great majority of business operations were conducted either by individuals or by partnerships. To-day, especially in conducting large business enterprises, corporations have replaced individuals and partnerships. Although (as we shall see later in the chapter on corporations) in law a corporation is deemed a separate, legal entity, distinct from the stockholders, in actual practice we know that there is no such distinct physical being as a corporation. It follows, therefore, that every act performed by a corporation must be performed through an agent. With the enormous increase in the number of corporations in the last twenty-five years, and that increase still continuing, we can see that the law of agency is a most important branch of commercial law and very closely connected with corporation law.

AGENCY DEFINED.—Merely for purposes of convenience, it may be best to divide the whole subject of agency into three branches: Principal and agent; master and servant; employer and independent contractor. The term "agency," when used in the broad sense, indicates a relation which exists where one person is employed to act for another. At the outset, we should keep in mind the distinctions between the agent, the servant, and the independent contractor. It is difficult to indicate these distinctions with absolute certainty by definition. An illustration, however, will show clearly what the difference is. I own an apartment house in New York, but as I am not in the city, except infrequently, I employ the real estate firm of Smith & Jones to manage the apartments and collect the rents. They are, of course, my agents, to act in the premises. I own an automobile and I employ a chauffeur to operate the car for me. He is my servant. I own a vacant lot in New York and on it plan to erect an office building. I employ the Smith Construction Company to erect the building. It is an independent contractor. What is the rule, then, to determine the distinction between these three persons? All three persons represent the principal, or the master, or the employer, but the line of distinction lies here: An agent is employed to bring the principal into new contractual obligations; a servant represents his master in the performance of ministerial, or mechanical acts or services, with no thought of bringing his master into new contractual relations with third persons. A person who is employed to perform ministerial or mechanical acts for another, as we have said, is a servant, but there are cases where the master retains no control or right of control of the means or methods by which such work is to be accomplished. In this latter case, the person performing the work is not a servant, but is an independent contractor.

HOW AGENCY MAY ARISE.—Although agency undoubtedly originated from the relationship of master and servant, and that relationship from the enforced service rendered by slaves to their master, to-day the law of agency in the broad sense is a contractual relationship. The agent or servant or independent contractor becomes such upon the express or implied request of the principal. Although agency may exist, in so far as third persons are concerned, without any formal contract between the principal and the agent, yet, in the great majority of cases, there is an actual contract between the parties to the relation. Compensation, although usually an element in the contract, is not necessarily a requisite. For instance, I may be liable for the negligent act of my son in running my automobile in connection with my business, although he is acting without any compensation. There are four methods by which the relationship of agency arises: (1) By contract; (2) by ratification; (3) by estoppel; (4) by necessity.

WHO IS OR MAY BE AN AGENT.—The law of agency, as between principal and agent, is simply an application of the general law of contracts, but as between third parties and the principal, or agent, new questions arise. The first question is, who is an agent and who is a principal? Any employer is a principal and any employee is an agent. The employer is a principal whether he employs the employee for a single act or whether he employs him for a period of time. Besides the ordinary cases that you will think of under the head of employer and employee, an officer of a corporation is an agent, the corporation being the principal. The president of a corporation is as much an agent as a clerk in the employ of the corporation. A partner is an agent—of the firm. These different kinds of agents are distinguished chiefly in the different scope of the authority which they possess.

DISABILITY.—In our discussion of contracts, we found that certain persons were under disability so far as making contracts was concerned. We mentioned the case of infants, married women, insane persons, and the like. The same disabilities do not exist in the law of agency, so far as the agent is concerned. Any person may act as an agent or servant. So infants, married women, slaves, and even lunatics, may be agents or servants whose acts will bind their principals. It has been held that even a dog may be an agent. As to who may be a principal, the ordinary rules of contracts, as we have discussed them, may be relied upon as giving the correct rule.

AGENCY BY CONTRACT.—Concerning agency which arises by contract, little need be said. A contract of agency must possess all of the elements of the ordinary contract, such as mutual assent, consideration, competent parties, legality of object, and in some cases, a particular form. The general principles of contract law as we have discussed them are applicable to this method of forming the agency relationship.

POWERS OF ATTORNEY.—In connection with the formation of agency by contract, special attention must be given to powers of attorney. A power of attorney must oftentimes be given in order to convince third persons that the agent really is an agent, with the powers which he claims to possess. A power of attorney is nothing more than a written statement that a particular person is the agent of another person, with the powers stated in the document. A power of attorney may be very broad, giving the agent very wide powers, or may be narrow, giving the agent or attorney power to do only a specific thing. Now, many powers, so far as the law itself is concerned, might just as well be oral as written, but you could not induce third parties to deal with the agent and believe that he had authority unless he showed as proof of it a power of attorney. That is why a power of attorney is generally given; not that the law requires it, but that the agent may have evidence of his agency which will satisfy third persons that he is really the agent. A corporation would not transfer stock without a written power presented to it; yet, if it chooses to run the risk, there would be nothing illegal in doing so. But it does not choose, and an attempt to compel it to transfer would be held unreasonable unless the authority of the person claiming to be empowered to transfer the stock were in writing and shown to it.

WITNESSED AND SEALED POWERS OF ATTORNEY.—A witness is not necessary on a power of attorney. A witness on a power of attorney has the same effect as on any other document where a witness is not absolutely required, and that is this: if the signature of a document is called in question and the signature is witnessed, the way which the law requires proof of the signature is by calling the witness to testify, and no other evidence is permissible until the witness is produced or his absence accounted for; that is, some adequate reason given and proved for not producing the particular man who witnessed the signature. For this very reason it is sometimes more difficult to prove a signature which is witnessed than one which is not. A signature which is not witnessed may be proved by anybody who has seen the person sign, or who is familiar with his signature, and who can testify that the signature in question is his. The object of a witness is to provide certain evidence that a signature is genuine. The testimony of a witness may be more convincing in case of a dispute than testimony of one who merely recognizes the signer's handwriting. A witnessed power of attorney might be, however, more difficult to prove if the power of attorney were contested than if it was not witnessed, that is, if the witness could not be found. On the other hand, if you had your witness within reach it would be easy to prove the signature by him. The whole matter of witnesses to deeds and other documents, where a witness is not absolutely required, may be thus summarized: it is a good thing to have a witness if the witness is a reliable, well-known person who can always or generally be reached. It is a bad thing to have a witness who is a servant or a person whom you may lose sight of after some time has elapsed. The question may also be asked: How does a power of attorney, when given under seal, compare with one without a seal? One is as good as the other, except that if it is desired that the attorney or agent shall execute any instrument under seal, such as a deed of real estate, the power must itself be under seal; but a power to do anything which does not require the execution of a sealed instrument is just as good without a seal as with one. This, however, is true; if the power contains an agreement by the principal not to revoke the power, this agreement will not be binding if there is neither seal nor consideration, but will be binding without consideration if under seal, in a State where seals still have their common-law effect. The principal will be able, it is true, even in such a case, to revoke the power, but he will commit a breach of contract if he does.

AGENCY BY RATIFICATION.—Where the assent of the principal to the act of the agent is given after the act is performed, it is in the nature of a ratification of the act, and is intended to clothe the act with the same qualities as if there had been a previous authority or appointment. Suppose, for example, A and B are acquaintances. Both are wealthy. A is a good judge of horses and knows B likes good horses. A discovers what he considers a good horse and buys it for B at a very low price. He tells B the next day what he has done and B goes to get the horse and tenders the price, but the dealer refuses to sell, as he has been offered a higher price. B has a cause of action for breach of contract, for by ratifying A's act, he has made a binding contract between himself and the dealer. Suppose in the same illustration, A had selected two horses for B, but when B saw them he decided to take only one of them. In that case, there would be no contract, for it is fundamental that a ratification, to be effective, must be of the whole contract, and not of a part. A ratification, once it is given, dates back to the original transaction and is irrevocable.

FORMATION OF AGENCY BY ESTOPPEL.—An estoppel may be said to arise where a person does some act which will preclude him from averring anything to the contrary. So, if one holds out another as his agent, he is estopped to repudiate the acts of such a person within the scope of his ostensible authority. In the case of Bradish v. Belknap, 41 Vt. 172, the facts were that for a long time prior to 1863, B was the agent of the defendants in selling stoves. This fact was generally known and was well known to the plaintiff. In 1863 B ceased to be the agent of the defendant, but continued to sell stoves, which he purchased of the defendants. No public notice of the termination of the agency was given, nor was the fact known to the plaintiff. B continued to represent himself as agent of the defendants and was in the habit of taking notes for stoves sold, payable to the defendants, and this was known to the defendants. The plaintiff, believing B to be the agent of the defendant, offered to buy a stove of him and pay him in pine lumber. To this B assented and the lumber was accordingly furnished to B and the defendants, together with other lumber which the plaintiff charged up to the defendants. The defendants later attempted to escape liability for the lumber furnished in excess of the value of the stove. The court, holding them liable, said: "B during all this time was perfectly poor and irresponsible, and this fact was known by both parties. B represented himself as the agent of the defendants, and the conduct of the defendants was such as to justify the plaintiff in regarding them as the principals; and we can hardly conceive it possible under the circumstances that the defendants did not understand that the plaintiff so regarded them. And to allow them now to deny the agency and thus defeat the plaintiff's right to recover for the balance of the lumber would be permitting them to perpetrate a palpable fraud on the plaintiff."

ESTOPPEL DEFINED.—This term will occur several times in the different topics of commercial law. An estoppel may be said to arise when a party by conduct or language has caused another reasonably to believe in the existence of a certain state of things and the other party acts on that belief, the first party is precluded from denying the existence of that state of things to any one who has justifiably relied on his language or conduct.

ILLUSTRATION.—There is a common saying in admiralty, that a seaman's claim for wages is nailed to the last plank of the vessel. So if boatswain John Silver is left unpaid by his vessel in London and he later finds the vessel in New York, although its ownership has entirely changed meanwhile, he may still file a libel for his wages and have the United States Marshal for the Southern District of New York seize the vessel. Suppose however you contemplate buying a vessel. You go on board with the present owner and while all the members of the crew are lined up on the main deck, you ask him in a voice loud enough to be heard by everybody whether there are any unpaid wage claims. He replies that everything is paid to date. The crew remain silent. You purchase the vessel and a few weeks later members of this same crew seek to collect from the vessel a wage claim of one year's standing. Their claims against the vessel or against you as owner are unenforcable. In other words, they are estopped because of their conduct when you purchased the vessel. If a person does not speak when he ought, at times the law will not allow him to speak when he wishes. Boatswain Silver had never done anything to preclude him from asserting his wage claim. His, therefore, is not a case of estoppel.

AGENCY BY NECESSITY.—The authority of the agent may be enlarged by some particular necessity or sudden emergency in which case it is the duty of the agent to act, even though he cannot receive the advice or directions of his principal. This method of creating the agency relationship is one upon which the courts are not agreed, and there is great conflict in the decisions. The case of Gwilliam v. Twist, (1895) 1 Q. B. 557, and 2 Q. B. 84, is a good illustration of how close the line may be drawn. The facts were that the driver of an omnibus belonging to defendants became intoxicated while on duty and was taken from his seat by a policeman. A man who happened to be standing near volunteered to drive the omnibus to the defendant's yard, and the driver and conductor acquiesced, the former warning him to drive carefully. The volunteer in negligently turning a corner ran over and injured the plaintiff, who brought action for damages against the defendants, owners of the omnibus. The trial court held, with considerable hesitation, that the defendants were liable for the injury, placing its decision upon the ground of agency by necessity; but the court of appeal reversed the decision on the ground that the necessity did not sufficiently appear, since the defendants might have been communicated with, and left open the question whether, if there had been an actual necessity, the defendants would have been liable.

RIGHT OF PRINCIPAL TO DILIGENT AND SKILLFUL SERVICE.—Let us consider, first, the rights of the principal and agent as between one another. The rights which the principal has against the agent are, first, a right to have the employee render reasonably diligent and skillful service. The amount of skill which the employer can fairly demand from his agent depends on the character of the contract between the two and on the circumstances justifying the principal in expecting a greater or less degree of skill. When a man employs an expert accountant to act for him he has a right to expect greater skill than if he were employing an ordinary bookkeeper. It depends on the character of the work and of the man employed. The amount of compensation paid to the employee may also have a bearing on the amount of skill the employer has a right to expect.

RIGHT OF PRINCIPAL THAT AGENT SHALL NOT EXCEED HIS AUTHORITY.—The second right that a principal has is to demand from his agent that the agent shall act in obedience to instructions and only within the limits of his authority. These limits may be fixed expressly in the contract between principal and agent, or they may be left wholly to implication from the nature of the employment. Perhaps more commonly they are partly fixed by express agreement and partly fixed by natural implications which arise from the nature of the employment.

RIGHT OF PRINCIPAL TO ACCOUNTING.—Thirdly, the principal has a right in financial dealings with his agent, or in regard to financial dealings of the agent with third persons, to demand an account from his agent. It is not enough that the agent actually expend money intrusted to him correctly; he must furnish a correct account of expenses and of collections.

RIGHT OF PRINCIPAL TO FIDELITY.—Finally, the agent is under a duty of fidelity or loyalty to his principal. The principal is entitled to demand that the agent, unless the contrary is agreed, shall make the employment or agency his sole interest in regard to that particular thing. Of course, in many agencies the agent is undertaking a great deal of outside business besides the particular agency in question, and he has a right so to do so long as the principal has not engaged his whole time, and so long as one agency does not interfere with another. But that last is an important point. An agent who undertakes one task for one principal which occupies only one-tenth of his time cannot take another employment which is inconsistent with that. An agent to sell a particular kind of goods for one principal, even though his agency is not expected to take the agent's whole time, cannot undertake an agency for a competing principal. The two things are inconsistent, and the agent would be disloyal if he accepted.

SIDE COMPENSATION.—Then, again, the agent must not get what may be called "side compensation" of any sort. His whole compensation as agent must be what is due him directly from the principal under the agreement. For instance, if a buyer for a department store gets paid a commission by a firm from which he buys goods, that is a side commission which the buyer as an agent has no right to take; and so strict is the law, that if an agent does take any such extra compensation the principal has a right to recover it from him. Of course, if the principal agrees to side compensation, it is all right for the agent to take it; when the principal agrees to it, it ceases to be what we have called side compensation and becomes part of the agent's direct compensation to which he is entitled under his bargain with his principal.

ACTING AS AGENT FOR BOTH PARTIES.—One of the most common difficulties that agents get into in regard to this requirement of fidelity, and sometimes with entirely good faith, is undertaking to act as agent for both parties. That cannot be done unless each party especially agrees that the agent may act for the adverse party. An attorney-at-law cannot represent two sides of a case. A real estate broker cannot represent buyer and seller, and a stock broker cannot represent buyer and seller. Stock brokers have one practice which perhaps may seem to infringe this rule. A customer comes into a broker's office and says he wants to buy 100 shares of New York Central. About the same time another customer comes in and says he wants to sell 100 shares of New York Central. Now, must a broker go on the exchange and make a purchase for one customer and then a sale for the other, or may he, so to speak, negotiate through himself a sale for the customer who wants to buy from the one who wants to sell? What he frequently does, in fact, is this: He buys and sells from himself, but publicly, giving other brokers the chance to buy or sell if they wish. The broker, according to the rules of the New York Stock Exchange, cannot execute this transaction secretly in his office, but must offer the securities in question on the exchange, and the purchase and sale must be recorded on the ticker. If the bidding and asking prices are more than an eighth apart, he may offer the New York Central at a price midway between the bidding and asking quotations and buy it himself and charge each customer a commission, but he must actually make the offer or bid aloud on the floor. The broker is technically acting for both parties, but he is not fixing the price. He makes an open bid on the exchange, and it may be that would save the transaction.

AGENT'S RIGHT TO COMPENSATION.—What are the rights of the agent against the principal? They are two. First, a right to compensation; that is, a right to the pay that has been agreed upon, or, if no pay was agreed upon but it was understood that there should be some compensation, then a right to reasonable compensation. It is perfectly possible to have an agency without compensation. Frequently one man agrees to act for another without pay, and an agent who is acting without compensation, so long as he acts as agent, is bound to the same obligations to his principal as if he were receiving compensation, only he can withdraw from his agency whenever he sees fit since he is not paid for it. But unless circumstances show that an agency was understood to be without compensation, it would be implied that reasonable compensation was to be paid to the agent for his services.

AGENT'S RIGHT TO REIMBURSEMENT.—The other right of the agent is the right to reimbursement and indemnity. As the agent is acting for the principal, the principal ought to pay all the bills of whatever kind incurred, so long as the agent is acting rightfully within his authority, and the principal is bound to pay all such bills. This obligation of the principal to pay all the bills of the agency means not simply that he must pay actual expenses, but that if liabilities of any kind arise by reason of third persons suing the agent or holding him liable, if the action of the agent was within his authority, the principal must indemnify against any loss.

PRINCIPAL BOUND TO THIRD PERSONS BY AUTHORIZED ACTS OF AGENT.—Now let us turn from the rights of principal and agent as between one another to the rights of third persons. When do third persons get rights against the principal? In the first place, whenever the agent, acting in accordance with his authority, enters into a transaction with a third person on behalf of the principal, the principal is bound to the third person to just the same extent as if he himself had entered into the transaction; but it is not only in cases where express authority is given to the agent that this principle applies.

IMPLIED AUTHORITY OF AGENT.—In many cases the authority given an agent is not expressly stated. One has to rely on the general course of business and on the nature of the employment to determine the extent of the agent's authority. A third person deals with a cashier of a bank, or deals with the paying teller, or he deals with the president; now whether the bank is bound by that dealing depends on what is by general custom, or course of business, the authority of a cashier or a paying teller or a president. If cashiers or paying tellers or presidents generally have certain authority, then it is a fair assumption that this particular officer has such authority.

AUTHORITY TO DO PARTICULAR ACTS.—An agent to sell has generally no authority to make a sale on credit or to receive anything but money; he cannot barter or exchange the property even in part, nor pledge or dispose of the property to be sold in payment of his own debts. For the sale of land an agent's authority ought always to be under seal, and the provisions contained in this power of attorney will be strictly construed. In a sale of personal property, an agent has implied authority to do whatever is usual and necessary in such transactions. He may receive payment if he has possession of the goods, but not otherwise, and warrant the quality, if such goods are customarily sold with a warranty by agents. He cannot sell on credit unless such is the custom, as in the case of commission merchants, nor pledge or mortgage the goods. The agent may not buy on credit unless so authorized, or it is the custom of the trade; but a principal's direction to purchase, without supplying the agent with funds, will imply authority to purchase on credit. The agent must purchase precisely as directed. An agent to manage has an authority co-extensive in scope with the business, and possesses the same power and authority as the principal, so far as management goes, but the agent may not sell or dispose of a business, nor mortgage the property used in carrying it on, nor engage in new and different enterprises. Public agents, i. e., public officers, cannot involve their principals, the municipal corporations whose officers they are, in contract liabilities with third parties unless actually authorized to do the act in question; and all persons dealing with them must inform themselves of the scope of their legal powers.

APPARENT AUTHORITY OF AGENT.—But it is not only in cases where the agent is expressly authorized, or authorized by such implication as we have just alluded to, that the principal is bound. There is the further case where the agent has apparent authority, although, as a matter of fact, he has no authority. Take the case of a cashier certifying a check. We will suppose that cashiers, generally, have authority to certify checks. With most cashiers that would be what we have called an implied authority, as it arises from the general nature of their positions though nothing was ever said about it by the bank directors. But suppose in a particular bank it was a rule of the bank, expressly stated and voted by the directors, that the cashier should not have power to certify checks. Now, no one can say that his power here is either express or implied; it is certainly not express, and any implication that might otherwise arise from his position is negatived by the express vote of the directors, and yet if that cashier should certify a check to any person ignorant of this limitation on his authority the bank would be bound by the certification because the cashier has apparent authority. He looks to the world as if he had authority, and seems to the public like any other cashier. Most of the difficult cases in agency, so far as liability of the principal to third persons is concerned, relate to this matter of apparent authority.

ILLUSTRATIONS.—Compare the following case with the case of the cashier above alluded to: A man who is giving some support financially to a book dealer writes a note in which he says, "I authorize A B to buy a stock of books not exceeding, at any one time, $5,000." The book dealer shows that written authority to persons from whom he wishes to buy books. They sell him books, and, unknown to the last person who thus sells him books, he has just before bought a quantity which makes the total largely exceed $5,000. Is the principal liable to the persons who last sold books to the dealer? The answer is no. And what is the difference between that case and the cashier case? In the book case the last seller saw the paper giving authority to the book dealer to purchase. He had no reason to know that the day before a large quantity of books had been purchased. He acted in entire good faith and the deception was natural. Still, the employer, or the writer of the letter, has done nothing here to make the last seller suppose that $5,000 worth of books had not already been bought, nor does the course of business justify the last seller in supposing they might not already have been bought. It was a hard question for him to find out, but on the face of the letter it was evident that any one who dealt with the bookseller might have to determine this question or rely at his peril on the bookseller's word. Here is another case: a town treasurer was authorized to borrow a certain sum of money. He gets a certified copy of the vote and goes to one bank and borrows the money, and goes to another bank with that same certified copy of the vote and borrows the money over again. Is the town liable to the second bank? No; on the face of the paper there was but one loan to the town authorized, and any one who lends the money must at his peril find out whether a loan has already been made. When we say, therefore, that a principal is bound if his agent had apparent authority, we do not mean that whenever a third person is deceived into the belief that the agent has authority, the principal is bound. Quite to the contrary, the principal must have in some way been the cause of that deception; he must have caused it either by some express representations, or he must have caused it by putting a man in a place where the general course of business would induce the public to believe the agent had greater powers than he had.

GENERAL AND SPECIAL AGENTS.—It is much easier to find a case of apparent authority, which will bind the principal, if the agent is a general agent than if he is a special agent. A special agent is an agent authorized to do one act, as this town treasurer was authorized to make one loan. The cashier is a general agent, authorized to do any of the great variety of acts which cashiers ordinarily do, and if the directors vote to take away one of the normal powers of the cashier, they must make the limitation public or the bank will be bound by the cashier's act.

UNDISCLOSED PRINCIPAL.—Not only may the third person hold the principal liable in cases where the agent purports to act for the principal, but also in cases where the agent does not disclose his principal at all and purports to act as a principal himself, so long as it is true that the agent really was acting in the principal's business. Suppose a selling agent for a manufactory enters into a contract for the sale of goods produced in the manufactory. The selling agent, we will further suppose, contracts—as selling agents often do—in his own name; but he contracts in regard to the sale of the product of the principal, the manufacturer, and on his behalf. Now, assume that this contract of the sales agent was authorized; the third person may sue the manufacturing company, though he did not know of the existence of the manufactory at the time he entered into the contract, and supposed he was contracting simply with the agent. As it is phrased in law, an undisclosed principal is liable, and conversely, the undisclosed principal may sue on this contract made by the sales agent.

RATIFICATION.—If an agent acts beyond his authority, the principal, if he chooses, may ratify the acts of the agent. Occasionally in an emergency it becomes necessary for an agent who has his principal's interest at heart to take a chance and act beyond the authority given him. In such a case, if the principal ratifies it, it is all right, both as far as the agent is concerned, and as far as the third person is concerned; but, of course, the principal is under no legal obligation to ratify.

RIGHTS OF PRINCIPAL AGAINST THIRD PERSONS.—Now, the right of the principal against the third person is the converse of the right of the third person against the principal, of which we have been speaking. Generally when a transaction is of such a sort that the third person would have a right of action against the principal, if the principal fails to do as he agreed, the principal will have a right of action against the third person if the latter breaks his agreement.

PRINCIPAL IS LIABLE FOR TORTS OF AGENT.—Not only is the principal liable for the contracts of his agent, but he is also liable for any tort which an agent may commit, so long as he is acting in the course of his business. Of course, accident cases present the commonest type of that sort of liability. A street railway is liable for the results of its motor-man's neglect, so long as the motorman was running the car. If the motorman got off the car on a frolic of his own, the street railway would not be liable for anything he might do then. The same principle may be found in other cases than accident cases. Suppose officers of a corporation wrongfully overissue stock. If those officers were the officers authorized to issue stock, and, therefore, were acting in the general course of their business, the corporation would be liable for that tortious act in overissuing stock.

AUTHORITY MAY GENERALLY BE ORAL AS WELL AS WRITTEN.—The authority given by a principal to an agent may in general be oral as well as written; it is just as good. There are, however, a few exceptions to that. In the first place, an authority given to an agent to execute an instrument under seal must itself be not only written but under seal. An oral or a written authority, if not under seal, given to an agent to convey land, which must be conveyed by a sealed deed, would not enable the agent to make a valid deed. Where the effect of seals is abolished this principle is of course no longer applicable. Generally an agent orally authorized to make a contract to buy or sell land may bind his principal by entering into such a contract. The contract the agent enters into, must, because of the Statute of Frauds, be in writing, and signed, but the agent's authority generally need not be written. In some States, however, written authority is required by statutes.

PROXIES.—A proxy is simply a written power of attorney to an agent, authorizing him to vote for a stockholder, and there, too, a corporation would be held justified in refusing to recognize any proxy that was not in writing, or any agent who did not have a written proxy even though proxies were not required to be in writing.

LIABILITY OF AGENT TO THIRD PERSONS.—How about the rights and duties of the agent as against the outside world? The agent is liable to a third person if he commits a tort. It does not make any difference that the principal is also liable, the agent is liable too. The third person may sue either the principal or agent as he prefers; he cannot get compensation for his injury more than once, but he can get that either from the principal or agent, whichever is more convenient. The third person may hold the agent liable if the agent contracts for an undisclosed principal. In the case of the sales agent referred to a moment ago, where the agent was really acting as agent for a manufacturer but did not say so, the third person might sue the manufacturer on the contract; but he might sue the agent, and if the agent was held liable the agent would have to seek reimbursement from the principal.

AGENT WARRANTS HIS AUTHORITY.—An agent is liable in one other case to the third person with whom he deals. If the agent did not have authority to do what he purported to do, the third person can sue him, though the third person could not sue the principal in this case, since the agent was exceeding his authority. An agent is said to warrant his authority to third persons with whom he does business.

AGENT CANNOT DELEGATE AUTHORITY.—An important rule in agency is that an agent cannot delegate his authority. If A is appointed to do certain work, A must do it himself, and cannot empower B to do it if it proves inconvenient to do it himself. There are three exceptions to this rule. The first is that if he is given express permission to delegate his authority, he may do so, and, of course, if the principal should ratify an unpermitted delegation of authority, the ratification would here, as always, serve as well as original authority. The second case is where the usage of business is such that the principal must be presumed to have understood that there was to be a delegation, or partial delegation, of authority, and in such a case, though the principal has not expressly authorized delegation, he will be treated as if he had authorized it by virtue of business usage. The third case where delegation is authorized is in regard to what are called ministerial or mechanical acts, that is, acts which involve no exercise of judgment or skill. The principal is entitled to the agent's judgment and skill, but if there are parts of the work that do not require skill and that, from their nature, any ordinary clerical assistant can do, then such acts may be delegated.

TERMINATION OF AGENCY BY ACT OF PARTIES.—The parties may have agreed in their contract that it should terminate at a certain time or on the happening of a certain event. The arrival of that time or the happening of the event would of course end the relation as between them. It would not so operate as between principal and third parties, however, unless the third parties were informed. So, performance of the purpose for which the relation was created terminates the relation as between principal and agent. The parties may make a subsequent agreement to terminate the relation, and such an agreement would be good, the abandonment of the rights of each party created by the original contract being a sufficient consideration for the promise of each to surrender his own rights.

REVOCATION.—Except in the case of irrevocable agency noted below, the principal may revoke at any time the agent's authority as to matters not already executed. Any other rule would enslave the principal to his agent by forcing him, at the agent's will, and against his own consent, into contracts with third parties. But, while the principal has this right, the exercise of it may subject him to liability to his agent. If the contract of employment is for a definite time, and the principal, without cause, revokes the agent's authority before that time arrives, the principal is liable to the agent for breach of contract; if no time is fixed for the termination of the agency, it is an agency at will, and the principal, with or without cause, may revoke at any time without incurring liability to his agent. The acts which will amount to a revocation by the principal are various. For instance, if an agent has exclusive authority to represent the principal, the appointment of another agent would amount to a revocation. As to making the revocation effective, a revocation operates on the agent from the time he has notice of it. It is effective as to third parties only when notice is given to those who have dealt with the agent that the agent's authority is revoked. Without such notice the principal does not escape liability to third persons by reason of further acts on his agent's part. Where an agent is appointed in a particular business, parties dealing with him in that business have a right to rely upon the continuance of his authority until in some way informed of its revocation. This notice must be actual to those who have dealt with the agent, and general, as by publication in newspapers, where persons have not before dealt with the agent.

RENUNCIATION.—The agent may renounce his employment at any time, but if he contracted to serve for a certain time, and renounce before that time arrives, he is liable to the principal for breach of contract, unless he has ground for renunciation, such as the principal's breach of faith with him. The sickness of the agent is a ground for renouncing the relation, even though the sickness be caused by his own negligence or wrong. The principal should inform third persons of the agent's renunciation if he would fully protect himself against further acts of the agent.

TERMINATION OF AGENCY BY OPERATION OF LAW.—As in the case of ordinary contracts, a contract of agency may be terminated by the rules of law upon the happening of certain events. Thus, the destruction of the subject-matter of the agency terminates the relation, if the parties contemplated the continued existence of the subject-matter as the foundation for what was to be done. A change in the law, as the enactment of a statute declaring illegal agencies of a certain nature, that previously had been legal, terminates the relation. So also certain changes affecting the parties to the relation—i. e., the principal or the agent—effect a termination. The death of the principal brings the relation to an end, and this is so although the agent had no notice of it and subsequently dealt on behalf of his principal with third persons; such contracts do not bind the principal's estate. The death of the agent necessarily ends the relation. The occurrence of the principal's insanity terminates the relation, and a judicial finding of insanity is notice to all; but without notice of the insanity third persons who deal with the agent in good faith are protected. The bankruptcy of the principal terminates the relation as to all matters affected by the bankruptcy. Impossibility to continue the relation brought about by restraint of law terminates the relation.

IRREVOCABLE AGENCIES.—An agency to do an act touching a thing in which the agent has an interest, or in which he is subject to an obligation, cannot be terminated by act of the principal alone. The principal cannot terminate the relation so as to leave the agent under obligations to third persons, thereby shifting his obligations upon the agent; nor can he do so when the agent has an interest in the subject-matter of the agency. It is difficult to state concisely what will constitute such an interest that the principal cannot terminate the relation, but it may be said to be some ownership or right in the matter dealt with, such that the agent may deal with it in his own name, and not a mere benefit to be obtained from the performance of the contract of agency, as a commission to be realized from sales. Possession of personal property with the right to sell, with authority to apply the proceeds to a debt due from the principal to the agent, is sometimes held to constitute an agency coupled with an interest such that the principal may not revoke it; on the other hand, an interest arising from commissions or the proceeds of a transaction, is not an interest which will prevent revocation. The courts carefully examine agencies claimed to be irrevocable because coupled with an interest, and are inclined to rule against them.

MASTER AND SERVANT.—As we have said, the function of the servant is to perform ministerial or mechanical acts for the master. The chief subject-matter under the law of principal and agent is contracts, while the chief subject-matter of the law of master and servant is tort. The servant, in performing acts for his master, may, inadvertently or wilfully, cause injury to a third person or to the property of a third person. The question arises: What is the master's responsibility? We shall consider this from two standpoints; the relationship of the master and servant, inter se (between themselves), and the relationship of the master and servant as to the outside world. For example: the driver of a delivery truck, operated by Lord & Taylor, negligently runs over a pedestrian. The truck was going at the rate of twenty-five miles an hour, although the instructions issued by Lord & Taylor to all their servants is not to run cars more than fifteen miles per hour in the congested parts of New York City. Is Lord & Taylor liable to the pedestrian? This question involves the relationship of master and servant as to outside parties. The same servant, while operating the delivery truck for Lord & Taylor is run into, negligently, by a delivery truck operated by R. H. Macy & Co. Is the master, Lord & Taylor, responsible to its servant for the injury which he suffers as the result of the collision? This question involves the relationship of master and servant inter se. We shall consider this latter relationship first.

THE COMMON LAW GOVERNING THE RELATIONSHIP OF MASTER AND SERVANT INTER SE.—What is the liability of the master towards the servant if the servant is injured? We shall see in the chapter on torts that a tort is defined to be a breach of duty imposed by law for which a suit for damages may be maintained. Hence it follows that the master's liability in tort flows from a breach of duty owed by him to his servant. If there is no legal duty, correspondingly there is no legal liability. These legal duties which the common law developed over a long period of years may be summed up as follows: (1) To provide a reasonably safe place for the servant to work. (2) To provide reasonably safe, suitable, and sufficient tools and appliances with which the servant is to perform his work. (3) To provide reasonably careful and competent fellow workmen and in sufficient number for the work in hand. (4) To warn the servant of any unusual dangers connected with the work. (5) Generally so to conduct the work as not to expose the servant to dangers which could be avoided by the exercise of reasonable diligence. From the servant's standpoint, it was said that he assumed the ordinary risks inherent to the kind of business in which he was employed. These rules of the common law were the outgrowth of conditions surrounding the small shop and involving the use of simple or no machinery. Under modern industrial conditions they have proved wholly inadequate. We have been unduly conservative in recognizing this. Strangely enough the Workmen's Compensation Acts, with which we are now so familiar, had their origin in Germany in 1884. Nearly all the countries of continental Europe recognized the situation about thirty years ago, and England in 1897, and the United States within the last few years.

THE OBJECTION OF THE COMMON LAW THEORY.—Under the old theory, if the master had observed the duties which we have mentioned, he had performed his whole obligation to his own servant; thus, if two fellow workmen were working on the twentieth story of a new steel skyscraper being erected by the Institute Construction Co., and through the carelessness of servant A, servant B was precipitated to the street and killed, there would be no recovery on the part of the estate of the deceased servant, although he may have left a wife and several children dependent wholly upon him for support. Even admitting that the Institute Construction Co. had exercised due care in selecting competent fellow servants for the deceased to work with, and had, therefore, performed all of its obligations on this score, nevertheless, it is better, from the standpoint of society, that the wife and children of servant B should receive fair compensation rather than be thrown upon the mercy of the public. The great object of the Workmen's Compensation Act is to shift the burden of such economic waste from the employer to the industry, in order that it may ultimately be borne by the consumer as a part of the necessary cost of construction and production. Thus we are asking the master to assume a greater financial responsibility for injuries to his servant under this new theory than he has assumed heretofore. This can be taken care of by the increased price he charges for his work and this in turn will ultimately pass the added burden to the community at large.

ILLUSTRATION.—Again, even if the servant did have a cause of action against his master, because of the master's failure to observe the common law requirements we have mentioned, nevertheless, the expense of litigation and the interminable delays connected with it, amounting at times to two or three years before the case was finally disposed of by the court of last resort, all tended to make litigation for the servant all but impossible. He would ordinarily have no money with which to begin this long litigation, and would be obliged to retain the services of a lawyer, who would take the case on a contingent fee basis, and often take from the workman, should the decision finally be in his favor, a third, a half, or even a greater portion of the amount that he recovers. Perhaps this was no greater compensation than the lawyer was entitled to because of the labor involved and the prospect of no pay if he lost the case, but regardless of this it was hard on the client. The Supreme Court of Washington, in the case of Stertz v. The Industrial Insurance Commission, 91 Wash. 588, has summed up the objections against the whole system as follows: "Both had suffered under the old system, the employers by heavy judgments of which half was opposing lawyers' booty, the workmen through the old defenses or exhaustion in wasteful litigation. Both wanted peace. The master in exchange for limited liability was willing to pay on some claims in future where in the past there had been no liability at all. The servant was willing not only to give up trial by jury but to accept far less than he had often won in court, provided he was sure to get the small sum without having to fight for it.... To win only after litigation, to collect only after the employment of lawyers, to receive the sum only after months or years of delay, was to the comparatively indigent claimant little better than to get nothing. The workmen wanted a system entirely new. It is but fair to admit that they had become impatient with the courts of law. They knew, and both economists and progressive jurists were pointing out, what is now generally conceded, that two generations ought never to have suffered from the baleful judgments of Abinger and Shaw."

WORKMEN'S COMPENSATION ACT.—To meet the objections we have just mentioned, the workmen's compensation act principle was developed on the continent of Europe. Practically all of continental Europe had placed laws of this character on its statute books before the end of the nineteenth century; in 1906 England passed similar legislation, and within the last few years, we have adopted the same principles. With the exception of a few Southern States, every State and territory of the United States has a Workmen's Compensation Act. We cannot consider these acts in detail. The principle underlying them is the same throughout the country. They are designed to compensate servants for "accidents" "arising out of," and "during the course of" their employment, and this, regardless of whether the servant was at fault or not. The whole theory of the common law had been that the master must be at fault in order that the servant may recover. The new theory is that the community at large can better stand the loss suffered by a servant than the individual servant. For example: a steel girder falls upon a workman engaged in structural steel work, through no fault on his part and also through no fault on the part of his employer. Under the common law, he would have to stand the loss himself. Under the Workmen's Compensation Act, such an event is an "accident"; it "arose out of" and "in the course of" his employment. Therefore, he is entitled to a fixed compensation, and he secures it almost immediately through a workmen's compensation bureau, or whatever body the act of the particular State creates for the purpose of settling such matters. This is a burden on the employer, it is true; he was in no way to blame. Neither was the workman. The employer may protect himself against the claims of his workmen by insurance under a plan provided by the State law, or if the State law does not provide for it, by arrangements with private companies the same as any other accident insurance is obtained, and by figuring his cost upon the particular job, he can charge as a part of his operating expense, the cost of his insurance and include that in his charge for work. The loss suffered by the individual workmen is then passed to the community at large. From an economical and sociological standpoint, this situation is undoubtedly better than that existing under the theory of the common law.

THE INTERPRETATION OF WORKMEN'S COMPENSATION ACTS.—Although these acts are comparatively new in this country, there has been a great amount of litigation, and it is not practical to enter into a discussion of all the close questions which are raised in interpreting such acts. A vast amount of the litigation has been concerned with the interpretation of the three expressions, common to almost all the acts, "accident" "arising out of" and "during the course of." While the courts have shown a broad-minded spirit in interpreting these expressions, it is undoubtedly true that some decisions will suggest further legislation in order to correct certain evils which exist at the present time. For example, in defining the term "accident," the leading English case said: "The expression 'accident' is used in the public and ordinary sense of the word, as denoting an unlooked-for event which is not expected or designed." And Judge Siebecker of Wisconsin says "accidental" contemplates "an event not within one's foresight and expectation, resulting in a mishap causing injury to the employee," and Mr. Justice Pound of New York says that the statute contemplates injuries "not expected or designed by the workman himself." To illustrate: A window-dresser is decorating the window in Woolworth's. He swallows a pin. This is an "accident" within the contemplation of the act, and entitles him to recovery. Again, a workman is employed in a white-lead factory. During his six months period of service in the factory, he contracts tuberculosis. This is not an "accident" because you must be able to put your finger upon a definite time when the unlooked-for event happened. This leads us to the general statement that Workmen's Compensation Acts in this country, as at present drawn, do not generally cover occupational diseases. Separate legislation is undoubtedly desirable to extend the principle in such cases, for if it is sound that the window-dresser in Woolworth's should recover, it should be equally sound that the workman who contracted tuberculosis should recover. Again, the other two expressions "arising out of," and "during the course of" have caused much litigation. Perhaps the most satisfactory statement about these expressions is in the leading Massachusetts case, In re McNicol, 215 Mass. 497. Here the court says: "The injury must both arise 'out of' and also be received 'in the course of' the employment. Neither alone is enough. It is not easy * * * to give a comprehensive definition of these words. * * * An injury is received 'in the course of' the employment when it comes while the workman is doing the duty which he is employed to perform. It 'arises out of' the employment, when there is * * * a causal connection between the conditions under which the work is required to be performed and the resulting injury. * * * If the injury can be seen * * * to have been contemplated by a reasonable person familiar with the whole situation, * * * then it arises 'out of' the employment. * * * The causative danger must be peculiar to the work and not common to the neighborhood. * * * It need not have been foreseen or expected, but after the event it must appear to have had its origin in a risk connected with the employment, and to have flowed from that source as a rational consequence." An illustration will show how these phrases are applied. The janitor of a building is alone in the building. An old enemy who has not seen him for years, learns his whereabouts, comes into the building, shoots him in the leg, causing him to have it amputated. Is the master liable? It is an "accident," and clearly it arose "during the course of" employment, but did it arise "out of" his employment? Manifestly not. The guilty party would have shot the man had he met him in Central Park, or any other place. It was purely personal vengeance on his part which caused the act. The night watchman in a bank is shot by a robber at night in the bank, while on duty. May he recover from his master? Clearly he can. It is an "accident." It arose "during the course of" his employment, it arose "out of" his employment also, because the robber would not have shot him were he not in the bank as a watchman, standing between the robber and the accomplishment of his purpose, the securing of money from the bank.

THE RELATIONSHIP OF MASTER AND SERVANT AS RELATING TO OUTSIDE PARTIES.—If the relationship of master and servant exists, the question arises, is the master responsible for the torts committed by his servant, resulting in injury to third parties? It is, of course, essential that the wrongdoer must be the defendant's servant. It does not follow that a wrongdoer is the defendant's servant simply because of a certain relationship, as that of parent and child, husband and wife, or employer and employee. Within the last few years, a great number of automobile cases have been decided by the courts, and they are commonly spoken of as the "family automobile cases." To illustrate: I own a car which is used by the various members of my family. My son, while running the car, for his own pleasure, negligently runs over some one. Am I responsible? Granting the relationship of parent and child, that would not constitute, per se (of itself), the relationship of master and servant. The injured man would have to show more than I have indicated in order to entitle him to recover for my son's negligence. Were members of my family in the car, being taken out for a ride by my son, I would be liable. Again, my wife, in discharging a servant, assaults her. Should the mere fact of the relationship of husband and wife make me liable on the theory of master and servant? Clearly not. Again, I employ John Smith as my chauffeur. I never operate my car on Sunday. John Smith, who lives in the town adjoining mine, is moving, and asks if he may borrow my car over Sunday to assist in the moving operations. While using the car for that purpose, he negligently runs over some one. Am I liable? Clearly not, for, although the relationship of master and servant exists between me and my servant at the time he did the injury, he was not acting for me as a servant. What is the rule to be applied to answer such questions?

THE SERVANT MUST BE ENGAGED IN HIS MASTER'S BUSINESS.—It is clear from the foregoing that, in order to make the master liable, the servant must be engaged in his master's business, and he must be acting within the scope of his employment. The New York case of Rounds v. The Delaware, etc., Railroad, 64 N. Y. 129, states the general rule: "For the acts of the servant, within the general scope of his employment, while engaged in his master's business, and done with a view to the furtherance of that business and the master's interest, the master will be responsible whether the act be done negligently, wantonly, or even wilfully." The Court of Errors and Appeals of New Jersey recently said in Holler v. Sanford Ross, 68 N. J. Law, 324: "The Supreme Court of Connecticut states the rule applicable to this class of cases about as clearly as it can be done, when it says: 'For all acts done by a servant in obedience to the express orders or direction of the master, or in the execution of the master's business, within the scope of his employment, and for acts in any sense warranted by the express or implied authority conferred upon him, considering the nature of the service required, the instructions given and the circumstances under which the act is done, the master is responsible; for acts which are not within these conditions, the servant alone is responsible.'"

LIABILITY OF A PUBLIC AGENCY FOR THE NEGLIGENT ACTS OF ITS AGENTS.—It is an old saying that "the King can do no wrong." This principle of the English common law we have applied in this country, and the Federal Government cannot be sued unless it gives its consent. While the Court of Claims has been established, Congress has generally provided that suits may be brought against the Federal Government only in contract actions, and not in tort actions, so that ordinarily, if a person is injured through the negligence of an employee of the Federal Government, he may not recover against that Government. Thus, my only remedy in case of an injury, received through the negligent operation of an elevator in a post-office building owned by the Government, would be the passing of special legislation by Congress compensating me. I would have no right to sue the United States for such injury. The same general principles are applied to the State governments. In regard to cities, the rule may be generally stated to be that a municipality is not liable for the negligence of its servants in those departments operated by the municipality in its governmental activities, as distinguished from its administrative activities, in which case it is liable. Thus, a city is not responsible for the negligence of its policemen or its firemen, although injury results from their negligence, these departments being examples of governmental activities of a municipality, while the city would be liable, generally, for the negligence of the employees of its water department, this being an illustration of its administrative activities. It is also generally held that public charities, such as hospitals, and the like, are not liable for torts committed by their servants, provided they have used reasonable care in the selection of their servants.

INDEPENDENT CONTRACTORS.—A distinction must be made between one whom we call an independent contractor and a master. When A desires a particular piece of work done, he has two options as to doing it. He may either hire a workman to do it, retaining control of the workman, and telling him how he shall do it, or he may let the work by contract, simply stipulating that it shall be done in accordance with plans and specifications which his architect has drawn up. He retains no control over the contractor or over his method of work. His sole interest here is to have the piece of work turned over to him in its completed state. In the first case, we call the workman a servant; in the second case, he is an independent contractor. One who employs an independent contractor is not liable for the negligent acts of the contractor or his servants, except in a few special cases. In Berg v. Parsons, 156 N. Y. 109, the majority of the court states: "There are certain exceptional cases where a person employing a contractor is liable, which, briefly stated, are: Where the employer personally interferes with the work, and the acts performed by him occasion the injury; where the thing contracted to be done is unlawful; where the acts performed create a public nuisance; and where an employer is bound by a statute to do a thing efficiently and an injury results from its inefficiency." A few, but not many courts, add to this list one further fact, that the employer must use due care in the selection of a competent independent contractor, otherwise he is liable. This would seem eminently sound.

CHAPTER V

PARTNERSHIP

RELATIONS ANALOGOUS TO PRINCIPAL AND AGENT.—There are a few relations, in the law, which are analogous to that of principal and agent. The one which we shall take up now is the relationship of a partner to a partnership, and also to the outside world. We shall consider in a subsequent chapter, the functions, duties and responsibilities of trustees, executors, and administrators.

THE IMPORTANCE OF PARTNERSHIP LAW.—There is a very common impression that partnership law is not as important now as formerly. This undoubtedly is true, as more and more large business enterprises are being conducted in the corporation form; but there is still a large amount of business done in the partnership form. What is most important, however, is the very informality of the type of business conducted under the partnership arrangement. Whether, in a given case, a partnership exists, becomes a vital question. Two friends, A and B, in an informal way, go into a business venture. The enterprise fails and A and B owe many debts. A has some property of his own; B has nothing. You are a creditor, but all your dealings have been with B. One simple point will show you whether your claim is worthless. If A and B were partners, you may hold A. If they were not partners, your claim probably never will be worth anything to you. The question, then, whether or not a certain relationship constitutes a partnership is a most important one, in the field of commercial law.

PARTNERSHIP DEFINED.—We shall have occasion, in the chapters on bills and notes, and personal property, to refer to the movement to codify certain branches of the law. This movement was begun by the Commissioners on Uniform Laws proposing the Uniform Negotiable Instruments Act, which has now been adopted in all of the States except Georgia. One of the most recent codifications is the Uniform Partnership Act which has been adopted in a number of the States, and which will undoubtedly follow the same course as the other acts drawn by the same Commissioners. We shall make frequent reference to the Uniform Partnership Act in this chapter. Although some of the writers on the law of partnership state that no satisfactory definition of the term partnership can be given, the Uniform Act defines it as follows: "A partnership is an association of two or more persons to carry on as co-owners a business for profit." It is undoubtedly true that even with this definition, a considerable amount of further explanation will be necessary to determine with any degree of certainty, just what is meant by partnership.

THE DIFFERENCE BETWEEN A PARTNERSHIP AND A CORPORATION.—While we may be anticipating our chapter on corporations, it is well, at the very outset, to understand the fundamental differences between a partnership and a corporation. We may mention six differences:

(1) When a partner dies, the partnership is automatically dissolved. If a partner sells or transfers his interest in the business, this works a dissolution of the firm. On the other hand, the situation is precisely the opposite in the case of a corporation. The death of a shareholder has no effect upon the corporation. In fact, if all of the shareholders of the United States Steel Corporation should die at once, the corporation would still exist. So also the transfer of stock from one owner to another has no effect upon the corporation's existence. Many thousand shares are dealt with on the exchange each day without the slightest effect upon any corporation.

(2) The doctrine of individual liability for the debts of a firm is a fundamental characteristic of partnership law. Each member of the firm is absolutely liable for all the debts of the firm. Thus, if the firm consists of A, B, and C, and the firm goes into bankruptcy and owes $50,000, and B and C are both individually worthless, and A has his own private fortune, A will be obliged to pay all of the debts, although, according to the arrangements that the partners made when forming the partnership, each was to share the profits and losses equally. Theoretically, A has the right to contribution from his fellow partners, and should they later acquire property, he will be able to enforce this right in a court of equity. In a corporation, a shareholder is liable only for the value of his share. If he subscribes to a share of stock, par value $100, and has paid only $50 on his subscription, and the corporation goes into bankruptcy, its receiver can compel him to pay the balance of his subscription, $50, but that would be the extent of his loss. If I buy a share of United States Steel Common, at $79, on the exchange, and the company goes into bankruptcy, my loss will be only $79. I would not be obliged to make up to the receiver the other twenty-one dollars. The only noteworthy exception to this rule as to the liability of a stockholder is in the case of a shareholder in a National bank, (this is true of some of the State banking laws also), where a shareholder is liable to an extra assessment equal to the par value of the stock he owns.

(3) In a partnership each member of the firm is a general agent for the partnership, and his acts bind the firm. In the case of a corporation, a shareholder, by virtue of the fact that he is a shareholder, has no power to bind the corporation. The position of a shareholder is very similar to that of a voter. The corporation is run by its board of directors. They are elected by the shareholders just as we elect a governor or president. If we are dissatisfied with the conduct of a governor or president, all we can do is to vote him out of office at the next election, except in unusual cases where a governor or president might be impeached. The same is true in the case of a board of directors.

(4) A partnership may be created by a formal contract, or a simple contract, in writing or by word of mouth; in fact it may be created in almost any way. A corporation, in order to do business, must comply with the corporation laws of the State in which it is incorporated. A regular formality must be observed. A certificate of

incorporation must be filed, generally with the Secretary of State, and with the county clerk of the county in which the corporation's principal place of business is located in the State.

(5) A partnership may do anything that is legal and which the members decide to do. A corporation exists by virtue of a charter, granted by the State. The sum total of the powers given in that charter gives the total of all of the activities the corporation may undertake. Engagement in activities not authorized in the charter may result in the forfeiture of the charter by the State.

(6) In legal theory, a corporation is looked upon as a separate entity. Most States require at least three persons to incorporate. A, B and C form a corporation under the laws of the State of New York. There are then four legal persons in existence: A, B, and C, and this separate person, or legal entity, the Green Corporation, if that is the name given the company. In the case of a partnership, the law does not, as a rule, consider the partnership as an entity distinct and separate from the members who make up the firm. Of course, the business man does, in a way, look upon the partnership as a separate commercial entity. The very fact that the members of the firm are all general agents for the firm, and that the members are individually liable for all of the debts of the firm, shows that the law does not carry the entity theory into practice in partnerships as it does in corporations.

DIFFERENT KINDS OF PARTNERSHIP.—What we have said applies to the ordinary partnership. There are certain forms of partnership which we can only mention. One of them is the limited partnership. Limited partnerships are created under the law of the State in which the business is to be conducted and in a general way, these limited partnerships are a combination of the principles underlying ordinary partnerships and corporations. The members may limit their liability to a certain amount, and in that sense, the limited partnership is like a corporation. On the other hand, the general principles of partnership, as we shall discuss them, apply with almost equal force to the acts of a limited partnership. A person should not undertake to give an opinion as to a legal problem relating to a limited partnership until the law of the State in which the limited partnership is organized has been consulted.

JOINT STOCK COMPANIES.—Occasionally we meet with organizations—joint stock companies—which occupy a sort of "No-man's land" between partnerships and corporations. The joint stock company issues shares of stock the same as a corporation. These shares are listed on the stock exchange, as for example, the Adams Express Company. The joint stock company, however, carries with it the individual liability of the shareholders for the debts of the company, which is technically a partnership attribute. The New York Court of Appeals in People ex rel. Winchester v. Coleman, 133 N. Y. 279, has put it this way: "More or less, they crowd upon and overlap each other, but without losing their identity, and so, while we cannot say that a joint stock company is a corporation, we can say * * * that the joint stock company is a partnership with some of the powers of a corporation."

HOW TO DETERMINE WHETHER A PARTNERSHIP EXISTS.—In a case,

not tried in court, the facts were: A Gloucester cod-fishing vessel made an unsuccessful fishing voyage. The sailors were to secure a certain portion of the profits of the voyage as their wages. When the ship returned to port, an attempt was made to collect bills incurred on the trip and to hold the seamen liable along with the owners of the vessel, as partners. It was contended that sharing in the profits made them partners. While this is true generally, this particular custom, whereby a laborer receives a certain portion of the profits of an undertaking as his wages, does not of itself constitute him a partner with the person operating the vessel. This point has been decided several times. Such questions as these arise and cause great difficulty in determining whether a partnership exists. At times it is very important, as in the case of the seamen, to know whether or not they can be made to assume the obligations pertaining to the partnership relations. While we cannot go into these relations in detail, the framers of the Uniform Partnership Act have laid down, with the utmost care, the rules which are to be used in determining whether a partnership exists or not. But, you say, why cannot the parties avoid all this difficulty by making a written agreement clearing up the entire matter? They could. It is the simplest matter in the world. But the trouble comes because a partnership arrangement is so easy to enter into, and requires so little formality, that it is taken for granted that it will come out satisfactorily, and the precautions which should be taken are sometimes forgotten. Hence, we have to have rules of interpretation to help us when the parties themselves have not taken the necessary precautions to make matters clear. These rules of interpretation are very clearly and very definitely laid down in the Uniform Partnership Act, in the following language:

(1) Except as provided by Section 16, persons who are not partners as to each other are not partners as to third persons.

(2) Joint tenancy, tenancy in common, tenancy by the entireties, joint property, common property, or part ownership does not of itself establish a partnership, whether such co-owners do or do not share any profits made by the use of the property.

(3) The sharing of gross returns does not of itself establish a partnership, whether or not the persons sharing them have a joint or common right or interest in any property from which the returns are derived.

(4) The receipt by a person of a share of the profits of a business is prima facie evidence that he is a partner in the business, but no such inference shall be drawn if such profits were received in payment:

(a) As a debt by installments or otherwise,

(b) As wages of an employee or rent to a landlord,

(c) As an annuity to a widow or representative of a deceased partner,

(d) As interest on a loan, though the amount of payment vary with the profits of the business,

(e) As the consideration for the sale of the good-will of a business or other property by installments or otherwise.

Section 16.—(Partner by estoppel.)—(1) When a person by words spoken or written or by conduct, represents himself, or consents to another representing him to any one, as a partner in an existing partnership or with one or more persons not actual partners, he is liable to any such person to whom such representation has been made, who has, on the faith of such representation, given credit to the actual or apparent partnership, and if he has made such representation or consented to its being made in a public manner, he is liable to such person, whether the representation has or has not been made or communicated to such person * * *.

FOR WHAT PURPOSES MAY A PARTNERSHIP BE CREATED.—A partnership may be created to carry on any lawful business, and whatever the individuals may do lawfully as such, two or more may do together in a group as a partnership. Professional occupations may be carried on in the partnership form advantageously. This is one case where a partnership has an advantage over a corporation. A group of lawyers may form a partnership and do business under a partnership name. But a group of lawyers seldom or never form corporations to practice law. The reason for this is that the corporation is a separate entity, and the corporation as such cannot pass a bar examination and be admitted to the bar. In fact, in a few States, there are statutes prohibiting a corporation from practicing law. There is, therefore, very little advantage in creating a corporation which cannot itself do the thing for which it was created.

ILLEGAL OBJECT.—A partnership which is formed to carry on any illegal purpose is, of course, not recognized by law. Thus, if A, B, and C form a partnership to engage in the gambling business and they elect C as treasurer and have a successful business so that they have a large amount of money on hand, A and B may not be able to reap the profits of the venture. C has the money. The agreement was that all were to share equally, but C insists on keeping it all. The law will allow him to do so, because it is beneath the dignity of the court to order an accounting in a transaction where all parties are equally guilty. The maxim is "in pari delicto, condicio defendentis potior est", that is, where the parties are in equal fault, the position of the defendant is the stronger. C, the guilty party, has the money; he is the defendant, therefore, he keeps it.

WHO MAY BE PARTNERS.—At common law, a married woman was incapable of becoming a member of a partnership because of her general incapacity to enter a contract. Statutes removing the disability of married women have been passed in practically all the States, and a married woman is generally free to become a partner, except, and this is true in many States still, husband and wife may not become partners. An infant may be a member of a firm on the same general principles as applied to ordinary infant's contracts. His entering the partnership agreement is not void, but voidable. When he becomes of age, if he affirms the contract of partnership, he will be liable the same as an adult. He has, however, the right to disaffirm his partnership agreement within a reasonable time after becoming of age, and if he does so, he will be absolved from all personal liability for the debts of the firm. It is very generally held that a corporation may not enter into a copartnership with another corporation or an individual. The reason for this is a general rule of public policy that in a partnership the corporation would be bound by the acts of persons who are not its duly appointed agents and officers. There may be any number of members in a firm, such matters being left to the choice and wisdom of those operating the business.

DELECTUS PERSONARUM.—While the foregoing is true, one must not reach the conclusion that an objectionable person may be forced into a firm. I am a member of a firm of three persons. I decide to withdraw, and tell my two fellow partners that I have transferred all my interest in the firm to John Jones. He will take my place. My two fellow partners believe Jones to be a crook, and do not wish to be in partnership with him. They would not be obliged to accept him. In other words, the doctrine of delectus personarum, or the choice of the person, is strictly applied in partnership, because a partnership relation is a very confidential relationship. Ordinarily the business cannot be conducted satisfactorily unless all of the partners have the confidence of each other. It is for this reason, that we have the rule, heretofore referred to, that the sale by a partner of his interest in the business works a dissolution of the partnership. John Jones, who purchased my rights in the firm, could not compel the other members to take him in, but the firm would have to be wound up and he would simply be able to recover what my share of the assets was. It is true that Section 27 of the Act does read that a sale by a partner of his interest does not of itself work a dissolution, but the doctrine of delectus personarum is fully preserved. That section reads: (1) A conveyance by a partner of his interest in the partnership does not of itself dissolve the partnership, nor, as against the other partners in the absence of agreement, entitle the assignee, during the continuance of the partnership, to interfere in the management or administration of the partnership business or affairs, or to require any information or account of partnership transactions, or to inspect the partnership books; but it merely entitles the assignee to receive in accordance with his contract the profits to which the assigning partner would otherwise be entitled.

(2) In case of a dissolution of the partnership, the assignee is entitled to receive his assignor's interest and may require an account from the date only of the last account agreed to by all the partners.

ARTICLES OF PARTNERSHIP.—We have learned that parties need not expressly declare themselves partners, or enter into an express contract, in order to become partners. So the framing of written partnership articles—a written contract of partnership—is not essential, though it is the ordinary and advisable course. We may note here a few rules governing the use and construction of such articles where they have been adopted. They should, of course, provide for as many contingencies as can be foreseen, such as the nature, name and place of business, when the relation is to commence and when to terminate, what capital shall be contributed by each, what the share of each in the profits and losses shall be, what the powers of the partners as between themselves shall be, whether the business shall be continued after the death of one or more of the partners and how it shall be wound up. But the important thing to note is, that if provision be not made, the general law, and particularly that part governing the powers and duties of partners to each other and to third persons, applies. In other words, the partners may, by their contract, determine what their rights as between themselves shall be; but if they do not, the rules of law will determine them. Thus they may determine that of two partners one shall have two-thirds and the other one-third of the profits; in the absence of such a clause the law determines the profits shall be divided equally. When articles have been once adopted they can be changed only by the consent of all the partners; this consent need not be formally expressed in words, but it may be implied from a long-continued course of conduct. The law provides no means to force a partner to live up to his contract except in a very few cases; the most it gives is a right of action for the breach caused by his failure to do as agreed.

FIRM NAME.—The adoption of a firm name is not an essential to a partnership, but is customary and advisable. The names of the partners may be combined, or a single name used, or a fictitious name, or any name, so long as the rights of other persons are not violated. In some States, notably New York, the use of the name of a person not a partner is forbidden, as is also the use of the expression "& Co.," unless a partner is represented by it. Ordinarily, contracts may be made in the firm name and by one partner, but contracts under seal should be made in the names of the partners "doing business as," etc., and cannot be made by one partner without authority from the others. Conveyances of real property should be made to or by the individual partners "doing business as," etc., for the law does not generally recognize the firm as a separate person or entity sufficiently to enable it as such to take or give a conveyance. If the deed ran to "John Doe & Co.," the title would be in John Doe only, though he would be said to hold it in trust for the firm, for if the partnership name is given as the grantee, the title goes only to those whose names appear, and if the partnership were doing business under a fictitious name, the deed would convey to no one. Whether land, the title to which is in the name of one partner, is held in trust by him as partnership property, is a question of intention, and that question is determined by asking with what money was the land bought, what use has it been put to, has it been carried on the books of the firm, with what money have the taxes, insurance, and other charges been paid, etc. If found to have been treated as partnership property, the fact that the title is in one person counts for little, as he will be said to hold it in trust for the firm; but the careful business man will avoid trouble by having the property conveyed to the firm in the manner indicated, if it is actually partnership property.

THE POWERS OF A PARTNER.—As a general agent, a partner has almost unlimited authority to bind the firm. Because of this, we have here one reason for not recommending the partnership form of doing business unless all the members of the firm have the utmost confidence in each other. These powers of the partners are so general that it is impossible for us to go into them in any detail. They are summarized in the most compact form in the Uniform Partnership Act. Sections 9 to 17 of that act are as follows:

9. (1) Every partner is an agent of the partnership for the purpose of its business, and the act of every partner, including the execution in the partnership name of any instrument, for apparently carrying on in the usual way the business of the partnership of which he is a member, binds the partnership, unless the partner so acting has in fact no authority to act for the partnership in the particular matter, and the person with whom he is dealing has knowledge of the fact that he has no such authority.

(2) An act of a partner, which is not apparently for the carrying on of the business of the partnership in the usual way, does not bind the partnership unless authorized by the other partners.

(3) Unless authorized by the other partners or unless they have abandoned the business, one or more but less than all the partners have no authority to:

(a) Assign the partnership property in trust for creditors or on the assignee's promise to pay the debts of the partnership,

(b) Dispose of the good-will of the business,

(c) Do any other act which would make it impossible to carry on the ordinary business of the partnership,

(d) Confess a judgment,

(e) Submit a partnership claim or liability to arbitration or reference.

(4) No act of a partner in contravention of a restriction on his authority shall bind the partnership to persons having knowledge of the restriction.

10. (1) Where title to real property is in the partnership name, any partner may convey title to such property by a conveyance executed in the partnership name; but the partnership may recover such property unless the partner's act binds the partnership under the provisions of paragraph (1) of Section 9, or unless such property has been conveyed by the grantee, or a person claiming through such grantee to a holder for value without knowledge that the partner, in making the conveyance, has exceeded his authority.

(2) Where title to real property is in the name of the partnership, a conveyance executed by a partner, in his own name, passes the equitable interest of the partnership, provided the act is one within the authority of the partner under the provisions of paragraph (1) of Section 9.

(3) Where title to real property is in the name of one or more but not all the partners, and the record does not disclose the right of the partnership, the partners in whose name the title stands may convey title to such property, but the partnership may recover such property if the partners' act does not bind the partnership under the provisions of paragraph (1) of Section 9, unless the purchaser or his assignee, is a holder for value, without knowledge.

(4) Where the title to real property is in the name of one or more or all the partners, or in a third person in trust for the partnership, a conveyance executed by a partner in the partnership name, or in his own name, passes the equitable interest of the partnership, provided the act is one within the authority of the partner under the provisions of paragraph (1) of Section 9.

(5) Where the title to real property is in the names of all the partners, a conveyance executed by all the partners passes all their rights in such property.

11. An admission or representation made by any partner concerning partnership affairs within the scope of his authority as conferred by this act is evidence

against the partnership.

12. Notice to any partner of any matter relating to partnership affairs, and the knowledge of the partner acting in the particular matter, acquired while a partner or then present to his mind, and the knowledge of any other partner who reasonably could and should have communicated it to the acting partner, operate as notice to or knowledge of the partnership, except in the case of a fraud on the partnership committed by or with the consent of that partner.

13. Where, by any wrongful act or omission of any partner acting in the ordinary course of the business of the partnership, or with the authority of his co-partners, loss or injury is caused to any person, not being a partner in the partnership, or any penalty is incurred, the partnership is liable therefor to the same extent as the partner so acting or omitting to act.

14. The partnership is bound to make good the loss:

> (a) Where one partner acting within the scope of his apparent authority receives money or property of a third person and misapplies it; and

> (b) Where the partnership in the course of its business receives money or property of a third person and the money or property so received is misapplied by any partner while it is in the custody of the partnership.

15. All partners are liable

> (a) Jointly and severally for everything chargeable to the partnership under Sections 13 and 14.

> (b) Jointly for all other debts and obligations of the partnership; but any partner may enter into a separate obligation to perform a partnership contract.

16. (1) When a person, by words spoken or written or by conduct, represents himself, or consents to another representing him to any one, as a partner in an existing partnership or with one or more persons not actual partners, he is liable to any such person to whom such representation has been made, who has, on the faith of such representation, given credit to the actual or apparent partnership, and if he has made such representation or consented to its being made in a public manner, he is liable to such person, whether the representation has or has not been made or communicated to such person so giving credit by or with the knowledge of the apparent partner making the representation or consenting to its being made.

> (a) When a partnership liability results, he is liable as though he were an actual member of the partnership.

> (b) When no partnership liability results, he is liable jointly with the other persons, if any, so consenting to the contract or representation as to incur liability, otherwise separately.

(2) When a person has been thus represented to be a partner in an existing partnership, or with one or more persons not actual partners, he is an agent of the

persons consenting to such representation to bind them to the same extent and in the same manner as though he were a partner in fact, with respect to persons who rely upon the representation. Where all the members of the existing partnership consent to the representation, a partnership act or obligation results; but in all other cases it is the joint act or obligation of the person acting and the person consenting to the representation.

17. A person admitted as a partner into an existing partnership is liable for all the obligations of the partnership arising before his admission as though he had been a partner when such obligations were incurred, except that this liability shall be satisfied only out of partnership property.

POWERS OF A MAJORITY OF PARTNERS. — If partners disagree, then a majority of them have power to decide what shall be done; but there are limits even to the power of a majority. They can only carry on the business of the firm, and any vote of the majority, or action of the majority, to change the character of the business for which the firm was organized, or to make any fundamental change in the original articles of the partnership, would be invalid.

RELATION OF PARTNERS TO ONE ANOTHER. — The rules determining the rights and duties of partners in relation to the partnership are concisely but fully set forth in the Act as follows:

18. The rights and duties of the partners in relation to the partnership shall be determined, subject to any agreement between them, by the following rules:

(a) Each partner shall be repaid his contributions, whether by way of capital or advances to the partnership property and share equally in the profits and surplus remaining after all liabilities, including those to partners, are satisfied; and must contribute towards the losses, whether of capital or otherwise, sustained by the partnership according to his share in the profits.

(b) The partnership must indemnify every partner in respect of payment made and personal liabilities reasonably incurred by him in the ordinary and proper conduct of its business, or for the preservation of its business or property.

(c) A partner who, in aid of the partnership, makes any payment or advance beyond the amount of capital which he agreed to contribute, shall be paid interest from the date of the payment or advance.

(d) A partner shall receive interest on the capital contributed by him only from the date when repayment should be made.

(e) All partners have equal rights in the management and conduct of the partnership business.

(f) No partner is entitled to remuneration for acting in the partnership business, except that a surviving partner is entitled to reasonable compensation for his services in winding up the partnership affairs.

(g) No person can become a member of a partnership without the consent of all the partners.

(h) Any difference arising as to ordinary matters connected with the partnership business may be decided by a majority of the partners; but no act in contravention of any agreement between the partners may be done rightly without the consent of all the partners.

19. The partnership books shall be kept, subject to any agreement between the partners, at the principal place of business of the partnership, and every partner shall at all times have access to and may inspect and copy any of them.

20. Partners shall render on demand true and full information of all things affecting the partnership to any partner or the legal representative of any deceased partner or partner under legal disability.

21. (1) Every partner must account to the partnership for any benefit, and hold as trustee for it any profits derived by him without the consent of the other partners from any transaction connected with the formation, conduct, or liquidation of the partnership or from any use by him of its property.

(2) This section applies also to the representatives of a deceased partner engaged in the liquidation of the affairs of the partnership as the personal representatives of the last surviving partner.

22. Any partner shall have the right to a formal account as to partnership affairs:

(a) If he is wrongfully excluded from the partnership business or possession of its property by his co-partners.

(b) If the right exists under the terms of any agreement.

(c) As provided by Section 21.

(d) Whenever other circumstances renders it just and reasonable.

TERMINATION OF THE PARTNERSHIP.—A partnership is terminated either by act of the partners, or by law. Under the first heading, we may mention such things as the partnership being terminated by the accomplishment of the object for which the same was formed, or by the termination of the time during which the partnership was to exist, or by mutual consent of all parties concerned. Under the head of termination by operation of law, we have such topics as the death of a partner, the insanity of a partner, or the bankruptcy of a partner, and a dissolution by a court, as for example, where it is absolutely certain, in the opinion of the court, that the business cannot be successfully continued longer. In such a case, although some of the partners may not wish to wind up the affairs of the business, the court may order it done in the interest of all parties concerned.

OWNERSHIP OF FIRM PROPERTY AND CREDITORS' RIGHTS.—The firm property is owned by all the partners jointly, but the interest of each individual partner is not an interest in each piece of firm property, but a right to have an accounting and to receive on the accounting such share of the assets as belong to him when all debts due from him to the firm and all liabilities to the outside world are settled. Consequently, a creditor of an individual partner cannot seize or attach or levy on firm property, because that firm property does not belong, nor does any part of it belong, to his debtor. The creditor must file a bill in equity asking that the partner's share be determined, and that on an accounting so much as is found due to the debtor partner be applied to discharge that partner's indebtedness.

THE DIVISION OF ASSETS.—Upon final dissolution, the question of division of assets comes up, and the Uniform Partnership Act gives us the general rule as to how the firm's assets are divided. Section 40 of the Act reads:

In settling accounts between the parties after dissolution, the following rules shall be observed, subject to any agreement to the contrary:

(a) The assets of the partnership are:

I. The partnership property,

II. The contributions of the partners necessary for the payment of all the liabilities specified in clause (b) of this paragraph.

(b) The liabilities of the partnership shall rank in order of payment, as follows:

I. Those owing to creditors other than partners,

II. Those owing to partners other than for capital and profits,

III. Those owing to partners in respect of capital,

IV. Those owing to partners in respect of profits.

(c) The assets shall be applied in the order of their declaration in clause (a) of this paragraph to the satisfaction of the liabilities.

(d) The partners shall contribute, as provided by Section 18 (a) the amount necessary to satisfy the liabilities; but if any, but not all, of the partners are insolvent, or, not being subject to process, refuse to contribute, the other partners shall contribute their share of the liabilities, and, in the relative proportions in which they share the profits, the additional amount necessary to pay the liabilities.

(e) An assignee for the benefit of creditors or any person appointed by the court shall have the right to enforce the contributions specified in clause (d) of this paragraph.

(f) Any partner or his legal representative shall have the right to enforce the contributions specified in clause (d) of this paragraph, to the extent of the amount which he has paid in excess of his share of the liability.

(g) The individual property of a deceased partner shall be liable for the contributions specified in clause (d) of this paragraph.

(h) When partnership property and the individual properties of the partners are in the possession of a court for distribution, partnership creditors shall have priority on partnership property, and separate creditors on individual property, saving the rights of lien or secured creditors as heretofore.

    (i) Where a partner has become bankrupt or his estate is insolvent, the claims against his separate property shall rank in the following order:

    I. Those owing to separate creditors,

    II. Those owing to partnership creditors,

    III. Those owing to partners by way of contribution.

LIQUIDATION OF PARTNERSHIP.—When a partnership is dissolved, it is common for the business to require liquidation, and frequently one or more of the partners are what are called liquidating partners. If a partnership is dissolved by death, for instance, the surviving partners have a right to be liquidating partners and liquidate the business. That means they may carry on existing contracts; they may dispose of the stock on hand to the best advantage. If this requires incidental purchases of new goods, they may be made, but in general, new business cannot be undertaken. The function of a liquidating partner is to satisfy existing contracts, reduce the property of the firm to cash, and then distribute it to those who are entitled to receive it.

LIMITED PARTNERSHIP.—Statutes, as we have learned, in many States permit the formation of limited partnerships, the object of which is to enable one or more partners to avoid unlimited liability for debts. Partners in a general partnership are each liable, individually, for the full amount of the firm's indebtedness. If one partner is thus compelled to pay more than his share, he may seek redress by demanding contribution from his fellow partners, and if they are not solvent, he will not be able to secure reimbursement. If there is one solvent partner, for instance, and two other partners, both of whom become insolvent, the result will be that the first partner will have to pay the debts of the firm and will have no redress except such as he may be able to get from the insolvent estates of his two partners. Now, in a limited partnership a limited partner does not stand to lose any more than the amount of money he actually puts in the firm. In order to create a limited partnership it is necessary to sign a certificate prepared for the purpose and stating the facts, file it in the office of the Secretary of State or other official, and also publish it so that the public may be informed of the circumstances and credit may not be given by the world at large to the firm on the assumption that the limited partner is a general partner. He puts a specified amount of money in the firm and that money may be reached by creditors of the firm, but they cannot hold him further liable. A good definition of a limited partnership follows: A limited partnership is one which consists of one or more persons called general partners and also one or more persons called special partners. Every general partner is an agent for the partnership in the transaction of its business and has authority to do whatever is necessary to carry on such business in the ordinary manner. Every general partner is liable to third persons, jointly and severally, with his general co-partners for all of the obligations of the partnership. A special partner may only advise as to the management of the partnership and he is liable for the obligations of the partnership only to the amount of capital invested by him therein.

SILENT PARTNERS.—A silent partner must not be confused with a member of a limited partnership. A silent partner is a general partner who takes no part in the active management of the business and frequently is a secret partner. A member of a limited partnership can never be a secret partner, since the terms of a limited partnership must be published. A member of a limited partnership should take no part in the management of the business, or he may render himself liable as a general partner. The limited partnership law requires, moreover, that he must have exactly complied with the law by making out, filing and publishing a certificate. The statutes of the State should be consulted on this point and closely adhered to.

LIMITED.—We often see also in print, so and so "Ltd." This does not mean a limited partnership. The word "limited" is used in the name of an English or Canadian company organized under the English or Canadian statutes, but such companies are rather analogous to corporations than to limited partnerships. The liability in such companies is limited altogether to the assets in the company's hands. There are no general partners. The liability of all stockholders is limited. The English and Canadian law requires that the word Limited be added to the name, so that the public may not be deceived into believing that the company is a partnership.

CHAPTER VI
CORPORATIONS

THE NATURE OF A CORPORATION.—The nature of a corporation is perhaps best understood by an illustration. In the case of People's Pleasure Park Co. v. Rohleder, 109 Va. 439, the facts were as follows: There was a large tract of land divided up into a number of lots, and in each deed, when a lot was sold, there was a covenant providing that title to the real property should never vest in a person of African descent, or in a colored person. Later, after the lots had been sold, several of them were conveyed to a corporation composed exclusively of negroes. The corporation knew, when it purchased the tract of land, of this restriction in the deed, and the land was bought by it for the purpose of establishing an amusement park for colored people. Suit was brought in a court of equity to compel the cancellation of the deed to the corporation. Stated boldly, the decision of the Virginia court amounts to an assertion that a corporation has no color. In other words, the corporation is an entity separate and distinct from its members, and so, although all the stockholders in this corporation were colored, that did not make the corporation a colored person. Thus, if A, B, and C, as incorporators, organize the X Corporation, although they are the sole stockholders, there are four persons, A, B, C, and the X Corporation.

THE ENTITY THEORY.—It may be doubted if any court would carry the entity theory to the extent that it would allow an individual who was the owner of a piece of real estate, which he was not permitted by the deed to sell to negroes, to deliberately go to a prospective negro purchaser and say: "I cannot sell my property to you because of a restriction in the deed, but I will pay the necessary expenses, if you, with two of your friends, will form a corporation to take title to this property, in which corporation each of your friends will own one share and you the balance, thus retaining control yourself. I will then deed the property to the corporation and will thereby get around the covenant in my deed preventing a transfer to negroes." We must not allow the entity theory to work a manifest injustice, as was said in Erickson v. Revere Elevator Co., 110 Minn. 443: "Where the corporate form is used by individuals for the purpose of evading the law, or for the perpetration of fraud, the courts will not permit the legal entity to be interposed so as to defeat justice."

RESULTS OF THE ENTITY THEORY.—Flowing from the entity theory is the result that the property of a corporation is owned by the corporation and not by the individual members. Therefore, all conveyances of such property, whether it is real property or personal property, must be made by the corporation, and cannot be made by the members or shareholders as individuals. It also follows that all suits against or by the corporation must be brought against the corporation or by the corporation as an entity and not against the individual members. Again, a corporation may take property from one of its individual members, and it may make a contract with one of them, and it may sue them and be sued by them.

KINDS OF CORPORATIONS.—Corporations are divided into public, quasi-public, and private corporations. The private corporation is such as is created for private enterprises, such as manufacturing, banking, and trading corporations. Religious and eleemosynary corporations are also included in this classification. The public corporation is such as is created for the purposes of government, such as cities, towns, villages, and institutions founded by the State, and managed by it for governmental purposes. Quasi-public corporations are such as are engaged in a private business which is affected with a public interest, such as railroads, both steam and electric, gas companies, water companies, lighting companies, and the like. The public, and generally the quasi-public, corporations possess the right of eminent domain, that is, the right to take private property for public purposes upon payment of just compensation to the owner. It is the private corporation with which we are usually concerned in commercial law, and this chapter will be devoted largely to a discussion of that class.

THE CREATION OF A CORPORATION.—A corporation must be created by legislative authority. Formerly, a corporation was created by special act of the legislature, but in recent years the growth in the number of corporations, and also the political wire-pulling necessary to get an incorporation bill through a legislature, have resulted in the almost universal practice of having the legislature pass a general corporation act, and then without further reference to the legislature, any group of persons, of the requisite number, may become incorporated by complying with the provisions of such an act. The formation of corporations under the laws of most States is a simple process, requiring in general the preparation of an official document sometimes termed the "certificate of incorporation" or the "charter," which paper sets forth the facts which are required under the laws of the State wherein the corporation is to be formed. These laws, while not uniform, generally require a statement as to the name to be used by the corporation, the names of the proposed directors and incorporators, a statement of the general purposes or objects of the corporation, the location of its principal office and place of business, how long it is to last, the amount of its authorized capital, the par value of its stock, as well as a statement in regard to any preferred stock which may be contemplated. Other details are sometimes required under the various State laws. This official document must generally be signed or executed by those persons who are the incorporators of the corporation. As a rule, three or more incorporators are required, although in some States five is the minimum. This official document, after it has been duly executed, is usually to be filed in the office of the Secretary of State, and usually also in that of the county clerk of the county wherein its principal office is to be. This procedure, however, is subject to some variations and the statutes of the State involved must always be closely followed. As soon as the official document has been properly filed and the other necessary steps taken the incorporators hold the first meeting and effect an organization, after which time the corporation is generally in a position to transact business, although in some States it is provided in effect that corporations should not commence business until a certain share of the capital has been paid into the corporation in cash.

CITIZENSHIP OF A CORPORATION.—Although a corporation is a separate entity, entirely distinct and apart from its members, such separate entity is not a citizen in the sense in which we use the term ordinarily. At a general election a corporation has no right to vote. Again, Article 4 Section 2, of the United States Constitution, provides that "citizens of each State shall be entitled to all of the privileges and immunities of citizens in the several States." A corporation is not a citizen in this sense. Hence a State may keep all insurance companies, incorporated outside of its area, from doing business in that State by discriminating legislation against foreign insurance corporations. Insurance is not looked upon as interstate commerce, about which the individual States may not legislate, and as a corporation is not a citizen within the meaning of Article 4, Section 2, such insurance companies have no redress. In one sense, however, a corporation is looked upon as a citizen. Where a suit is between citizens of different States, and the amount involved is over the prescribed sum, either party may bring the action in the Federal courts, if he so desires, instead of in the State courts. In this sense, a corporation is to be regarded as if it were a citizen of the State in which it is created. If I live in New York and the American Tobacco Co. is incorporated in New Jersey, suit between us may be brought in the Federal courts on the ground of diversity of citizenship on the part of plaintiff and defendant.

POWERS OF CORPORATIONS.—A corporation is unable to do anything beyond such powers as are granted it by law. As to the extent of the powers possessed by a corporation, we may conveniently divide corporate powers into those which are express and those which are implied. Express powers may be considered as including those which are mentioned in the official documents used or granted upon the beginning of the existence of the corporation. These official documents are spoken of as "charters" or "certificates of incorporation." Whatever term may be applied to them there is generally in such documents a statement of the general purposes or objects for which the corporation is formed; in other words, of the general business in which it is to engage. There is also a statement of the general powers of the corporation which is to engage in the business mentioned. The powers so mentioned in such official documents may be termed, as we have stated, express powers of the corporation. Needless to say, however, it is not usual or possible to attempt to indicate in any such official documents all the details of the operations of business. Therefore, it is necessary to imply that in addition to such express powers the corporation has power to do such acts as may be reasonably necessary or incidental to the carrying on of the business mentioned. Powers so implied, without words, are termed "implied powers." Therefore, the total powers of a corporation consist of the express powers, namely, such as are named in the official documents containing a statement of its purposes and the business in which it is to engage, and the powers which would be reasonably implied under the rule just mentioned, as necessary and incidental to the carrying out of the express powers. Such implied powers do not give the corporation any power to do acts which are not reasonably necessary and incidental in its regular business. To allow validity to acts not so reasonably necessary and incidental would be in reality allowing the corporation to engage in outside business, which, under its charter, it has no power to engage in. As an illustration of this let us assume that the X company was incorporated to build, run and operate a railroad between two towns named A and B. The official charter of the corporation may state further details of the corporation's powers or it may not. But, if such details are not stated, the corporation would, obviously, have as express powers, the power to build the road and to operate it between the towns mentioned. It would also have as implied powers the power to do any act reasonably necessary or incidental to the operation of a railroad, such for example as the purchase of rails, ties or other railroad supplies, the hiring of employees, erection of stations and the power also to give negotiable paper in payment for such supplies or the raising of money by mortgaging its property or otherwise where necessary to carry on its business. In other words, the corporation may be said to have as implied powers all the powers which an individual would reasonably and usually exercise if he were operating the railroad. However, the corporation would have no power, express or implied, to do any act not reasonably necessary to the railroad business, such, for example, as the purchase of a stock farm or the operation of a steamer line or a grocery store, or the leasing of its line. If the corporation, then, should make any contract with relation to engaging in these outside matters—the corporation having no power to engage in them—a valid contract could not arise and therefore the corporation could not be held liable thereon.

ULTRA VIRES ACTS.—Where a corporation attempts to do an act which is clearly beyond its express or implied powers, such act is generally termed an "ultra vires" act, and it may frequently consist in an attempted contract by a corporation. Hence we must consider with some care contracts of corporations which may be termed ultra vires. As the corporation lacks power it is generally said that the contract does not arise and hence neither the corporation nor the person with whom it attempted to contract would theoretically be bound thereon. Yet, in many States, a special rule has been adopted whereby a corporation may be held upon such contract in certain cases even though it had no power to make it. This may be termed the "doctrine of estoppel," and generally includes cases where the corporation has assumed to make a contract which was ultra vires or beyond its powers but which would appear to an outsider as incidental to the corporate business and therefore as within its corporate powers. In such circumstances, if the outsider with whom the corporation assumed to make the contract does in fact rely reasonably upon the corporate power to make it, having been deceived by appearances and having no warning that the corporation actually lacked power, and having paid over money or delivered goods or performed services or parted with other value under the contract, he may generally enforce the contract against the corporation. In other words, under such circumstances, the corporation is estopped or forbidden to evade its obligation by asserting the point that it had no power to make such contract. However, this is strictly limited to cases where the corporation appeared to have the power to make the contract and where the person dealing with it had no reason to suspect or doubt its power in that regard, and where the person dealing with the corporation had parted with some value of the kind mentioned, in his reliance that the contract was within the corporate powers of and therefore binding upon the corporation. Thus, where such person has done nothing toward carrying out his duty under the contract he would have no claim or right to enforce the same as a binding obligation of the corporation. Many courts also treat him somewhat differently and take the attitude that an outsider who has dealt with the corporation is entitled not to enforce the attempted contract, but is entitled only to recover from the corporation the reasonable value of such goods or service as it has voluntarily accepted from him.

DE FACTO AND DE JURE CORPORATIONS.—It sometimes happens that a group of persons may attempt to organize a corporation and fail to comply with all the provisions of the law in the State in which they attempt to organize. The question arises then: What have we? Of course, we do not have a full completed organization, which we would call a corporation de jure (by right of law). We may have what is called a corporation de facto (in fact). In order to constitute a corporation de facto, it is generally held that the following requisites must exist: There must be a valid law which authorizes the formation of such a corporation; a colorable attempt to organize under the provision of such law; and an assumption of corporate power, or, as is sometimes called, a user. If these facts exist, we then have a corporation de facto, and persons dealing with such a corporation are usually held to the same responsibilities as though it was an actual de jure corporation. The State, ordinarily, is the only person which can question the existence of such a body, and this is usually done in a suit by the attorney-general. If the parties have not even complied with the requisites of a de facto corporation, the authorities are divided as to what kind of an organization it is, although, perhaps, the best decisions would hold the parties liable as partners. They must have contemplated some kind of liability and failing to create even a corporation de facto, a partnership liability is all that is left, except individual liability, and that is apparently just what they did not intend.

PROMOTERS.—A promoter is a very common person in the modern industrial world. He is a person who brings about the organization of corporations, gets the people together who are interested in the enterprise, aids in procuring subscriptions, and takes general charge of all the matters incident to the formation of the corporation. In other ways, he is governed by the rules of agency and his position is that of a fiduciary. The majority of the courts hold that there is no liability on the part of the corporation to pay for his expenses and his services, in promoting the organization, unless the corporation as an organization expressly promises to pay or otherwise clearly recognizes the obligation. Because of the fiduciary relationship, which a promoter occupies, he is not permitted to make any secret profits at the expense of the corporation. If he secures property for $1,000,000, he may not turn it over to the corporation for $1,500,000 and pocket the profit himself. A corporation cannot be liable for the acts of a promoter before the corporation came into existence. It may, however, after coming into existence adopt the acts of the promoter and thereby render itself liable. If, knowing the terms of an agreement made by a promoter, the corporation takes advantage of the agreement or recognizes it, it thereby in effect itself becomes a party to the agreement. Unless the terms of a promoter's agreement expressly state the contrary, the promoter is personally liable upon it as a contractor.

POWER OF THE STATE OVER A CORPORATION.—It must follow, that if a State creates a corporation, then it should have certain control over it. The United States Supreme Court has recognized the right of visitation as residing in the State. Visitation is, in law, the act of a superior or superintendent officer who visits a corporation to examine into its manner of conducting business and its observance of the laws. The visitation of National banks by the Comptroller of the Currency is a common example of the exercise of this authority. One of the most famous cases in the United States Supreme Court is the Dartmouth College case. In 1769, the King of England granted a charter to twelve people under the name of "The Trustees of Dartmouth College." They were authorized to conduct a college and they founded Dartmouth College in Hanover, New Hampshire. In 1816, the legislature in the State of New Hampshire undertook to amend the charter in many ways, among other things, increasing the number of trustees to twenty-one. A furious conflict ensued between the State and the trustees. The State finally brought suit to recover the corporate seal and records which were held by a Mr. Woodward, who held them under the amendatory act to which we have referred. The case is known as Dartmouth College v. Woodward, 4 Wheaton 518. The Dartmouth College trustees were represented by Daniel Webster, and this is one of his famous cases before the Supreme Court. He took the position that the charter granted by the King of England and afterwards recognized by the State of New Hampshire, was a contract between the State and the trustees. This being so, it was protected by the provision in the United States Constitution which provides that no State shall pass any law impairing the obligation of contracts. The United States Supreme Court upheld this position. The act of the legislature of New Hampshire was held invalid. We then found ourselves in the position of having States creating corporations and then not being able to control them. Whatever may be said in regard to the law as laid down by the United States Supreme Court, this situation was unfortunate. Shortly thereafter in the various State legislatures, a method to meet the situation was devised, and this is what was done: When a general corporation law is passed, the State inserts in it a clause to this effect: "The State hereby reserves the right to alter, amend, or repeal the charter of any corporation organized under this act." This, then, makes this clause a part of the contract when a new corporation is organized. It knows that it is subject to having its charter amended or repealed without its consent. The effects, therefore, of the Dartmouth College decision have been practically nullified by such clauses inserted in the various incorporation laws. Such incorporation acts do not relate to corporations organized before such act was passed. Under this method of procedure, the legislature today surely has an efficacious method of controlling the corporations which it creates.

LIABILITY FOR TORTS AND CRIMES.—A corporation is ordinarily liable, the same as an individual, for all torts committed by its agents in the scope of their authority. A corporation may even be liable for acts which are beyond its authority. For example, in the case of Hannon v. Siegel-Cooper Co., 167 N. Y. 244, it was held that the department store of the Siegel-Cooper Company, a corporation, was liable for mal-practice in dentistry. The charter of the company did not give the company the right to practice dentistry, but space in the store was rented to a dentist who conducted a dental parlor. Because of his negligent treatment of a patient, the court held that the corporation was liable for the negligent acts of its agent. Corporations may also be held liable for such torts as involve a mental element, like fraud and libel. A corporation may be criminally responsible for failure to perform a duty imposed upon it by law, and in many States there are statutes which make it a criminal offense for a corporation to do or fail to do certain acts. It is generally held, however, that a corporation cannot commit a crime which involves a mental operation, as for example, murder. Murder involves a mental operation; it is "killing with malice aforethought." Then again, it would be difficult to punish a corporation for the crime of murder, because under our State constitutions, the punishment for murder is either death or life imprisonment. Although a corporation is a separate person, there is no way to kill it or imprison it for life. You surely would not do so by inflicting this penalty on all the stockholders. It is generally provided, then, by statute that such crimes that a corporation can commit are to be punished either by a fine or by imprisonment of the directors.

SHERMAN ANTI-TRUST ACT.—On July 2, 1890, the Sherman Anti-Trust Act was passed by Congress. The first section of this act reads: "Every contract, combination in the form of trust or otherwise, or conspiracy, in restraint of trade or commerce among the several States, or with foreign nations, is hereby declared to be illegal. Every person who shall make any such contract, or engage in any such combination or conspiracy, shall be deemed guilty of a misdemeanor, and, on conviction thereof, shall be punished by a fine not exceeding $5,000, or by imprisonment not exceeding one year, or by both said punishments, in the discretion of the court." The second section of this act reads: "Every person who shall monopolize, or attempt to monopolize, or combine or conspire with any other person or persons to monopolize any part of the trade or commerce among the several states, or with foreign nations, shall be deemed guilty of a misdemeanor, and on conviction thereof shall be punished by a fine not exceeding $5,000, or by imprisonment not exceeding one year, or by both said punishments, in the discretion of the court."

It would be impossible, in a small amount of space, to call attention, except in a general way, to the importance of this act and the difficulty of understanding it, without carefully reading the various conflicting decisions of the United States Supreme Court handed down since the passage of the act. The act, being a Federal act, relates only to interstate commerce. That kind of business, conducted by corporations, which is intrastate, if controlled at all by similar legislation, would be by virtue of a State act. Perhaps the most famous of the Sherman Anti-Trust Act cases decided by the United States Supreme Court is that of the United States v. Standard Oil Co., 221 U. S. 1, where the majority opinion was written by the late Chief Justice White, and in which he enunciated the so-called "rule of reason" which brings the interpretation of that act very much in harmony with the rules of the common law in regard to illegal contracts and monopolies.

BY-LAWS.—A by-law is a permanent rule for the government of a corporation and its officers. The purpose of a by-law is to regulate and define the duties of the members of the corporation toward the corporation and between themselves. The power to make the by-laws is vested in the stockholders. There are certain qualifications which all by-laws must possess. They must be reasonable and not inconsistent with law or any rule of public policy. It would not be possible for a majority of the stockholders at a regular stockholders' meeting to pass by-laws which would deliberately deprive the minority stockholders of rights which belong to them. The by-laws are, of course, always subject to the provisions of the charter of the corporation, and if a corporation is authorized to operate a railroad, it could not, by passing a by-law, to the effect that it was deemed wise to enter into the steel manufacturing business, change the nature of the corporation in that manner.

STOCKHOLDERS' MEETING.—In order that the acts of the majority of stockholders shall be valid, they must be authorized at a regular stockholders' meeting. This must be held in the principal office of the company, and the notice required by the by-laws must be given to all of the stockholders. After this is done, the majority of the stockholders may transact business and bind the corporation. Of course, in a large corporation with a hundred thousand shareholders, as is the case with some of our bigger corporations like the United States Steel Corporation and the Pennsylvania Railroad, very few of the stockholders actually attend the meetings. The directors usually send out with the notice of the meeting, a proxy, and the stockholders who are not able to be present send in their proxy authorizing certain persons to vote for them. In this way, a majority of the stockholders are present at the meeting, either in person or by proxy. In certain cases stockholders may interfere with the action of directors in connection with the general management of a corporation, or may even oust the directors from their positions. These cases are extremely rare, since the power of directors is supreme as to all corporate matters as to which the statutes or by-laws do not provide for concurrence or other action by the stockholders. Where proof is offered, however, of fraud, violation of law or gross negligence of the directors whereby loss has been caused or is threatened, stockholders may in some cases obtain the ousting of directors. This sometimes results in placing a receiver in temporary charge of the corporation or in the holding of a special election of new directors. No complaint, however, will generally be entertained against directors merely because their judgment does not agree with that of the stockholders even if some action of the directors may not have resulted favorably to the corporation, provided such action was taken honestly and with all due care and regard to law. As an illustration, the directors of the X Company made a certain contract on behalf of the corporation whereby it was agreed with Y that property of the corporation should be transferred to the latter for much less than its evident actual value. This operation would usually indicate fraud on the part of the directors, or at least such gross negligence as would in many cases justify stockholders in asking a legal inquiry into the action of the directors, which would result, if sufficient facts were proved, in their removal and an injunction against the performance of the contract. However, if the value of the property were doubtful and the directors had used all due care and effort to ascertain its true value and to obtain the best available price, no complaint could usually be made although it should later develop that a better price might have been obtained.

FOREIGN CORPORATIONS.—A foreign corporation is one which is organized under the laws of some foreign country or some other State. Foreign corporations are not necessarily confined to doing business in their own State; they may enter other States. As for example, a company organized in New Jersey may enter the State of New York and do business. If, however, the New Jersey corporation comes to New York and makes a regular practice of doing business, it must comply with the provisions of the corporation law of New York, and secure a license to do business in New York. It is not uncommon to enforce this provision in an indirect method by providing that if a foreign corporation does not take out this license, it shall not be allowed to sue in the courts of the State where it is doing business.

MANAGEMENT OF CORPORATIONS.—The management of any corporation rests directly with the board of directors and they may be considered as the agents of the corporation to direct its business affairs. The directors, however, are subject in their action to any limitation upon their power which may have been included in the charter or certificate of incorporation or which may have been adopted in the by-laws. The directors are also subject to any provisions in the statutes of the State, which frequently provide that they shall not take certain important actions, such as the mortgaging of corporate property, etc., without special procedure involving a meeting and vote of the stockholders. Where, however, the directors' authority is not limited by the statutes or the charter or by-laws, they may be considered as having full power to manage the affairs of the corporation. In connection with that power they may elect a president and other corporate officers and may appoint any other agents or employees at their discretion. They may also define the powers to be exercised by the president and the other officers and employees. This would give them power to limit the authority of the president or any other officer. However, where a person deals with the president or any other officer of a corporation in behalf of the corporation, he may usually rely reasonably upon the president or other officer having similar power to that generally possessed by such an officer, and in many cases the corporation would be held bound by the acts of such officer even though he actually violated some limits placed upon him by the directors. This may be illustrated by assuming that the X Company was in the business of manufacturing furniture, and A, the president thereof, had made a contract with B, an outsider, for the purchase from the latter of certain wood to be used in the corporate business. As a matter of fact, however, A, the president, had no power to make such contract, since the directors had passed a resolution forbidding him to purchase any raw materials without first having the proposed purchase approved by the board of directors. Therefore, A, as a matter of fact, would have no power to make the contract with B, on behalf of the corporation. Yet, B had not in any way been warned of this limitation upon A's power, and as the purchase of materials would be a usual one for the president or executive head of such a corporation to make, B might reasonably assume that A had power to make the contract. Therefore, B would be able to hold the corporation to the contract under the principle of apparent authority, considered in connection with the law of agency. Naturally, in turn, the directors would have a claim against the president for any loss sustained, as he had not only violated his duty but had also disobeyed and disregarded explicit instructions. The by-laws of a corporation are generally adopted by the stockholders and provide for all matters relating to the corporate management which are not provided for in the charter or certificate of incorporation. Such by-laws are binding upon all persons who know of them, or reasonably should know of them, provided they are not in violation of law and are reasonable. It is the general rule that meetings called to adopt new by-laws or to alter previous by-laws should be announced in some special way so that all interested parties may receive due notice and thus have an opportunity to arrange to be present and vote on the matters to be taken up at such meeting.

ELECTION OF DIRECTORS.—The directors of a corporation are elected by the stockholders and the election generally takes place at the regular annual meeting of stockholders of the corporation. Either the entire board of directors is elected at that time for the ensuing year, or a portion of them. In this connection it is provided by the statutes of many States that at least a certain proportion of the total number of directors shall be elected annually. The method of electing such directors at the annual meeting is usually provided for by the statutes of the various States, but it is commonly the rule that each stockholder shall have one vote for each share of stock owned by him, although in some States they also allow what is termed "cumulative voting." This method of voting generally allows each stockholder to have as many votes as he owns shares of stock multiplied by the number of directors to be elected at the meeting and he may cast all of his votes for one or more of the candidates. In other words if five directors are to be elected he may concentrate all his votes upon one or more of the candidates and is not compelled to vote for each one. This cumulative voting is authorized for the purpose of allowing the minority stockholders to concentrate their votes upon one or two of the candidates and thus have some representation upon the board of directors. As an illustration of this, let us assume that the X Company had an authorized capital stock of $100,000, composed of 1,000 shares at the par value of $100 per share, and that all these 1,000 shares are issued and fully paid up. Let us further assume that six individuals each own 100 shares of stock and act in unison, thereby constituting a majority, the other 400 shares of stock being held by the minority stockholders. Each stockholder would usually have one vote for each share of stock owned by him, and therefore, if five directors were to be elected under the usual method of voting, those individuals composing the majority of the stockholders would succeed in casting a majority of votes for each of the five directors. This would leave the minority without representation upon the board. If, however, cumulative voting were used, the minority having a total of 2,000 votes (400 multiplied by 5, the number of directors to be elected) could concentrate 2,000 votes upon one or two of their candidates and this would probably insure the election of such candidates to the board, thus giving the minority representation. In the case of a non-stock or membership corporation, each member has simply one vote for directors or for other purposes. It may be noted that the directors themselves, in their meetings, have also one vote each and this is entirely independent of the amount of stock which they may own in the corporation. It should also be noted that the directors in their meetings may not vote by proxy, but sometimes the members of a membership corporation may vote in this way. Voting by proxy is a usual practice in stock corporations. A proxy is merely a power of attorney or agency given in writing by one stockholder whereby he authorizes another person as his proxy to vote, at a corporate meeting, his shares of stock in his place. A proxy should be in writing and in a form in accordance with the statutes of the State involved, and is often, but not necessarily, under seal. A stockholder who has given a proxy may revoke it whenever he chooses and this would prevent the holder of the proxy from voting on it. This would be entirely independent of whether the person giving the proxy had by revoking it violated his contract with the person to whom it was given. That contract would be only a private matter between them.

VOTING TRUSTS.—The proxy principle is involved in what are termed "voting trusts." These arrangements involve the placing by a number of stockholders of their stock in the hands of certain persons, giving to the latter the right to vote on the stock; in other words, it is a concentration of the stock of a number of persons in the hands of one or a few persons. The latter are termed "voting trustees." It is necessary to consult the statutes of the various States with regard to the legality of such voting trusts, but they are generally permitted, with the restriction, however, that the agreement under which the stock is deposited with the voting trustee or trustees must be in writing and that any stockholder may have the right to deposit his stock with such trustee or trustees and become a party to the voting trust. The statutes also frequently limit the time during which such a voting trust may continue.

ISSUE OF STOCK.—The stock of a corporation is in theory issued for an amount of money or property equal to the par value of the stock. In practice, however, in many States there is no limitation on the valuation which the promoters of a corporation may put upon the property or rights which are transferred to the corporation. The stock is regarded as fully paid in if property transferred to it is transferred as having the assumed value of the corporation's capital, however little the property may actually be worth. In other States, however, an official must approve the valuation put upon property transferred as payment for stock, and in such States it may be assumed that the assets of a corporation when it begins business represent at least approximately the amount of its capital stock; even in such States, however, there is no difficulty in promoting a corporation which shall have a large capital though its property is of slight value. All that is necessary is to incorporate under the laws of another State which allows greater freedom. Corporations organized in one State are in general allowed to do business in other States; so that a corporation which is intended to carry on business in New York, may be incorporated in another State, where it is not expected to do business.

PROCEDURE IN ISSUING BONDS.—It is sometimes difficult for the investor fully to appreciate the vast amount of detail work involved in the bringing out of a new bond issue. Before the investment banker underwrites the issue, or makes his purchase from the corporation—before the bonds are offered to the public—there is always a painstaking and minute investigation of the new security from many different viewpoints, made by and in behalf of the banker. The investor can never know from the banker's printed circular, descriptive of the issue, the great amount of original work which underlies it and of which it is a meager reflection. The circular is a summary of the banker's investigation; it contains the salient features of the issue and of the issuing corporation, reduced to terms that are intelligible to the average layman. It is a statement of the principal facts which led the banker to make an investigation of the business and upon which investigation he bases his recommendation of the security offered by him to his clients.

WHAT IS A BOND?—This can be explained best by comparing it with a real estate bond and mortgage, the nature of which has already been discussed. When money is loaned on real estate, the mortgagor, or the one who borrows, executes two papers in favor of the mortgagee, or the lender. The first is either a promissory note or a bond. The bond is a sealed writing whereby the borrower binds himself, his heirs, administrators or executors, or assigns, to pay the lender a given sum of money at a specified time, together with interest. The second paper given as security for the note or bond, is a mortgage, which conveys the title to the property to the lender, with the provision, however, that if the borrower satisfies the conditions imposed in the bond—that is, the payment of a certain sum of money at a given time, together with interest as agreed—this conveyance (mortgage) is to be held null and void.

WHAT IS A CORPORATION INDENTURE?—The indenture is a more lengthy instrument than the bond, and, as will be noted, it is called an "indenture" and not a "mortgage." The mortgage strictly is only that portion of the indenture whereby the property is conveyed or deeded to the mortgagee, with the provision that the deed so given is to be held null and void in the event that the conditions named in the bond are faithfully carried out. The indenture is broader than the mortgage; it contains provisions other than those bearing directly on the mortgage. An indenture is a sealed agreement between two or more parties and any number of provisions may be inserted in it, in addition to the mortgage clauses, as may be deemed necessary or desirable. It is always possible for the individual to obtain a loan secured by a lien on his property, provided the security is good and considered ample. If, however, his property was of so great value that he desired to obtain a loan of several millions of dollars, he would find it difficult, or even impossible, to find any one person willing to lend him so large an amount. If, however, the borrower could find a number of persons who could and would jointly contribute enough money to equal the amount of the loan, he could divide this total amount into equal parts and each lender could have such a proportionate interest as might be desired. This, then, is the case with large corporations, which are legalized persons. Owing to the fact that the holders of the bonds have only a fractional interest in the loan and therefore in any property that may be pledged to secure it, it is impossible to create separate mortgages in favor of the individual bondholders on any particular part of the property. No portion of the property can be specifically designated—the interests of the bondholders are in common. For this reason and others, corporations are obliged to create what is known as a Mortgage Deed of Trust—making the mortgage to secure the many bonds in favor of some responsible individual or trust company, who holds it on behalf of the various bondholders in accordance with the definite terms of the trust, and who is therefore known as the Trustee. The indenture of the corporation must in addition to covering the mortgage, contain other related and necessary covenants, especially as to the trust that must be created. As there are so many covenants or provisions necessary in order to fully protect all interests concerned, the corporation indenture becomes bulky, but its form in substance is not very different from that of the bond and mortgage of the individual, which we have already analyzed, and which for this reason it is well for us to keep in mind as we follow the corporation indenture.

ANALYSIS OF INDENTURES. — The indenture, or agreement, must of necessity be made between certain parties, the mortgagor or the corporation and the mortgagee, in this case the Trustee who holds the security given in trust for the various bondholders. It is, therefore, proper that we recite at the very beginning of the indenture the parties in interest, giving their legal residence, or as in the case of corporations the names of the States wherein they are incorporated. It is quite essential that we know in what State a corporation was incorporated, as its rights and privileges are determined by the statutes of the State which created it and by the charter which has been granted to it. What are our reasons for creating the indenture? The very first premise is that the corporation is legally able to borrow money by law. If it did not have this right we could proceed no further. To borrow money and mortgage or pledge property as security therefor is a common law right of corporations, but the amount which may be borrowed is sometimes limited by State statutes. In the event that the corporation desired to borrow in excess of the limitation, additional capital stock is sometimes authorized thereby creating a larger basis for borrowing. If this premise is not incorporated, its omission does not affect the status of the indenture, but it is generally placed, as many other premises are, in the indenture, for the sake of logic, and to show that the matter has been considered, and that the fact is admitted by the parties to the indenture. The purpose for which the bonds are to be issued is sometimes duly set forth, as for instance, to refund certain maturing obligations, to construct a certain extension, to build new terminals, etc. While the purpose may not always be mentioned in the indenture, nevertheless it must accord with the charter of the corporation and the laws of the State. The company cannot exceed the powers that have been granted to it. We next want to know whether the authority to borrow money and issue bonds therefor has been obtained in lawful manner. Provisions covering the manner of securing this authority will be found in the by-laws of the corporation, and the counsel must examine this matter carefully in order to see whether all legal formalities have been strictly observed and whether the resolutions are in proper order. There are certain essential facts that must be stated in the bonds themselves and which are elaborated in the covenants of the indenture. These facts are embodied in the resolutions of the Board of Directors and of the stockholders and are, therefore, incorporated in the premises of the indenture. These facts include the total amount of bonds authorized, title, denomination, form, date of issue and maturity, rate of interest and where payable. In order that there may be uniformity in the wording and form of the bonds, so that no one holder will perchance receive an undue advantage over any other bondholder, the form of the bond, its coupons and trustee's certificate must be duly set forth in the indenture.

LIMITATION OF POWERS OF DIRECTORS.—There are various matters wherein directors of any corporation do not usually have power to act on behalf of the corporation without special authorization. Such matters include the amendment of the corporate charter (thereby changing the purposes of the corporation), the change of the name of the corporation, the increase or decrease of authorized capital stock, the sale of the total corporate assets and franchise, the consolidation of the corporation where permitted by statute, and the giving of mortgages upon the corporate property. This last point is especially important since the validity of a corporate mortgage as security for a loan of money depends upon whether the mortgage was authorized and given in all respects pursuant to statute of the State involved. As these corporate mortgages not only are given as security for a single loan of money but also furnish security often for very large amounts of bonds, the matter of the authority of the directors and the validity of the mortgage becomes of great importance. Therefore the statutes of the State involved must be followed closely as to the procedure in connection with the giving of a mortgage. It may be stated, however, with regard to this matter and the other special matters mentioned, the statutes generally provide that some form of authorization should be obtained from the stockholders, generally through their vote at a special meeting called for that purpose, of which proper notification and announcement have been given; that some form of certificate as to the proceedings at such meeting be made and filed by the secretary and treasurer or other designated officer of the corporation; that it should also be filed in the office of the county clerk of the county involved and in the office of the Secretary of State; and that some notification of the act in question be also given to the directors as well as the stockholders. It is, of course, impossible to take up the details as to such matters, the only safe course to pursue being to follow with extreme care the statutes of the State wherein such action is to be taken. From the foregoing, however, the general purpose and effect of prevailing law may be seen.

DIVIDENDS ON STOCK.—Dividends on the stock of corporations are declared by the directors, who have power to use their discretion as to the amount to be disbursed in this way. The statutes are, however, very explicit in prohibiting the declaration of any dividends except out of the surplus profits of the business conducted by the corporation. With respect to dividends properly declared, the declaration of the directors generally provides that they shall be paid to all stockholders registered upon the books of the company at a specified date in the future. Hence, if a stockholder should sell or otherwise transfer his stock, after that date to another person, the latter, while becoming the owner of the stock, would not be entitled to the dividend when paid. It would be payable to the former stockholder, although he might, pursuant to the agreement made with the person to whom he sold the stock, turn over to the latter the amount of the dividend.

CUMULATIVE DIVIDENDS.—It frequently happens that a corporation does not earn any dividends in a particular year. The question arises, is the holder of a 7% preferred stock in a position to demand that the dividend be paid the following year. Suppose the corporation earns nothing in 1921 and earns 14% in 1922. The holder of one share of a non-cumulative preferred stock would receive the usual

7% dividend only in 1922. If the stock were cumulative he would receive 14%. In other words the unearned dividends accumulate and become a charge which the corporation must pay when sufficient is earned in prosperous years before the holders of common stock are entitled to receive any dividend. Usually the stock certificate and the articles of incorporation specify whether stock is cumulative or non-cumulative. If they do not, then reference to the law of the State where the company is incorporated, is necessary to decide such a question.

LIABILITY OF OFFICERS AND DIRECTORS TO THE CORPORATION.— Whether a corporation becomes liable by virtue of action taken by its officers or directors depends upon principles of agency applied to the law of corporations. These principles have already been stated. Whether the directors or officers are themselves personally liable is another matter. Conceivably they may be liable either to their employer (the corporation) or to creditors of the corporation. They are not directly liable to the shareholders as such. Any injury or wrong they may indirectly do to shareholders is directly done to the corporation, the shareholders being injured only because the corporation in which he is interested is injured. Shareholders may, however, institute proceedings against directors or officers if, as not infrequently happens, the corporation itself, being controlled by the wrong-doers, fails to take proceedings. The shareholders in such a case, however, demand redress for the corporation, not for themselves; and whatever may be recovered, is recovered for the benefit of the corporation. The duty of the directors and officers of the corporation is analogous to the duty of any agent to his principal. That is, each officer or director must exercise reasonable diligence in the performance of his work and must observe fidelity to his principal. The application of these principles to particular fact is not always easy, but the principles themselves are plain. Especially the degree of care which directors are bound to use presents a troublesome question of fact. In a small business it may be the duty of a director to take active control of the policy of the company and supervise with some minuteness each business operation. Such direction is impossible where a great railroad or industrial corporation is concerned. In such a case directors necessarily derive their information from subordinate agents and cannot investigate facts for themselves. Directors are not liable for mistakes of judgment if they use reasonable care; if, however, they wilfully do an act which they know is not authorized by the charter or by-laws of the corporation, they will be liable for the consequences. Directors who are cognizant of wrongs committed by their co-directors and fail to take available measures to prevent the wrongs, become liable themselves. Directors may terminate their liability for future acts by resigning, but resignation will not destroy liability for acts already done even though the resulting damage does not happen until after resignation. The corporation requires that a director or other officer shall not act on behalf of the corporation in a matter in which he has a personal interest at variance with that of the corporation. Should matters of this sort arise, as they often do, the interested officer or director should not take part in the decision of the question, and may render himself liable if he does so.

LIABILITY OF OFFICERS TO CREDITORS.—So long as a corporation is solvent, creditors of the corporation have no reason or right to seek redress from any one but the corporation itself. Creditors of an insolvent corporation, however, may enjoin action by the company's officers which is unauthorized or likely to prove detrimental to the assets of the corporation. If the officers knowingly misapply the assets of an insolvent corporation they are personally liable to the creditors for the injury caused thereby. They are liable sometimes by statute, but also even apart from statute, for false statements of the condition of the corporation in reliance upon which credit is given the corporation. Like other agents, the officers of a corporation impliedly warrant to persons with whom they deal their authority to do the acts which they undertake; and if authority is lacking, they are liable personally. The only qualification of this principle is that if the facts from which authority, or lack of it, may be determined, are known to the person dealing with them, they are not liable; that is, they do not warrant the correctness of an inference of authority from known facts.

LIABILITY OF BANK OFFICERS.—The principles governing the liability of bank directors and other officers of a bank are the same as those which govern similar questions regarding other corporations. The bank laws, however, impose certain duties and penalties which affect the application of general principles. It may be worth while to enumerate briefly some of the duties of different bank officers, a violation of which renders them personally liable. As to directors it has been said that "It is not necessary to show directly that the directors actually had their attention called to the mismanagement of the affairs of the bank, or to the misconduct of subordinate officers. It is sufficient to show that the evidence of the management or misconduct were such that it must have been brought to their knowledge unless they were grossly negligent or wilfully careless in the discharge of their duties." They are liable for the consequences not only of their own fraud but of their ultra vires acts. They are liable for approving the discount of notes known to be worthless or of so doubtful value as to be obviously unsafe. If guilty of negligence in failing to discover that such paper was worthless they may also be liable. They are guilty of negligence and may thereby render themselves liable if they wholly neglect to ascertain the condition of the bank from its books, though a thorough examination of the books of a bank, especially of one transacting a large business, cannot be expected of every director; and the law would require no more than would be demanded by the standard of reasonableness.

THE PRESIDENT.—The duties of the president, and consequently his liabilities, must be determined by general law, the charter of the particular institution, its by-laws, and by general business usage. Thus, if the usage exists for the president to draw and sign checks in the absence of the cashier, the president will have authority so to act. He has authority to conduct the litigation of the bank; he may employ counsel. He may generally indorse negotiable paper of the bank. On the other hand, he will be personally liable if he permits improper loans or over-drafts; if he fails to give proper instructions to inferior officers; if it is his duty to require a bond from an inferior officer, and he fails to do so; and, generally, if he commits a breach of duty to the corporation which causes damage. He has no power to execute deeds of real estate without authority of the directors and, generally, an instrument which must be executed under the seal of the bank must be authorized by the board. The discount of negotiable paper also is a duty of the directors.

THE CASHIER.—The Supreme Court of Maine has thus expressed the functions of the cashier of a bank: "A cashier, it is well known, is allowed to present himself to the public as habitually accustomed to make payment for its bills or notes payable to other persons; to make payment for bills and notes discounted by the directors; to receive payment for bills of exchange, notes, and other debts due to the bank; to receive money on deposit and to pay the same to the order of the depositors. He is presented as having the custody of its books, bills of exchange, notes, and other evidences of debt due to it, and, indeed, of all its movable property; as making entry in its books and as keeping its accounts and a record of its proceedings. In many banks these duties are performed in part by tellers, clerks, or assistants, but generally, it is believed, under his superintendence, and he might at any time assume the performance of them and perform them, if able to do so, without such assistance. His true position appears to be that of a general agent for the performance of his official and accustomed duties. While acting within the scope of this authority he would bind the bank, although he might violate his private instructions." He must exercise proper oversight over subordinate officers; he must use reasonable care and skill. He may become liable personally for failure to observe instructions as to a special deposit; for the improper sale of stock held as security for a loan; for improperly making loans, for failure to give essential information to the directors; for failing to exercise proper oversight over inferior officers or agents, as well as in the more obvious case where he has taken advantage of his position to commit intentional fraud upon the bank.

BLUE SKY LAWS.—The term "blue sky" has become very familiar to the corporation lawyer in the last few years. The so-called "blue sky" legislation is a well meaning, if partly futile, attempt to meet an existing evil in connection with the sale of corporate securities. We shall find later that five elements are necessary to constitute the action of fraud or deceit: (1) a false representation of a material fact; (2) made with knowledge of its falsity; (3) with intent that it be acted upon; (4) that it be acted upon; (5) damage follows. The courts have almost universally held that a mere statement of opinion does not give rise to a cause of action for fraud, whereas a mistatement of fact does. Hence if I state to you when selling you 100 shares of the Bonanza Gold Mining Corporation that the company has never paid less than 20% in dividends during the last five years and you purchase the stock relying on this misrepresentation of fact (the situation actually being the company has never paid a dividend) you would have a cause of action in deceit against me. If, however, I had simply said in selling you the stock that the outlook for the company was the brightest in its history, that the president had told me that dividends of 30% a year were assured indefinitely and that this stock was by far the best bargain which had been on the market in over a year, although I know when I made such statements that there was little or nothing to substantiate them, nevertheless, I would not be liable in deceit. My statements were merely matters of opinion or what we call "seller's talk" or "puffing one's wares."

THE FINANCIAL PROSPECTUS.—If you will examine the average financial prospectus of a new stock being offered for sale to the public, you will find that when most of the high sounding terms and flattering statements are analyzed carefully that they will fall in this second class of non-actionable statements. There are few statements of fact but many glowing statements in the nature of "seller's talk." We all know, however, that enormous quantities of worthless stock are sold each year by this method. When business conditions are good it sometimes seems as if the wilder the scheme the easier it is to find a gullible public ready to purchase such securities. To prevent the perpetration of such frauds on the public is the object of the so-called "blue sky" legislation.

THE LAW ANALYZED.—The first "blue sky" law was passed in Kansas in 1911. The evil sought to be remedied was so prevalent that the idea spread rapidly and now similar legislation, of one type or another, has been enacted in a majority of the States. Some of the acts are crude, some have been held unconstitutional, and many are difficult of enforcement. Recently, however, more care has been taken in drafting such legislation, and many of the earlier laws will undoubtedly be amended to conform with this later legislation. We may take the Illinois statute of 1919 as a good sample of a drastic yet fairly workable Act. The law may be briefly considered from three standpoints: (1) the persons affected; (2) the securities affected; (3) the penalties provided for violation of its provisions.

AS TO THE PERSONS AFFECTED.—Generally any person offering any securities, and any seller's agent or broker, the issuer, or any agent or director of the issuer, or any owner or dealer, is covered by the Act. Illinois fiscal corporations such as banks, trust companies, insurance companies, building and loan associations and the like are practically exempt from the provisions of the Illinois securities law.

THE ILLINOIS ACT.—The Illinois act covers the following securities:

Section 3. For the purposes of this Act securities are divided into four classes as follows:

(1) Securities, the inherent qualities of which assure their sale and disposition without the perpetration of fraud, which shall be known as securities in Class "A";

(2) Securities, the inherent qualities of which, or in the nature of one or both parties to the sale thereof, assure their sale and disposition without the perpetration of fraud, which shall be known as securities in Class "B";

(3) Securities based on established income, which shall be known as securities in Class "C";

(4) Securities based on prospective income, which shall be known as securities in Class "D";

Section 4. Securities in Class "A" shall comprise securities:

(1) Issued by a government or governmental agency, or by anybody having power of taxation of assessment;

(2) Issued by any National or State bank or trust company, building and loan association of this State, or insurance company organized or under the supervision of the Department of Trade and Commerce of this State;

(3) Issued by any corporation operating any public utility in any State wherein there is or was at the time of issuance thereof in effect any law regulating such utilities and the issue of securities by such corporation;

(4) Appearing in any list of securities dealt in on the New York, Chicago, Boston, Baltimore, Philadelphia, Pittsburgh, Cleveland or Detroit Stock Exchange, respectively, pursuant to official authorization by such exchanges, respectively, and securities senior to any securities so appearing;

(5) Whereof current prices shall have been quoted from time to time for not less than one year next preceding the offering for sale thereof, in tabulated market reports published as news items, and not as advertising, in a daily newspaper of general circulation, published in this or in an adjoining State, including the State of Michigan, not including any trade paper or any paper circulating chiefly among the members of any trade or profession;

(6) Issued by any corporation organized not for pecuniary profit or organized exclusively for educational, benevolent, fraternal, charitable or reformatory purposes;

(7) Being notes or bonds secured by mortgage lien upon real estate or leasehold in any State or territory of the United States or in the Dominion of Canada, when the mortgage is a first mortgage on real estate, and when in case it is not a first mortgage lien or is on a leasehold, the mortgage and notes or bonds secured thereby (not including interest notes or coupons) shall each bear a legend in red characters not less than one-half inch in height, indicating (1) that the mortgage is on a leasehold, if that be the case, and (2) that the mortgage is a junior mortgage, if that be the case;

(8) Being a note secured by first mortgage upon tangible or physical property, when such mortgage is assigned with such securities to the purchaser;

(9) Evidencing indebtedness due under any contract made in pursuance to the provisions of any statute of any State of the United States providing for the acquisition of personal property under conditional sale contract;

(10) Being negotiable promissory notes given for full value and for the sole purpose of evidencing or extending the time of payment of the price of goods, wares or merchandise purchased by the issuer of such notes in the ordinary course of business, and commercial paper or other evidence of indebtedness running not more than twelve months from the date of issue;

(11) Being subscriptions for the capital stock under any license issued to commissioners to incorporate a company under the laws of this State where no commission or other remuneration paid for the sale or disposition of such securities;

Securities in Class "A" and the sales thereof shall not be subject to the provisions of this Act.

Section 5. Securities in Class "B" shall comprise securities:

(1) Sold by the owner for the owner's account exclusively when not made in the course of continued and repeated transactions of a similar nature;

(2) Increased capital stock of a corporation sold or distributed by it among its stockholders without the payment of any commission or expense to solicitors, agents or brokers in connection with the distribution thereof;

(3) Sold by or to any bank, trust company, or insurance company or association organized under any law of this State or of the United States, or doing business in this State under the supervision of the Department of Trade and Commerce; or of the auditor of Public Accounts; or by or to any building and loan association organized and doing business under the laws of this State, or any public sinking fund trustees; or to any corporation or dealer or broker in securities;

(4) Sold or offered for sale at any judicial, executor's or administrator's sale, or at any sale by a receiver or trustee in insolvency or bankruptcy, or at a public sale or auction held at an advertised time and place;

Securities in Class "B," when disposed of by the persons and in the manner provided by this section, shall not be subject to the provisions of this Act.

Section 6. Securities in Class "C" shall comprise the following:

Those issued by a person, corporation, firm, trust, partnership or association owning a property, business or industry, which has been in continuous operation not less than two years and which has shown net profits, exclusive of all prior charges, as follows:

(1) In the case of interest-bearing securities not less than one and one-half times the annual interest charge upon all outstanding interest-bearing obligations;

(2) In the case of preferred stock not less than one and one-half times the annual dividend on such preferred stock;

(3) In the case of common stock not less than 3% per annum upon such common stock.

Section 7. Securities in Class "C" may be disposed of, sold or offered for sale upon compliance with the following conditions, and not otherwise:

A statement shall be filed in the office of the Secretary of State:

(1) Describing the evidence of indebtedness, preferred stock or common stock intended to be offered or sold;

(2) Stating the law under which and the time when the issuer was organized;

(3) Giving a detailed statement of the assets and liabilities of such issuer and income of profit and loss statement, and giving an analysis of surplus account;

(4) Giving the names and addresses of its principal officers and of its directors or trustees;

(5) Giving pertinent facts, data and information establishing that the securities to be offered are securities in Class "C."

Such statement shall be verified by the oath of not less than two credible persons having knowledge of the facts. Not less than twenty-five copies of such statement, wholly printed or wholly typewritten, shall at the time of filing the original statement be filed with the Secretary of State. The printed or typewritten copies so filed shall bear at the top in bold faced type the expression:

"Securities in Class 'C' under Illinois Securities Law," followed by the expression, also in bold-faced type:

"This statement is prepared by parties interested in the sale of securities herein mentioned. Neither the State of Illinois, nor any officer of the State, assumes any responsibility for any statement contained herein nor recommends any of the securities described below."

Section 8. All securities other than those falling within Class "A," "B" and "C," respectively, shall be known as securities in Class "D."

Section 9 gives the requisites of the statement required to be filed with the Secretary of State before securities of Class "D" may be sold. Such statement is even more complete than that required in Section 7.

SALES AND CONTRACTS VOID.—Every sale or contract in violation of the act is void, and the fines vary from not less than $100 to not more than $25,000, and the imprisonment from six months to five years. Although there is great need for a Federal incorporation act there is even greater need for a Federal blue sky law. With different acts in the different States, the Illinois act being simply an example, even the most careful business man may unwittingly find himself in a position where he has violated one of these laws with their severe penalties.

CHAPTER VII

TRANSFER OF STOCK

UNIFORM TRANSFER OF STOCK.—Turn now to an entirely different matter, the transfer of stock. A stock certificate is one of the quasi-negotiable instruments of commerce, at common law not fully negotiable like bills and notes, but, nevertheless, having some of the attributes of negotiability, especially in States where what is called the Uniform Transfer of Stock Act has been enacted. This statute applies only to corporations of those States which have passed the statute.

TWO METHODS OF TRANSFERRING STOCK.—Stock may be transferred in two ways: first, by delivery of the certificate with the indorsement upon it of the owner of the stock, indicating that he assigns or authorizes the assignment of the stock, and second, by delivery of the certificate, with a separate document of assignment attached stating that the owner of the certificate assigns or authorizes the transfer of the stock. This second method is not so completely good as the first, where the assignment is on the certificate itself, because if for any reason the separate document should become detached from the certificate, the transferee's right would not be apparent, and therefore the Transfer of Stock Act provides that if a purchaser should get possession of the stock certificate with an indorsement upon it, he would take precedence over even a prior assignee who had a separate paper assigning the certificate to him. Of course, after the transfer is duly registered on the books of the company, then it makes no difference whether that transfer was secured by means of a separate power or assignment or by means of one written on the certificate itself.

EFFECT OF TRANSFER ON THE BOOKS OF THE COMPANY.—What is the effect of transfer on the books of the company? Under the common law, stock was originally transferable just like any intangible right, merely by agreement of the parties, to which requirement was added, as a necessity when stock certificates became common, the delivery of the certificate itself. But it was convenient for the company to know who was owner of its stock. It was inconvenient to have stockholders buy and sell without any notice to the company, and therefore a common by-law was that stock should be transferred only on the books of the company. The Uniform Transfer of Stock Act goes back partially to the old rule, since the transfer of the certificate with the indorsement or separate assignment is what transfers the stock, not the transfer on the books of the company; but in order that the corporation may not be inconvenienced it is provided that the corporation shall have the right to pay dividends to any one registered on the books of the company, such persons being the apparent owners, and that only such persons have the right to vote. An analogous custom that shows the importance of registration of stock transfers on the books of the company is the registry of deeds in the transfer of real estate. It is the deed, not the record of it, which creates a title, but an unrecorded deed may be defeated by creditors or purchasers without notice, so that to protect himself fully the owner of land is obliged to record his deed.

OWNERSHIP OF STOCK, INDIVIDUALLY, IN COMMON, JOINTLY AND BY FIDUCIARIES.—Stock may be owned by a man individually, it may be owned by several persons in common, or it may be owned by several persons jointly, or it may be owned by a person in a fiduciary capacity, as trustee, executor or guardian. What is the difference, may be asked, between the case of ownership of stock by several persons in common and ownership by several persons jointly. The common law drew this distinction between joint right and rights merely held in common; that a joint right survived to the survivors when one of them died, whereas a right held in common passed, on the death of one of the owners, pro rata to the personal representatives of the deceased. Therefore if A, B and C own stock jointly, when C dies A and B are the owners. If A, B and C own the stock in common, A, B and the executors of C would own it on the death of C. Generally where several persons own a right now, they own it in common, but there are two notable exceptions—the case of partnerships and the case of trustees. Stock held in the name of A, B and C, when A, B and C are either partners or trustees, will pass to A and B on the death of C. C's executor will not have to join in the transfer.

DIFFICULTIES IN TRANSFER AFFECT PURCHASER AND ALSO CORPORATION.—The difficulties in the transfer of stock may be looked at (1) from the standpoint of a purchaser of the stock, including within the name of purchaser one who lends money on the stock as well as one who buys it, and (2) from the standpoint of the corporation whose duty it is to transfer the stock on its books. Generally the difficulties which confront the purchaser are the same which confront the corporation when it is asked to transfer. If the purchaser should get a defective right when he bought, then the corporation, if it should transfer, would generally get into trouble also.

LEGAL AND EQUITABLE DIFFICULTIES IN TRANSFERS.—The main difficulties which arise may be divided into legal and equitable difficulties. By legal difficulties are meant cases in which the purchaser will not get a good legal title. By equitable difficulties, cases in which the purchaser will get a good legal title but which will be subject to an equitable right in favor of some other person. The person who has an equitable right cannot reclaim the stock from one who is, or succeeds to the rights of, a bona fide purchaser for value without notice.

LEGAL DIFFICULTIES—FORGED CERTIFICATE.—First, in regard to legal difficulties. The certificate of stock may be forged. The purchaser of a forged certificate of stock, of course, gets nothing in the way of stock. He does get the right, however, to sue the person who sold him the stock on an implied warranty of genuineness. Analogous to the situation of the purchaser is the situation of the corporation if, on receiving a forged certificate with a request for a transfer, it should transfer ownership on the books, completing the transfer by issuing a new certificate; for any person who took the new certificate, even though he was a bona fide purchaser for value, would not get any stock in the corporation, if all authorized stock had previously been issued. The corporation has no power to overissue stock; it cannot emit any more even if it tries, and therefore the purchaser gets no stock. He does, however, get a right against the corporation. The corporation has issued what purports to be new stock to him, or if he is a remote purchaser he has paid for stock in reliance on a certificate which the corporation has issued. The corporation is estopped, as the legal phrase is, to deny the validity of that certificate as against one who has thus relied on its acts. The result is that the corporation is bound to pay to him value equivalent to that of real stock, because the corporation has put out something which seems to be good stock, and owing to the act of the corporation the purchaser has been deceived.

FORGED ASSIGNMENTS.—A second legal difficulty arises where the indorsement or assignment of the certificate is forged. Only the owner of stock can sell it. Consequently, if anybody else attempts by forgery or otherwise to make a transfer, the transfer will be ineffectual. The result will be the same as though the whole certificate were forged. The purchaser under the forged indorsement will get nothing. If the corporation relies on the forged indorsement and issues a new certificate, it will, in the same way as in the case of a new certificate issued for a wholly forged one, be liable to a purchaser for value. It is, of course, of vital importance, therefore, to make sure that indorsements are correct, and generally it is desirable to take indorsed certificates only from reliable persons. If you take such a certificate from a reliable person, even though there is no express guaranty of signatures by a brokerage house or other third person, as there often is, you will be practically safe because of the implied warranty of genuineness by the seller which applies to the indorsement on certificates as well as to cases of wholly forged certificates.

ASSIGNMENTS BY UNAUTHORIZED AGENT.—A third case is where the indorsement is made by an agent, and the agent has no authority to act. A corporation transferring stock should require, and a purchaser should require, the clearest evidence of an agent's authority if the signature of the transferor is made by an agent. It is not only necessary to be sure that the agent's authority originally existed, but it is necessary to be sure that his power has not been revoked, either by the death of the principal or by express revocation during his life. A question that sometimes is troublesome, in regard to the agent's authority to make such an indorsement, arises where the terms of the power given the agent are general; where he is authorized to do a very broad class of acts for the principal, but no specific mention is made of the particular certificate which he seeks to transfer. Such a power, if it certainly includes the transfer of that certificate, is legally good, but a corporation would object to make a transfer under a power which did not specifically mention the particular certificate, unless it was absolutely certain from its terms that this certificate in question was included.

LACK OF CAPACITY TO ASSIGN.—A fourth case is lack of capacity on the part of the owner of the stock to make a transfer. This lack of capacity may arise from a variety of causes, insanity or infancy, for instance. A totally insane person is as incapable of transferring stock as of transferring other property. An infant, that is, a minor, though not wholly without capacity, if not under guardianship, becomes, presumably, wholly without capacity to transfer stock if under guardianship. An elderly person under the charge of a conservator would be incapacitated to transfer his property. An infant who has had no guardian appointed, though he could make a transfer, could also, by virtue of his infant's privilege, revoke that transfer, which, therefore, would be too insecure either for a purchaser to take or for a corporation to allow. If stock is owned by an infant, a purchaser or a corporation should require that a guardian be appointed and that the transfer be made by the guardian.

LACK OF DELIVERY—THEFT OF CERTIFICATE.—A fifth case is where the signature on the back of the certificate of stock is genuine, but where there has been no valid delivery by the owner. This is rather a troublesome case to detect. In the case of full negotiable instruments, like bills and notes, if the signature of an indorser is genuine, a purchaser for value of the instrument will get title even though he purchases from a thief, or though for any reason there was no intention on the part of the owner who wrote his name on the back to make a transfer of the instrument. But by the common law stock certificates were not negotiable to this extent. This case occurred in a law office in Boston: the head of the firm rather carelessly kept "street certificates" for stock (that is, certificates made out in the name of the brokerage firm which was the former owner and indorsed in blank), not having the certificates transferred to his own name. The stock was not at the time dividend-paying, so that a transfer on the books seemed unimportant. He put the certificates into the office safe to which the office boy had access. This boy took the certificates and sold them through a broker, and the loss was not discovered for several years. After it was discovered the loss was traced by the numbers of the certificates, and action was brought against the brokers who were unfortunate enough to have taken the stock from the office clerk. Now, if the certificates had been negotiable paper, the brokers would not have been liable, but under the law then existing it seemed so probable that they were liable that they settled the case by paying more than half the value of the stock. The only thing that could have prevented their being liable was that, under the circumstances, the contention was possible that the owner of the stock had been so negligent in his dealing with the certificates as to preclude him from asserting any right. Now the Transfer of Stock Act changes the law in this respect so far as Massachusetts stock certificates are concerned. The act makes them fully negotiable, but the common law would apparently still apply to certificates of stock of corporations incorporated in other States. And similar principles would be applicable in other States which have passed the same statute.

DEATH OF OWNER OF INDORSED CERTIFICATE.—A somewhat similar case is this: suppose that after the owner of stock has written his name on the back of it, he dies; that is a common enough case. Many men have used their stock certificates to borrow money on, and therefore, after paying the loan they have them in their possession with their signatures on the back. They put those certificates back in their safe deposit boxes. Then suppose the owner dies and an attempt is made to transfer the stock by virtue of that signature written on the certificate.

That is not a valid transfer at common law. The certificate was owned only up to the time of his death by the man whose name is on the face; on his death his executor becomes the owner and the executor's signature is necessary to transfer the title, and the signature of the man himself written before his death is not effective for that purpose; and yet a purchaser may not be aware that that signature is invalid; he may not know that the man who signed it is dead, and similarly the corporation may allow the transfer to go through in ignorance that the signer is dead. If the money which is the proceeds of the stock actually reaches the executor of the estate, of course he could not object to the validity of the transfer, and he could not object if he were in any way a party to the transfer of the stock by means of the signature of the dead man; but if the proceeds did not get to the hands of the executor and he was in no way responsible for the transfer, he could assert that the transfer was invalid and that that stock belonged to him. This, again, is changed by the uniform law so far as applies to corporations in the States which have enacted that law. To avoid misapprehension it should be said that if an indorsed certificate has been delivered for value by the owner, during his lifetime, to a purchaser or lender, the death of the indorser does not impair the validity of the signature even at common law. The purchase of the stock or a loan made on the stock gives the purchaser or lender a power which cannot be revoked by death or otherwise.

BANKRUPTCY OF THE OWNER OF STOCK.—One other important case, in which a genuine signature of one who was the owner cannot transfer a good title, is the case of bankruptcy. The Federal bankruptcy law provides absolutely that title to property which a bankrupt has at the time of his bankruptcy shall be vested in his trustee. If, therefore, after A's bankruptcy, A seeks to transfer stock which he had owned, and which was in his own name, he cannot do so, for he is no longer the owner of the stock, and he has no power to transfer it. Therefore, even a bona fide purchaser from a bankrupt will get nothing.

ATTACHMENT OF STOCK.—A sixth difficulty in regard to transfer of stock—attachment of the stock by a creditor of the registered owner—is eliminated in States where the Uniform Transfer Act has been enacted. Such attachments created considerable difficulty before the passage of the act. Suppose this case: A is the owner on the books of the company of 100 shares of Boston & Albany stock. He knows a creditor is about to attach that stock, and in order to get ahead of the creditor he sells the stock on the exchange. If he makes the sale before the attachment, undoubtedly the sale everywhere would prevail over the subsequent attachment; but suppose the attachment preceded by a little while the sale of the stock. A still has the certificate, and brokers and purchasers are accustomed to rely on the certificate as evidence of ownership. They take the certificate and pay A money for it; then when the purchaser goes to transfer the stock he finds that an attachment has been put upon the books of the company. Where the uniform law governs the case the only way to make an attachment of stock effective is to seize the certificate itself. But in other States this difficulty may still arise, of a purchaser being deceived by the certificate itself, and paying money on the faith of it when there has been an attachment levied by a creditor immediately before on the books of the company.

TRANSFERS BETWEEN HUSBAND AND WIFE.—One other matter of transfer deserves attention, and that is a transfer between husband and wife, or wife and husband. A married woman can contract in most States as fully as a married man, but generally, though not universally, neither of them can contract with the other or make a conveyance directly to the other. A promissory note from wife to husband, or husband to wife, or any other conveyance or transfer or contract was at common law and still is in many States invalid. A husband can, however, appoint his wife his agent, and a wife can appoint her husband her agent, and when such an agent acts, his act will be legally that of the principal, just as in any other case of agency. Accordingly, if a husband draws a check payable to his wife, though he does not become liable as drawer to his wife, and could not be sued by her if the check was not paid, the bank runs no risk in paying the check because the husband has authorized the bank to make a payment to the wife. Similarly, if a husband authorizes a corporation to transfer stock to his wife it seems that the corporation is protected, having acted under the authority of the owner, and that the wife would get a good title to the stock. This question has, however, been somewhat disputed by lawyers. Therefore it is very probable that a corporation would, as a matter of precaution, refuse to run any risk by transferring directly from husband to wife or vice versa, but would require that the transfer should be made through a third person in any State where husband and wife cannot contract with one another. So much for difficulties arising out of defects caused by the lack of legal title to the stock.

STOCK HELD IN TRUST.—Now let us consider equitable defects. Such defects chiefly arise where stock is held in trust. It would be the simplest and pleasantest thing for a corporation if it could refuse to register stock in trust at all, but it has been decided that it cannot do this, that it is bound, if requested, to register stock in favor of a trustee and issue stock to trustees. Now trustees hold under an appointment by the court. A trustee may cease to be such at any time by removal of the court as well as by death. Suppose stock in the name of D, trustee. If D has ceased to be trustee because he has been removed from office, a transfer by him will not be valid. Accordingly, it is essential for a corporation and for a purchaser to be certain, not simply that D was trustee, but that D is trustee at the time he attempts to make the transfer. We may suppose the case of a certificate which does not state that there is a trust. Not infrequently trustees, to avoid complications, do not specify in the certificate that they are trustees. If the corporation or if the purchaser of that stock has no notice that D is really holding that stock in trust, the corporation or the purchaser will have the same rights as if there were no trust. But if either the corporation or the purchaser learns, from extrinsic sources, that the stock is really held in trust, they will be bound to make certain that the seller is still empowered to act as trustee, in the same way as if the certificate specifically stated on its face that the stock was owned by D in the capacity of trustee.

ONE HAVING NOTICE THAT STOCK IS HELD IN TRUST MUST ASCERTAIN THE TERMS OF THE TRUST.—Even if the supposed trustee is actually the trustee he may not have power to give a good title to the stock. He has the legal title, undoubtedly, but if the certificate contains notice that he holds the legal title as trustee, every one is bound at his peril when purchasing the stock, and also the corporation is bound at its peril before it allows the transfer of the stock, to make sure that the trustee is authorized by the terms of his trust to transfer the stock.

A TRUSTEE HAS POWERS NECESSARY TO CARRY OUT TERMS OF TRUST.—Generally when a transfer of stock is attempted by a trustee it means that the trustee is selling the stock, though that is not necessarily the case. A trust may be terminated; that is, a trust may be created for twenty years, with directions to the trustee to transfer the trust property at the end of twenty years to certain beneficiaries. A transfer by the trustee at the close of the twenty years to the beneficiaries would not be a sale of the stock; it would be a transfer for the purpose of carrying out the trust, and a trustee always has implied power to make any transfer of stock that is necessary to carry out the purpose of the trust.

A TRUSTEE HAS NO IMPLIED POWER TO SELL.—A trustee has no implied power to sell. The general duty of a trustee is to keep the property which is left to him in trust or conveyed to him in trust in its existing form, and no power is implied to change the form to something else. Accordingly, if no power to sell is in terms given in a trust created by deed or will, a corporation will require, and a purchaser should require, the trustee to obtain the authority of the probate court to make the sale. Carefully drawn trusts generally contain a power for the trustee to sell if the purpose of the trust is to produce an income-bearing fund for a long period of years. For that purpose a change of investment is frequently desirable, and therefore trustees are expressly given that power. But the corporation which has issued a certificate to a trustee and a purchaser from the trustee must find out at their peril whether such a power is given.

A TRUSTEE HAS NO IMPLIED POWER TO PLEDGE.—Another power, and one which is not commonly given, is the power to borrow on stock, to pledge it or use it for collateral security. Such a power is not implied and is not commonly given in trust deeds or wills. Therefore, a bank or other lender should not lend on certificates of stock which are made out to the borrower as trustee, or made out to any one as trustee. Of course, it is improper, even though the trust did give power to borrow, to allow the trustee not only to borrow money on trust securities but to use the money borrowed as part of his own assets; that is, to put it in his own general account. It is his duty to keep trust money separate, and therefore if the trustee has power to borrow he should keep the funds which he borrows earmarked as trust property; but as has been said, he will rarely have power given him expressly to borrow even for trust purposes.

A TRUSTEE CANNOT TRANSFER TO HIMSELF.—Suppose a trustee is by a deed or will given power to sell and he asks the corporation to make a transfer of the stock to himself. The corporation should not do it. He has power to sell to any one else but himself. A fiduciary cannot make a bargain with himself in regard to his trust property, and therefore he should not be allowed to transfer the stock to himself.

A TRUSTEE CANNOT DELEGATE HIS POWER TO SELL.—A trustee cannot delegate his powers, and therefore he cannot give a general power of attorney to another, to sell trust stock or any trust property whenever it may seem wise to the agent to do so. Even though the trustee has himself power to sell, he must exercise his own discretion as to the occasion when it is proper to sell.

PURCHASER FROM A TRUSTEE IS NOT BOUND TO SEE TO APPLICATION OF PURCHASE MONEY.—Though the corporation and though the purchaser from a trustee are bound to see, if they have notice of the trust by the form of the certificate, that the trustee is not making an unauthorized sale, neither the purchaser nor the corporation is bound to see that the trustee does not make an improper application of the money received from sale of trust stock. In the current legal phrase, neither the purchaser nor the corporation is bound to see to the application of the trust money; but if either the purchaser or the corporation had notice of a proposed misapplication of the trust money to be received for the stock, it would be improper to allow the transfer knowing that the proceeds would be misapplied, and the corporation or the purchaser would be liable if the transfer was carried out.

AN EXECUTOR HAS IMPLIED POWER TO SELL.—Stock held by a guardian or by an executor is in many respects treated similarly to stock held by a trustee. There is this difference, however, in the executor's position, that as it is his duty to reduce the estate to cash he has in most, but not all States, an implied power to sell; it does not have to be given to him in the will. The will, however, may restrict an executor's right to sell certain stock, and therefore even in the case of an executor it would be proper for a corporation to make sure that the executor's power had not been restricted by the will before allowing the transfer.

TRANSFER BY AN EXECUTOR TO A LEGATEE.—Generally the executor will seek to reduce the property to cash and therefore seek to transfer the stock in the estate to a purchaser, but he may try to transfer it directly to a legatee. He may himself be a legatee and endeavor to transfer to himself. Unless he is a residuary legatee or a legatee of the specific stock in question it is as improper for him to transfer to himself as for a trustee to transfer to himself. Even though the executor is a pecuniary legatee or is entitled to payment for commissions, he would have no right to take stock in lieu of such pecuniary legacy or commission, for he cannot make such a bargain with himself though he might in regard to the legacy of another. If the executor is a specific or residuary legatee the question of a right to transfer to himself is the same as to transfer to any other legatee, and that right is only subject to one qualification. Creditors of an estate have the first right; legatees do not get their legacies paid unless creditors are taken care of first. Creditors have a fixed period from the time when executors or administrators give bonds within which to assert their claims. If they have not asserted their claims in that period the claims are barred. After that time has expired it is generally known whether the assets of the estate are sufficient to pay legacies, and it is usually then proper to allow a transfer to a legatee. Prior to that you run the risk—which may be in a particular case a very small one or it may be a very large one—that the creditors of the estate may exhaust the assets and the legatees not be entitled to anything.

LOST CERTIFICATES.—Occasionally a question arises in regard to a lost certificate. The Uniform Law provides for this case in substantially the same way as the common law would deal with it if there were no statute, namely, the corporation may demand a bond to indemnify it before it issues a new certificate. This bond is essential because should the old certificate turn up and be transferred to a bona fide purchaser for value, the corporation would be liable on the old certificate, and as it would also be liable to a purchaser for value of the new certificate it is necessary that it should have a bond to protect it.

INTERPLEADER OF SEVERAL CLAIMANTS FOR STOCK.—If there are several claimants for stock, as sometimes happens, the corporation should file a bill of interpleader, as it is called, against the several claimants, asking the court to determine which one is rightfully entitled. An instance of that kind would be where A asks a corporation to transfer stock to him, presenting a certificate indorsed by B, but B notifies the corporation that he has been defrauded out of that stock by A, and that he elects to rescind the transfer to A and demands the certificate back. The corporation cannot undertake to determine which of these parties is in the right; it must ask the court to do so. Not infrequently the same situation arises in a bank where money has been lent on stock, and notice is given to the bank not to return that security to the borrower because he obtained it fraudulently or otherwise has acted in violation of the rights of a third person in pledging it to the bank. The bank, if it is a bona fide lender, is, of course, entitled to hold the stock for its own security so far as it may be necessary to repay the loan; but perhaps the bank can get the loan repaid out of other securities unquestionably belonging to the borrower. In that event the bank should do so and then ask the court who is entitled to the disputed stock.

EFFECT OF DELIVERING UNINDORSED CERTIFICATE.—In order to transfer stock, as previously said, it is necessary that the stock should be either indorsed or that on a separate paper an assignment or power to transfer should be written. What is the effect of giving a certificate without either of these formalities? It virtually protects the person who receives the certificate, for though he has not title to the stock and cannot get title without an indorsement, he has the certificate in his possession which prevents any other person from getting title; and, furthermore, he has the right to require an indorsement from the person whose indorsement is needed, provided, of course, that the holder of the certificate took it from the owner, who impliedly or expressly agreed that he should have title. If somebody not an owner of a certificate delivered it without indorsement to a bank, and borrowed money on it, the bank would not be protected. The true owner could say, "That is mine," and take it away.

CHAPTER VIII
PERSONAL PROPERTY

PROPERTY DEFINED. — Property in the strict legal sense, is the aggregate of rights which one may lawfully exercise over particular things to the exclusion of others. "If a man were alone in the world," says Kant, "he could properly hold or acquire nothing as his own; because between himself, as Person, and all other outward objects, as Things, there is no relation. The relation is between him and other people, whom he excludes from the thing." All things are not the subject of property, because, the sea, the air, light, and similar things, cannot be appropriated.

ILLUSTRATION. — An illustration that gives us the idea of property will make our definition clear. A takes his shoes to a cobbler to be repaired. When he calls for them, he does not have the price for the work, and the cobbler refuses to give them up. Both A and the cobbler have a property right in the shoes. The right to absolute ownership is in A, that is his property right. The temporary possession, however, is in the cobbler, and he may hold the shoes under the lien for repairs indefinitely and until he receives his compensation. The lien is his property right. When we use the term property in its lowest form we mean by it the right of possession. In our illustration, the cobbler's lien gives him the right of possession. When we use the term in its highest form, we mean the right of exclusive ownership; in our illustration, A's shoes after he has paid the repair bill and secured the shoes again.

THE RIGHTS OF OWNERSHIP. — Exclusive ownership implies:

1. The right of exclusive possession for an indeterminate time.

2. The right of exclusive enjoyment for an indeterminate time.

3. The right of disposition.

4. The right of recovery if the thing be wrongfully taken or withheld.

But, you say, this is not the idea one ordinarily has of the term "property." One speaks thus of his watch: "I own this watch. It is my property." The answer is, property is a term with a double meaning. In the ordinary sense "property" indicates the thing itself, rather than the rights attached to it. Therefore it is that we have a law of personal property, and a law of real property.

PERSONAL PROPERTY AND REAL PROPERTY DISTINGUISHED. — Real property has been defined to be co-extensive with lands, tenements, and hereditaments; to put it more simply, we may say that it consists of land and anything that is permanently affixed to the land. Personal property embraces all objects which are capable of ownership except land. One fundamental difference between the two is that real property is generally considered to be immovable, while such property as is movable is usually termed personal property. It is important that the distinction between the two forms of property be kept in mind because different results follow where the property is held to be one or the other. For example, on the death of the owner of real property, it passes to his heir or devisee, while in the case of personal property, it goes to the personal representative, the executor or the administrator, and through him to the legatee or distributee. Again, in settling the estate of the deceased person, personal property is always to be used first to pay the decedent's debts. The modes of transferring personal property and real property differ. Real property is transferred by deed. Personal property may be transferred without any writing and even in the case of a transfer of personal property, by a bill of sale, the requirements for recording it are generally quite different from those relating to the recording of deeds. Again, the transfer of real property is governed by the law of the place where the real property is situated, whereas the transfer of personal property is governed by the law of the domicile of the owner. Taxation is another subject where the distinction is most important.

SALES OF PERSONAL PROPERTY.—The most important branch of the law of personal property, in the field of commercial law, is that relating to the sale of personal property. We shall confine the balance of this chapter to a consideration of that subject. As we have a uniform Negotiable Instruments Law, so we also have a Uniform Sales Act which has now been adopted in many of the States. The Sales Act defines a sale and a contract to sell as follows: (1) A contract to sell goods is a contract whereby the seller agrees to transfer the property in goods to the buyer for a consideration called the price. (2) A sale of goods is an agreement whereby the seller transfers the property in goods to the buyer for a consideration called the price. (3) A contract to sell or a sale may be absolute or conditional. (4) There may be a contract to sell or a sale between one part owner and another.

SALES AND CONTRACTS TO SELL.—Sales are to be distinguished from contracts to sell. A sale is an actual transfer of property, whereas a contract to sell is an agreement to make a sale in the future. Sales at a shop, for instance, are made without any contract to sell, but orders for goods at a distance, and agreements to ship them, frequently precede the actual sale of the goods, which is made in pursuance of the prior contract to sell. The sale of personal property is subject to different rules from the sale of real estate. In the transfer of real estate, formalities of deed and seal are necessary, which are not required in personal property, and the subjects must be considered separately.

A SALE DISTINGUISHED FROM SIMILAR TRANSACTIONS.—At the outset, a sale must be distinguished from several other similar transactions. The law of sales is a branch of contract law, hence consideration is necessary in a sale. A gift, on the other hand, which may result in the transfer of personal property in practically the same manner as a sale, does not require any consideration. Hence, an agreement to sell goods is unenforceable if not supported by consideration. A promise to make a gift is always unenforceable because the very idea of a gift negatives any idea of consideration. A sale and a bailment must also be distinguished. A bailment is the rightful holding of an article of personal property by one, for the accomplishment of a certain purpose, with an obligation to return it after the completion of that purpose. Where there is a sale, the entire property right passes to the new buyer, and if the article is destroyed, providing title has passed, the new buyer must pay the purchase price if he has not already done so, although he gets nothing for it. In a bailment, the title does not pass. The case of the cobbler repairing the shoes is an illustration of a bailment. If, while the shoes are in his possession, his shop is burned, through no fault of his, the owner of the shoes would stand the loss. If I borrow a person's automobile, and while using it the car is struck by lightning and totally destroyed, the loss falls on the owner because this also is a bailment. On the other hand, had I bought the car and temporarily kept it in the seller's garage, awaiting the completion of my own garage, and it is burned while in his garage, the loss is mine. By such a transaction, I become the owner when the sale is made, and the former owner becomes the bailee.

FORMALITIES NECESSARY FOR THE COMPLETION OF A SALE.—The Sales Act provides in section 3, subject to a few provisions, that "a contract to sell or a sale may be made in writing (either with or without seal), or by word of mouth, or partly in writing and partly by word of mouth, or may be inferred from the conduct of the parties." The main qualification of the right to make an oral sale or contract to sell is found in the next section (Section 4) which is virtually a copy of a similar provision in the English Statute of Frauds in regard to the sale of personal property. Section 4 reads as follows:

"(1) A contract to sell or a sale of any goods or choses in action of the value of five hundred dollars or upwards shall not be enforceable by action unless the buyer shall accept part of the goods or choses in action so contracted to be sold, and actually receive the same, or give something in earnest to bind the contract, or in part payment, or unless some note or memorandum in writing of the contract or sale be signed by the party to be charged or his agent in that behalf.

"(2) The provisions of this section apply to every such contract or sale, notwithstanding that the goods may be intended to be delivered at some future time or may not at the time of such contract or sale be actually made, procured, or provided, or fit or ready for delivery, or some act may be requisite for the making or completing thereof, or rendering the same fit for delivery; but if the goods are to be manufactured by the seller especially for the buyer and are not suitable for sale to others in the ordinary course of the seller's business, the provisions of this section shall not apply.

"(3) There is an acceptance of goods within the meaning of this section when the buyer, either before or after delivery of the goods, expresses by words or conduct his assent to becoming the owner of those specific goods."

THE CAPACITY OF PARTIES.—The Sales Act provides in section 2 that "capacity to buy and sell is regulated by the general law concerning capacity to contract, and transfer and acquire property. Where necessaries are sold and delivered to an infant, or to a person who by reason of mental incapacity or drunkenness is incompetent to contract, he must pay a reasonable price therefor. Necessaries in this section mean goods suitable to the condition in life of such infant or other person, and to his actual requirements at the time of delivery."

IMPORTANCE OF DISTINGUISHING SALE AND CONTRACT TO SELL.—Why is it important to distinguish between a contract to sell and a sale; what difference does it make whether title has passed or not? The primary reason that it makes a difference is because as soon as the title has been transferred from the seller to the buyer the seller is entitled to the price. Prior to the transfer of title, if the buyer refused to take the goods, the seller would be entitled only to damages, which would be the difference between the value of the goods which the seller still retained and the price which was promised. If the goods were worth as much or more than the amount of the price promised, the seller would not be entitled to any substantial damages. But after title has passed the buyer must pay the full price, and the seller may recover it if the buyer refuses to accept delivery. Another consequence flowing from the transfer of title is that the goods are thereafter at the risk of the buyer. If they are destroyed by accident the buyer must nevertheless pay the price, for the right to the price accrued before the goods were destroyed, and when they were destroyed they were at the buyer's risk. Bankruptcy is another circumstance which makes it important to determine who holds title to the goods. If the buyer becomes bankrupt, after title to the goods has passed to him, his trustee in bankruptcy takes the goods for his creditors, but if he becomes bankrupt before title has passed that would not be true. The bankruptcy of the seller would make a similar difference.

WHEN TITLE IS PRESUMED TO PASS.—There are several presumptions in the law as to when title will be presumed to pass if there was no specific agreement between the parties as to when it should pass. If they simply bargain for the goods without saying anything about the time when the buyer is to become the owner, the first presumption is that title passes as soon as the goods are specified and the parties are agreed on the terms of the bargain, even though no part of the price has been paid and though the goods have not been delivered. It is often assumed that delivery is essential to transfer title to goods, but that is not so, though delivery is strong evidence of intent to transfer title. If the parties have made their bargain, and definitely agreed on the terms of the bargain, title passes even though possession of the goods still remains in the hands of the seller. The seller, however, has a lien for the price though he has parted with title. As long as the goods are in his possession he may refuse to surrender until he is paid the price, unless he agreed to sell on credit.

TITLE PASSES WHEN PARTIES AGREE.—It is only a presumption that, where the terms of a bargain are fixed and the goods are specified, title passes at once, for if the parties agree that title shall not pass at once it will pass when and as they agree. Their intention in regard to the transfer of title may not be stated in express terms, and it may be gathered only from the acts or words of the parties. If something remains to be done to the goods by the seller, to put them in a deliverable condition, that indicates an intent that title shall not pass until they are in the condition agreed upon. If the parties provide that the goods shall be stored at the expense of the seller, for a time or at the risk of the seller, that indicates title is not intended to pass, for if they are at the seller's expense and risk, presumably they are still his goods. On the other hand, delivery of the goods indicates an intent to pass title, although it is possible, if the parties so agree, that title does not pass even though the goods are delivered. Again, payment of the price is evidence tending to show an intent to pass title, for buyers do not ordinarily pay the price in advance. It is not uncommon for credit to be given by the seller, but it is uncommon for the buyer to pay first; but even that is not impossible, and therefore, though payment of the price is evidence of an intent to transfer title immediately, it is not conclusive evidence.

TRANSFER OF TITLE BY SUBSEQUENT APPROPRIATION.—Suppose title does not pass immediately, which may be due to the fact that the parties so agreed, or to the fact that the goods were not specified at the time the bargain was made. That is a common case. A and B contract for the sale of 100 cases of shoes to be made by A. At the time the parties make their bargain the shoes have not yet been made, but the parties expect that they will be made later, and appropriated to the bargain, as the legal phrase is. Or title may not pass at the time the bargain is made, although the goods are specified. The parties may have expressly agreed that title should not pass; or though the goods are specified, something may remain to be done to them by the seller to put them in a deliverable condition. Now, if title for any of these reasons does not pass when the bargain is made, it may pass by an express agreement of the parties, made later, that the buyer shall take title and that the seller shall give title; or frequently it may pass by what is called an appropriation of the goods by the seller to the buyer, without any express later assent of the buyer, by virtue of an implied assent of the buyer given in the original agreement that the seller should appropriate the goods. What is meant will be understood by one or two illustrations.

APPROPRIATIONS BY DELIVERY TO A CARRIER.—Suppose A contracts to sell and ship to the buyer 100 cases of shoes, and B contracts to receive and pay for them. That shipment to the buyer is an appropriation of the goods. The very 100 cases with which the seller intends to fulfill the bargain are indicated by the delivery of them to the carrier, and the buyer, since he agreed in the first place that they should be shipped, has assented to the appropriation. Therefore, in such a case, as soon as the goods are delivered to the carrier the presumption is that title passes to the buyer. This is by far the commonest case of appropriation by the seller in accordance with authority given by the buyer in his original agreement, and it is so common that it deserves a little further treatment.

ILLUSTRATION.—This kind of appropriation can be very well illustrated by the case of a supposed sale of tobacco to a minor. A, a minor, lives in an outlying suburb of Boston where the sale of tobacco to a minor is not permitted. He buys goods of S. S. Pierce Company in Boston and wants to buy some cigars from them. He can buy cigars of them in Boston and send them out to his home, but the title must pass to him in Boston. If the title passes in the suburb it is an illegal sale by S. S. Pierce Company, and consequently they do not want to make it. Of course the buyer can go and get the goods and pay for them in Boston and send them himself to his residence. But suppose he sends an order by mail; if S. S. Pierce Company are willing to charge goods to him, giving him credit, they can send the goods by express, because on their shipment of the goods the title will pass and the buyer will become a debtor for the price of the goods in Boston; but they must not send the goods by their own wagon, as their carrying the goods themselves out to the buyer's residence leaves them in their possession until delivery, and the delivery does not take place until the goods are delivered from their wagon at his house. That would not do. Whereas if the goods are delivered to a public carrier in Boston the carrier would be the buyer's agent and title would pass in Boston.

THE SELLER MUST FOLLOW EXACTLY AUTHORITY GIVEN HIM.—Suppose the buyer specified that the goods are to be shipped by a given route, and the seller shipped them by a different route. Title would not pass then because the buyer had not authorized the seller to appropriate them to him, the buyer, in that way. It may be that the seller's way of sending them was better than that originally assented to by the buyer, but the seller, if he wishes to hold the buyer, as owner of the goods from the time of shipment, must get his approval of that better way. Still more important than the method of shipment is the character of the goods themselves. The seller cannot, by putting any goods on the train, transfer title. He must put on the train the very kind of goods which the buyer agreed to receive, and that will mean not simply, in the case supposed, that the goods must be shoes, but they must be merchantable shoes of the character and sizes which the buyer agreed to take. The goods must be properly packed and all usual precautions in regard to them taken. In so far as the original agreement specified what was to be done, those things must be done. In so far as the original agreement does not specify how the goods are to be shipped, or what shall be done in regard to them, the seller has discretion to do anything which is customary and proper for a careful business man.

SHIPMENT OF GOODS C. O. D.—There has been considerable litigation in regard to the effect of shipping goods C. O. D. Suppose goods were ordered and goods of the sort ordered were shipped in accordance with the directions in the order, but were marked C. O. D. Those letters mean, as you know, collect on delivery, and two possible explanations may be given of their effect. One, that the seller retains not only control of, but also title to, the goods until they are delivered and the price paid. According to that view the carrier is made the seller's agent, to hold the title to the goods and transfer it to the buyer when he pays for the goods. But the better view is that the carrier merely retains a hold on the goods, a lien on behalf of the seller, while title to the goods passes on shipment.

EFFECT OF THE FORM OF A BILL OF LADING.—One cannot speak of title passing or being retained on shipment of goods without referring to bills of lading, for the general rules which have been given must be qualified by this statement, that by means of a bill of lading the title may be at will retained or transferred (if the buyer has authorized a transfer). The proper way to indicate a transfer of title when goods are shipped is to have the buyer named as consignee in the bill of lading. A bill of lading is very much like a promissory note; the carrier promises to deliver the goods to somebody who is called the consignee, and who corresponds to the payee of a note. There is this further feature in a bill of lading: the carrier acknowledges receipt of the goods from the consignor, that is, the shipper, and the carrier promises to deliver them.

ILLUSTRATIONS.—Now, when S. S. Pierce Company decide to ship goods to a buyer, it may consign them to the buyer or it may consign them to itself; that is, the same person may be consignor and consignee. That is very common in business, in order that the shipper may retain title to the goods until he receives payment. He takes the bill of lading in his own name and then, generally, attaches a draft on the buyer of the goods, and sends the bill of lading and the draft together through a bank. The bank notifies the drawee of the draft, who is the man who has agreed to buy the goods, that the bill of lading with the draft are at the bank, and that the buyer may have the bill of lading when he pays the draft. The buyer pays the draft and gets the bill of lading, and then for the first time does he become the owner of the goods. On the other hand, if the shipper—S. S. Pierce Company—had consigned the goods directly to the buyer, the buyer would have become the owner of the goods on shipment, provided the buyer had authorized that shipment. The seller cannot, however, by naming a buyer consignee, make the buyer owner of any goods which he has not agreed to receive. So much for appropriation of the goods to the buyer by shipment. In another chapter fuller reference will be made to bills of lading as documents of title and as bank securities. In this connection they are referred to merely as indicating an intention to transfer or retain title as between buyer and seller.

IMPORTANCE OF DELIVERY IN SALES OF GOODS.—Title to chattel property, it has been said, may pass without delivery. This is true as between the parties, but as against creditors and third persons delivery is necessary. Suppose A sells a horse to B and does not deliver the horse, and A afterwards sells the horse to C and does deliver the horse to C. B comes around to C and says, "That is my horse. I paid A the full price." C may say, "I bought him in good faith. I thought it was A's horse. I have got him and I am going to keep him." C may keep him.

PLACE OF DELIVERY.—Certain contractual rights between the buyer and seller are implied from the nature of the bargain of sale. A seller is under an implied obligation not only to transfer title to the buyer, but to deliver possession to him. Where must the seller deliver possession? If the contract states the place, the terms of the contract decide that question. If the contract does not expressly state where the place is to be, the place of the seller's residence is the place where the seller is bound to deliver, unless the goods are too heavy for easy transportation, and in that case the place of delivery is the place where the goods are at the time of the bargain. That may be the seller's place of business, and it may not.

DELIVERY AND PAYMENT ARE CONCURRENT CONDITIONS.—Concurrently with the seller's duty to deliver possession, the buyer is under a duty to pay the price, unless the contract provides for a period of credit. The delivery and the payment of the price are, in the absence of contrary agreement, concurrent conditions. The seller must offer to deliver if he wants to get a right of action for the price, and the buyer must tender payment if he wants a right of action for the goods. The tender of price and delivery must be at the place where payment and delivery is due. It may be asked, how is the seller to tender the goods at the place delivery is due if that is the seller's place of business and the buyer does not appear? The answer is, that it is in effect a tender for the seller to have the goods in the place where they are to be delivered, he being ready and willing to deliver them. If the buyer does not come there the buyer must, nevertheless, pay the seller. By the seller's readiness to perform, at the place where performance is due, and deliver, if the buyer with his money is at the place where payment is due, there is in effect a tender.

RIGHT OF INSPECTION.—The buyer and seller have certain other implied rights and duties. A right which the buyer always has, in the absence of agreement to the contrary, is a right to inspect the goods, to see that he is getting what he bargained for, before he accepts title and pays the price. He may, however, waive this right of inspection; he may agree to pay the price without seeing what he is getting, and in modern business this is not uncommon. One sort of bargain frequently made contains this term: "Cash against bill of lading." That means the buyer is to pay the price of the goods on receiving the bill of lading. The bill of lading will usually reach him before the goods, and, therefore, before he has a chance to inspect; and by the terms of his bargain he has agreed to pay cash against the bill of lading and he must do so. Of course, if the goods when received turn out not to be what he bargained for, he has a right to sue for breach of contract or recovery of the price paid. But in the first place, when the bill of lading comes he has to assume that the goods are going to be right and pay for the bill of lading. Another case where a right of inspection is waived is where goods are sent C. O. D. You order goods to be sent in that way and the expressman brings them. You say you want to open the package and see if the goods are right. You will find the expressman will not let you. He will say, "No, you must pay for the sealed package," and until you do so, you will have no right to the possession of the goods. If the goods are not all right you have redress by suing the seller, but you must pay your money first.

WARRANTIES.—Another and most important right which the buyer has is the enforcement of warranties. Warranties of a chattel may be either express or implied. An express warranty is a promise or an obligation imposed by the law because of a representation which the seller has made in regard to the goods. The simplest form of warranty is where the seller says, "I warrant this horse is sound," or, "I warrant this piano will stay in tune for a year." These warranties are promises and are subject to the same rules as other promises. They are contracts for consideration, the consideration for the promise being in each case the purchase of the goods. But we have warranties which are not based on promises, strictly so called, and yet are express. A tries to sell a horse. He says the horse is perfectly sound, four years old, broken to harness, and has trotted a mile in three minutes. Those are in form representations rather than promises; they are assertions of fact, and when A makes them it is possible he does not understand that he is binding himself for the truth of his statements; and yet if they are made as positive statements of fact, the seller is held to warrant the truth of those statements.

REPRESENTATIONS OF FACT AND OF OPINION.—The great distinction, between warranties by representation and statements in regard to property which do not amount to express warranties, is that between statements of opinion and statements of positive fact. If the buyer said, "I believe the horse can trot a mile in three minutes any day," it is not a warranty; even the statement, "The horse can trot a mile in three minutes" would probably not be a warranty; but the statement, "The horse has trotted a mile in three minutes," is a direct assertion of fact, and the element of opinion does not occur, and therefore that would be a warranty. Statements of value do not amount to warranties. Those are necessarily to some extent matters of opinion. General statements of good quality do not, ordinarily, amount to warranties. The courts, however, are getting stiffer and stiffer in regard to these matters. It used to be the law that a seller could represent nearly anything he chose in regard to his goods, and not be bound, so long as he did not expressly say, "I warrant," or make a promise in terms in regard to them. That was called the rule of "caveat emptor"—"let the buyer beware"—but this rule is almost wiped out so far as representations of fact are concerned. Now, the seller had better beware of what he says, for he may find himself liable as a warrantor.

NO WARRANTIES IMPLIED IN SALES OF REAL ESTATE.—There are certain warranties implied, although the buyer does not bargain for them and although the seller makes no express representations regarding them. In this respect sales of personal property differ entirely from sales of real estate. In the case of real estate you get no warranty but what you bargain for. If you get a deed without words of warranty, and it turns out that the seller had no title, in the absence of fraud you have no redress; you cannot get your money back though you have no title to the land.

WARRANTY OF TITLE IMPLIED IN SALES OF PERSONAL PROPERTY.—In the case of personal property it is otherwise. The first implied warranty that exists in the case of a sale of personalty, unless the contrary is expressly agreed, is the implied warranty of title. The seller impliedly warrants that he has title to the property and will transfer title to the buyer. The only exception to this is where a sale is made by a person in a representative capacity, as by a sheriff or an agent. In that case the person making the sale does not impliedly warrant title. In the case of an agent, however, if the agent was authorized to make the sale, the principal would be liable as an implied warrantor of title; and if the agent was not authorized to make the sale, the agent would be liable as warranting his authority—not as warranting title to the goods, but warranting that he had a right to bind his principal. Even in the case of a sale by an agent, therefore, the purchaser gets substantial redress if the title turns out to be defective. It is possible, of course, by express agreement, for a buyer to buy and a seller to sell merely such title as the seller may have; but there must be an express agreement, or very special circumstances, indicating that such was the intention of the parties, in order to induce a court to give this construction to a bargain.

IMPLIED WARRANTY OF QUALITY IN SALES BY DESCRIPTION.—Not only are there implied warranties of title, but there are also implied warranties in regard to the quality of goods. The fundamental principle at the bottom of implied warranty of quality of goods is this: if the buyer justifiably relies on the seller's skill or judgment to select proper goods, then the seller is liable if he does not deliver proper goods. We may distinguish in regard to implied warranties of quality, sales of specific goods—that is, sales of a particular thing—and sales of goods by description. In the case of sales by description there is always an implied warranty that the buyer shall have not only goods which answer that description, but merchantable goods which answer that description. Suppose a seller contracts to sell so many hogsheads of Manila sugar. The law formerly was that the seller could tender to the buyer, in fulfillment of that contract, the worst article that he could find which bore the name of Manila sugar. The law at present is that the seller must furnish to the buyer merchantable Manila sugar; that is, Manila sugar of average and salable quality. It does not have to be the best, but it must be ordinarily salable as merchantable Manila sugar.

IMPLIED WARRANTY IN SALES OF SPECIFIED GOODS.—Contrast with that case a contract to sell a specific identified lot of Manila sugar before the buyer and seller. Is the buyer bound to take without objection that specific lot, whether or not it turns out to be merchantable? Or suppose you go to a shop where they sell bicycles and buy a bicycle; you pick out a specific bicycle, and it turns out that, owing to defects in manufacture, it is not good for anything. It breaks down the first time you ride it. May the seller say, "You looked at what we had in stock and this is the machine you agreed to buy"? It is in this class of cases that the question of justifiable reliance by the buyer on the seller's skill and judgment becomes important, and in determining whether the buyer justifiably relied on the seller's skill and judgment several things must be considered.

INSPECTION AS AFFECTING IMPLIED WARRANTY.—Was the defect open to inspection and was there opportunity to inspect the goods? If there was, there is less reason to suppose that the buyer was relying on the seller's skill and judgment than if the defect was latent and not open to inspection.

IMPLIED WARRANTY WHERE THE SELLER IS A MANUFACTURER.— What was the nature of the seller's business? Was he a manufacturer of the goods in question? The strictest rules of implied warranty of quality are applied against manufacturers, and this is, you will see, reasonable, because the manufacturer ought to know about the goods and the buyer naturally relies on the manufacturer, as knowing about the character of the goods, to give goods of proper quality. Therefore, unless the buyer pretty clearly assumes the risk himself of picking out what is satisfactory to himself, a seller who is a manufacturer will be held to warrant the merchantable quality of the goods which he makes and sells.

IMPLIED WARRANTY WHERE THE SELLER IS A DEALER.—The next grade below a manufacturer is a dealer in that sort of goods. He cannot have the same knowledge as a manufacturer, but still, a dealer in goods of a particular kind is much more competent to judge of their quality than an ordinary buyer and therefore a dealer also, unless there is special reason to suppose the buyer did not rely on his own judgment, will be held to warrant that the goods are merchantable.

IMPLIED WARRANTY OF FITNESS FOR A PARTICULAR PURPOSE.— Sometimes there is a warranty of still greater scope than a warranty of merchantability; that is, a warranty of fitness for a particular purpose. A buyer agrees to buy glue of a manufacturer. The buyer is, as the glue manufacturer knows, a furniture manufacturer. The glue manufacturer sells the buyer glue which is merchantable glue, but it not good furniture glue, as furniture glue must be of unusual tenacity. The seller is liable here under an implied warranty. He knew that furniture glue was wanted. He was a glue manufacturer, and he ought to have understood that the buyer was looking to him to furnish glue of a sort that would not only be salable as glue but would fulfill the purpose which the buyer had in mind when he made the purchase.

KNOWN, DESCRIBED AND DEFINITE ARTICLES.—On the other hand, if the buyer orders what is called a known, described and definite article, he takes upon himself the burden of determining whether the thing which he buys will fulfill his purpose or not. For instance, a buyer in Missouri ordered of a boiler manufacturer two boilers selected from the catalogue of the boiler manufacturer, describing them by number. The boilers were good boilers, under ordinary circumstances, but the amount of mud in the Missouri River, on the banks of which the boilers were to be used, was so great that they could not be successfully used there. The buyer had no redress against the seller in that case. He had taken upon himself to specify the particular kind of boilers he wanted; he got them and they were merchantable boilers. The only trouble was that they were not fit for use in the place where the buyer was intending to use them. If the buyer had simply ordered boilers for a factory on the Missouri River, the result might well have been the other way, for that would have put the duty on the seller to furnish something that was suitable for that purpose.

RELIANCE ON THE SELLER IS THE ESSENTIAL ELEMENT.—The great thing to remember throughout the whole subject is that the implied warranty of quality depends on the justifiable reliance of the buyer on the seller's skill. If the goods are not merchantable under circumstances where the buyer does rely, he can recover from the seller, even though the seller was not guilty of negligence. A warranty is not dependent on negligence of the seller.

REMEDIES FOR BREACH OF WARRANTY.—One of the remedies, allowed in many but not all States, for breach of warranty, is to return the goods and demand the purchase money back; but that is only one remedy. Another remedy, which is universally allowed, is to sue for whatever damage the breach of warranty may have caused, and one or two cases will show how serious these damages may be. A seller sells a pair of sheep to a buyer with a warranty, express or implied, of their soundness. They have an infectious disease, and when put with a large flock of the buyer's sheep they infect the whole flock, and the damage is the loss of the whole flock. Another actual case was based on an implied warranty of the quality of rags sold to a paper manufacturer. The rags came from Turkey and were infected with smallpox. They gave smallpox to the operatives in the buyer's mill, and the mill had to be closed down, which caused great loss to the manufacturer. All that loss can be recovered from the seller of the rags, even though he was not negligent in bringing the result about.

ONLY ORIGINAL BUYER CAN RECOVER ON A WARRANTY.—Nobody, however, can recover on a warranty except the original buyer. For instance, the operatives who caught smallpox could not sue the seller unless the seller was negligent. If he had been careless or negligent in disregarding their safety, they could sue him in an action of tort, though they had no contractual relation with him. And if the buyer resells the goods the purchaser from him cannot sue on a warranty given to the original buyer.

EFFECT OF ACCEPTING DEFECTIVE GOODS.—Another matter that has caused considerable litigation in regard to warranty and the obligation of the seller in regard to the quality of goods, is the effect of acceptance by the buyer of goods which are offered to him. Suppose a certain quantity of Manila sugar is offered to one who has agreed to buy, and he takes from the seller that quantity of sugar, but finds it is not of as good quality as it ought to have been. The buyer subsequently objects, but the seller says, "You should have objected to that at the outset and refused to take it. Your taking it is an assent or acceptance of it as a fulfillment of the contract, and any right you may have had is now gone." It is settled law that if the defect was not observable with reasonable care, the buyer does not lose any right by taking the goods, provided he gave prompt notice of the defect as soon as it was discovered. Further, even though at the time of delivery the buyer observed the defect or might have observed it, it is the law of most but by no means all States, that taking the goods does not necessarily indicate assent to receive them as full satisfaction of the seller's obligation. The buyer may receive the defective goods as full satisfaction, but the mere fact of taking them does not prove it. It is advisable, however, for the buyer as soon as he sees the defect to protest against it. He may in most States safely take the goods if he says in taking them, "These goods are defective and I do not take them in full satisfaction;" or, if he does not discover the defect immediately on taking the goods, he ought to give notice as soon as he does discover that the goods are defective, and state that, though he proposes to keep them, he does so subject to a claim for their defective quality.

SELLER'S RIGHTS WHERE BUYER FAILS TO ACCEPT GOODS.—Now the seller has some rights, also, that should be referred to. In the first place, if the buyer refuses to take title to the goods when they are tendered to him, the seller has a right to recover damages. The amount of damages will be the difference between the value of the goods which the seller still retains, because the buyer will not take them, and the contract price which was promised. If the goods are worth as much as the price promised for them, the seller's damages will be only nominal, for he still has the goods and may sell them to somebody else for as good a price as was stipulated in the original bargain.

SELLER MAY RECOVER PRICE WHERE TITLE HAS PASSED.—If the title to the goods has passed, the seller may sue for the price. This right to the price is secured by a lien on the goods as long as the seller retains possession of them. If the seller has parted with possession and with title, he cannot get the goods back except in one narrow class of cases.

STOPPAGE IN TRANSIT.—If the goods are in the hands of a carrier, or other intermediary between the seller and buyer, even though title passed on delivery to the carrier, the seller may stop the goods in transit if the buyer becomes insolvent before they are actually delivered to the buyer. The right is exercised by notifying the carrier to hold the goods for the shipper since the buyer has become insolvent. The right of lien and of stoppage in transit is given the seller to enable him to secure the price, which is the thing of interest to him in the contract.

LEGAL AND EQUITABLE TITLES.—A legal title is a full right of ownership against everybody. The legal owner can take his goods wherever he finds them. An equitable title is a right to have the benefit of the goods or property, and, also, it frequently involves a right to have the legal title transferred to the equitable owner, making him full legal owner. The peculiar feature of an equitable title, however, is that it is good only against the particular person who, as the phrase goes, is subject to the equity, and also against any person who has acquired the property, either without giving value or with knowledge of the equity. To put the matter conversely, an equitable title is not good against a purchaser for value without notice, or, in the language of the Negotiable Instruments Law, against a holder in due course.

FRAUDULENT SALES.—This principle is important in other branches of the law besides that governing negotiable instruments. The most common case of equitable rights in sales arises in fraudulent sales. Where a sale is induced by fraud of the buyer, he gets the legal title to the goods, but the seller has an equitable title or right to get the goods back. Let us see how this works out. The buyer procures goods by fraud and he sells them to A. Now, the defrauded seller cannot get the goods back from A if A paid value for them in good faith. If A did not pay value in good faith, then the defrauded seller may get the goods from him or anybody who stands in the same position. If the defrauded seller can reach the goods before they have left the hands of the fraudulent person, he may replevy them or he may seize them if that is possible. It is not worth while to go into the various kinds of fraud that may be practiced in the sale of goods, but there is one specific kind that comes up very commonly which is worth mentioning; that is, buying goods with an intention not to pay for them. Generally, in order to create a fraudulent sale, it is necessary that the fraudulent person shall have made some misrepresentation in words, but here is a case where, though it may be said there is a misrepresentation, it is not put in words. It may be said there is a misrepresentation, for it is fair to say that every buyer when he buys goods not only promises to pay but represents that his intention is to pay for the goods, and perhaps that his financial condition is not so hopeless as to make the expectation utterly impossible of fulfillment. If the situation actually was that the buyer either had a positive intention not to pay, or was so hopelessly insolvent that any reasonable person would know he could not pay for the goods, the transaction is fraudulent; the seller still retains an equity, and may reclaim the goods from the buyer who has acquired a legal title or from any other person except a bona fide purchaser. (A draft of a statute to punish the making or use of false statements to obtain property or credit, jointly prepared by the General Counsel of the American Bankers Association and Counsel for the National Association of Credit Men, has been enacted in the form recommended, or with more or less modification, in a majority of the States. This statute provides, in substance, that "any person who shall knowingly make or cause to be made any false statement in writing, with intent that it shall be relied upon, respecting the financial condition, or means or ability to pay, of himself, or any other person, for the purpose of procuring in any form whatsoever, either the delivery of personal property, payment of cash, making of a loan, extension of credit, etc., for the benefit of either himself or of such other person, shall be guilty of a felony, and punishable, etc.") This question often arises in bankruptcy: Suppose the buyer goes bankrupt and the goods come into the hands of the buyer's trustee in bankruptcy. The trustee in bankruptcy is in legal effect, in such a case, the same person as the bankrupt; he is not a bona fide purchaser from him, and thus the seller may reclaim the goods from the trustee in bankruptcy just as he might from the bankrupt. In the case supposed the seller has been fraudulently induced to part with his title and may reclaim it. A case may be supposed, however, where the seller fraudulently retains his title, and here the buyer's creditors may seize the goods as if the title were in the buyer. Thus it is a fraud to make a conditional sale of goods to a person who intends, and who is understood to intend, to sell the goods again. The reason why it is a fraud is because it is inconsistent on the part of the wholesaler to say, "I retain title to the goods until paid for, yet I give them to you, knowing that you are going to put them in your stock of trade."

DESTRUCTION OF GOODS SOLD.—The question sometimes arises as to the effect of the destruction of the goods sold or contracted to be sold. The Sales Act in Sections 7 and 8 governs this:

Section 7. (1) Where the parties purport to sell specific goods, and the goods without the knowledge of the seller have wholly perished at the time when the agreement is made, the agreement is void.

(2) Where the parties purport to sell specific goods, and the goods without the knowledge of the seller have perished in part or have wholly or in a material part so deteriorated in quality as to be substantially changed in character, the buyer may at his option treat the sale:

(a) As avoided, or

(b) As transferring the property in all of the existing goods or in so much thereof as have not deteriorated, and as binding the buyer to pay the full agreed price if the sale was indivisible, or to pay the agreed price for the goods in which the property passes if the sale was divisible.

Sec. 8 (1) Where there is a contract to sell specific goods, and subsequently, but before the risk passes to the buyer, without any fault on the part of the seller or the buyer, the goods wholly perish, the contract is thereby avoided.

(2) Where there is a contract to sell specific goods, and subsequently, but before the risk passes to the buyer, without any fault of the seller or the buyer, part of the goods perish or the whole or a material part of the goods so deteriorate in quality as to be substantially changed in character, the buyer may, at his option treat the contract:

(a) As avoided, or

(b) As binding the seller to transfer the property in all of the existing goods or in so much thereof as have not deteriorated, and as binding the buyer to pay the full agreed price if the contract was indivisible, or to pay the agreed price for so much of the goods as the seller, by the buyer's option, is bound to transfer if the contract is divisible.

CONDITIONAL SALES.—Certain transactions in which personal property is held as security, which are somewhat analogous to mortgages and which are very common, may now be referred to. They may be classed thus: Conditional sales, consignments, leases and chattel mortgages. A conditional sale, as that term is commonly used, is a transfer of the possession of personal property under an agreement to sell, the seller expressly retaining the title. Here we have possession and title divided. If it were not for the express agreement that title should remain in the seller, the delivery of the goods to the buyer, with his agreement to pay for them, would indicate a transfer of title to the buyer. The purpose of the seller in making a conditional sale is to retain security for the price which the buyer cannot pay all at once. Conditional sales are most common in regard to furniture and machinery of various kinds. Creditors of the buyer naturally suppose that the goods in his possession are his, and it is to avoid deception, or possible deception, that most States require that the conditional sale be recorded, so that creditors and everybody else may have notice that, although the buyer seems to be owner of this property, he is not so in reality. But, in Massachusetts, record is not required, and conditional sales, other than those of household furniture, need not even be in writing. The seller is secured by this sort of bargain in several ways. If the buyer does not pay the price when it is due, the seller may take the goods back. They are his goods and therefore he may reclaim them. Or the seller may conclude that it is better to sue for the price, and may decide to let the buyer keep the goods and himself collect a judgment for the price by levying on any property the buyer may have, including that which was conditionally bought. Even though the buyer has paid a large part of the price of the goods, the seller may, nevertheless, reclaim the goods. The seller's course will be dictated largely by how much of the price has been paid. If a large part has been paid, the seller will very likely prefer to reclaim the goods unless they are household furniture. Why, it may be asked, does a buyer enter into a conditional sale, which is rather a poor bargain as far as he is concerned? The reason, of course, is that he cannot pay cash and he wants the use of the goods at once, and the conditional sale enables him to get them. By statute, in some jurisdictions, the conditional buyer is protected after he has paid a considerable portion of the price; either by extending the time within which he may pay the balance due, or by requiring a sale of the goods and the return to the buyer of any surplus.

CONSIGNMENT.—How does a consignment differ from a conditional sale? When goods are sent or consigned it means that the person to whom they are sent is agent for the person who sends them. The consignment is like the conditional sale in this respect, that the person who has possession of the goods has not the title. The consignment differs vitally from a conditional sale in this respect, however, that the consignee is not a debtor for the price. If the consignee sells the goods, then he, of course, must turn over the price to the consignor less such commission as he takes, or if the transaction was not on commission, then the consignee must pay to the consignor the price it was bargained the consignor should receive. But until the goods are resold they remain the consignor's and at his risk. If goods conditionally sold are destroyed, the conditional buyer must, nevertheless, pay for them. They are at his risk and he is an absolute debtor for the price; but the consignee merely holds the goods as agent until a purchase takes place.

LEASES OF CHATTELS.—Sometimes goods are leased. Here, again, we have the same point of similarity, that the person who has possession of the goods is not the owner. The lessee, like a consignee, is not a debtor for the price; he is a debtor for rent, but he is not a debtor for the price of the goods. Often leases contain an option to purchase, and a lease with an option to purchase is used by piano dealers and others as an alternative mode of dealing with customers unable to pay cash, instead of a conditional sale; but it is not the same thing, for if a piano were destroyed without fault of either party after it had been leased with an option to purchase, the loss would be on the seller. If the option to pay had been exercised, of course, the loss would be on the buyer.

CHATTEL MORTGAGES.—The goods are here owned originally by the mortgagor, and they ordinarily remain in his possession after he has transferred them by the mortgage. The fundamental principles governing chattel mortgages are the same as those which govern mortgages of real estate. Chattel mortgages must be in writing and recorded, or the mortgaged property must be delivered to the mortgagee; otherwise they are invalid against the creditors or trustee in bankruptcy of the mortgagor; that is, one may mortgage his chattels, either by delivering them to the mortgagee or by making a writing and having that recorded. Even without record or delivery it is good between the parties, but it is not good in case of bankruptcy against the trustee in bankruptcy of the mortgagor, nor is it good against attaching creditors if there is no bankruptcy.

MORTGAGES OF FUTURE GOODS.—An agreement is sometimes made to make a mortgage of goods which do not at the time exist, or are not at the time defined. This is especially common in regard to a stock of goods. A wants to borrow money on his stock of goods in his shop. His stock may be worth $25,000 and A has not capital enough to get along without mortgaging it. Of course, he can mortgage the existing stock of goods without difficulty, but the trouble is he wants to keep on doing business, and sell in regular course of business the mortgaged stock of goods. That, too, would be easy enough if the mortgagee were willing to agree to it, but the mortgagee is not willing to agree unless equal security is substituted for any goods that are sold. What they would like to provide is that the mortgagor shall have power to sell the existing goods if he chooses in the ordinary course of business, provided he always keeps a stock of goods on hand equal to that on hand at the time the mortgage was made, the idea being that as one thing is released from the lien of the mortgage other things, of at least equal value, shall replace it. It is not an unreasonable transaction, from a business standpoint, but the law generally does not allow it validity except to this extent. It is valid as between the parties so far as to give the mortgagee a power at any time to take possession, and when he does take possession the mortgage is valid as to the goods of which he takes possession against creditors or anybody else. The mortgagee may thus take possession right up to the time of the mortgagor's bankruptcy, or at any time prior to actual seizure of the stock of goods on an attachment. This gives the mortgagee some security if the mortgagor will be good enough to give the mortgagee a hint when it is wise for the mortgagee to take possession, because, as the mortgagee can take possession just before bankruptcy or just before an attachment, the mortgagee will be protected. But, of course, there is a chance that the mortgagee may not get the goods, and therefore this form of security, in most States, is not now advised, although it has been much attempted in the past. In some States, however, such a mortgage gives a right against goods afterwards acquired, which is superior to that of attaching creditors or of a trustee in bankruptcy, even though the mortgagee does not take possession.

GIFTS.—A gift is the immediate voluntary transfer of personal property. To make a valid gift, therefore, it must be voluntary, gratuitous, and absolute. As has been explained, a gift is distinguished from a sale or a contract to sell by the fact that it is gratuitous. Gifts are usually divided into two classes: gifts "inter vivos" and gifts "causa mortis." There is no distinction between these two kinds of gifts, so far as the necessity of the intent to deliver title and delivery of the property are concerned, but the distinction lies in the fact that in gifts "causa mortis," the change in title is defeasible upon certain conditions. The ordinary gift "inter vivos," "between living people" is irrevocable when completed. The gift "causa mortis," that is, one made by a person in immediate apprehension of death, is always subject to the condition that if the person recovers, the title to the property, which he has given away, reverts to him. For A, who is in his last illness, to say to B, who is sitting near his bedside, "I wish you to have my gold watch when I am gone, but my brother is wearing it now in Europe" would not be a gift "causa mortis." There is no delivery. It would not pass title, upon his death, to his friend because in order to dispose of property after one is dead, a will is necessary. Even between the parties gifts are invalid unless accompanied by delivery, or made by deed under seal. The transaction without delivery or deed is, in effect, a promise to give, and there being no consideration the promisor may subsequently refuse to keep his promise. If a savings-bank book, a bond, a stock certificate, a life-insurance policy, a note or check of a third person (but not one made by the giver), or any chattel property is delivered to the donee, the gift is binding and irrevocable; but otherwise the donee gets absolutely nothing and the donor's executor is entitled to the property attempted to be disposed of by gift, and must treat it as part of the assets of the estate.

ILLUSTRATION.—A recent case in New Jersey shows clearly the effects of the application of the rules just described. In Bailey v. Orange Memorial Hospital, 102 Atl. 7, the facts were that the testatrix died about June 10, 1893, leaving a will, which had been duly probated, and under which the complainants had qualified as executors. Among the papers, which the executors found in the testatrix's safe deposit box after her death, was a certificate made in her name for fifty shares of the capital stock of the United N. J. Railroad and Canal Co., bearing the following indorsement, "For value received I hereby assign and transfer unto the Orange Memorial Hospital fifty shares of the capital stock represented by the within certificate and do hereby irrevocably constitute and appoint .... attorney to transfer the said stock on the books of the within named corporation with full power of substitution in the premises.

Mary Campfield.

"Dated Oct. 28, 1911.

"Witnessed by James C. MacDonald."

In the same envelope containing this certificate the executors also found the following letter in the handwriting of Mrs. Campfield: "To my executors: The accompanying certificate of fifty shares of the United, etc. Co. is my gift to the Orange Memorial Hospital for a bed to be called the 'Mahlon Campfield Bed.' The stock has been retained since its date of transfer because I desire to be benefited by the dividends thereon as long as I live.

Mary Campfield.

"Dated Oct. 28, 1911."

In this box Mrs. Campfield kept her bonds and mortgages, stock certificates, and other valuable papers relating to her own property and to the estate of her husband, of which she was executrix. There were two sets of keys to the box, one of which was in Mrs. Campfield's possession, and the other in the possession of one of her executors, who assisted her for some time in the management of her affairs. Shortly before the indorsement on the certificate was made, and the letter written, Mrs. Campfield requested Mr. Everett, the executor, to take the stock certificate from her box and deliver it to her attorney, stating that she would let her attorney know in a few days what to do about it. A few days later the attorney handed Mr. Everett an envelope containing the stock certificate, and told him there was a letter with it. Mr. Everett saw the certificate but did not see the letter, and he placed the envelope containing the certificate in the safe deposit box. The attorney had sealed the envelope after showing him the certificate. After Mr. Everett had told Mrs. Campfield what had been done, she said, "Well, that is for the hospital and that settles it," and she added: "It is in an envelope, as you probably saw, and addressed to my executors, and they will find a letter inside telling them what to do with it." After this, Mrs. Campfield continued to receive the dividends paid on these shares, and there is some evidence to indicate that she had access to the safe deposit box and examined its contents during the winter preceding her death. The court, in its opinion, said: "I do not think there can be any doubt of Mrs. Campfield's donative intention regarding these shares of stock, and it is equally clear that she never consummated that intention to make the gift, by the actual delivery of the stock to the hospital, or to any one as trustee for it; and it also appears that she intended the gift should be effective only after her death. She expressly retained the ownership and dominion over the stock for the purpose, at least, of collecting and enjoying the dividends paid thereon. * * * The gift of the stock not having been completed by delivery, or by the relinquishment of control over the certificate representing it, the stock must be declared to be an asset of the estate."

CHAPTER IX
REAL PROPERTY

DISTINCTION BETWEEN THE LAW GOVERNING SALES OF REAL AND PERSONAL PROPERTY.—The main distinction between the law governing real and personal property is the increased formality necessary in transactions governing real estate. Contracts for the sale of real estate must be in writing and actual conveyances of an interest in land must not only be in writing, but, except where seals have been abolished by statute, must be executed under seal. In order to make the transaction valid against third persons, record in the Registry of Deeds in the county where the land is situated is also requisite. Unless a contract for the sale of real estate is recorded, a subsequent conveyance to a purchaser, for value and without notice, will destroy the right of the buyer under the first contract to get the land, though he will still have an action for damages against the seller. So, in many jurisdictions, creditors of the man contracting to sell may by attaching the land as the seller's property satisfy their claims from it to the detriment of the buyer's right. Therefore, an actual conveyance of real estate must be recorded in order to protect the grantee. As a pre-requisite for record it is generally required that contracts and deeds of real estate shall be acknowledged before a notary public or other official authorized by law.

DUTIES OF BUYER AND SELLER UNDER CONTRACT TO CONVEY REAL ESTATE.—The primary duty of the seller in a contract to convey real estate is to transfer a good title. It is important for the buyer to determine before the time for performance whether the seller's title is good in order to determine whether he himself will accept the deed and pay the price. Accordingly, the buyer has the title examined by search in the Registry of Deeds. If the search discloses that the seller's title is defective the buyer does not on that account necessarily have a right to rescind the contract. The defect of title may be removed before the time of performance, and if the nature of the defect is such that this is possible, the buyer can only give notice of the defect and request its removal. If the title of the seller is so defective that it cannot be cured, or if the seller manifests by his conduct an intent to repudiate the contract, as by selling the land to another, the buyer need not wait for the time for performance, but may at once give notice that he rescinds the contract. Unless the seller has expressly contracted to convey by warranty deed, his obligation is generally satisfied by a quit claim deed. It is well, therefore, for a purchaser, when he contracts to purchase a piece of real property, to insert in the contract a clause to the effect that the seller agrees to convey by a sufficient warranty deed. The seller is also bound not to commit waste on the premises between the time of the contract and the time of performance. The rule in regard to accidental injury is stated hereafter, but as to intentional or negligent injury of the premises, the law is clear that such an injury is a breach of duty by the seller. The buyer's duty is to pay the price according to the terms of the contract. The obligations of the seller to convey, and of the buyer to buy, are concurrent, unless the contract expressly provides the contrary; that is, the buyer in order to acquire a right against the seller must tender payment, as he demands a deed; and the seller in order to acquire a right against the buyer must tender a proper deed when demanding payment. The obligation of either party to tender may, however, be excused by circumstances showing that tender would be useless. Thus, if the buyer is insolvent, the seller need not tender a deed, and if the buyer has repudiated the contract or committed waste to a material extent, or conveyed the premises to a third person, the buyer need not tender payment, in order to acquire a right of action. But if there is any doubt at all, the purchaser or the seller, as the case may be, should make a tender, so as to preserve his legal rights.

DOWER AND CURTESY.—By the common law a wife on her marriage acquired a right in her husband's land, which, though not vesting until his death, encumbered the title immediately. On his death she became entitled to a life estate in a one-third interest of all the lands of which he had been possessed since the date of their marriage. Accordingly, where the common law rule of dower still prevails, a husband cannot give an unencumbered title to real estate unless his wife joins in the conveyance. Similarly a husband was entitled at common law to a life interest in the lands of his deceased wife if they had had a child born alive. This was called the estate by curtesy. Its extent, it will be observed, is not the same as that of dower. The husband's life interest extended to all the lands of the wife, but on the other hand, it did not arise at all unless there was a child born alive; whereas the wife's dower right arose immediately on marriage. The rules of dower and curtesy have been changed by statute to a greater or less extent in most States, but it is still almost universally important that a wife should join in her husband's conveyance of real estate, and that a husband should join in a wife's conveyance of her real estate.

DEFAULT IN PERFORMANCE.—The law regards more leniently a default in time in carrying out contracts for the sale of real estate than it does a similar default in the sale of personal property. In sales of personal property, especially if it is of a character which rapidly fluctuates in value, time is said to be "of the essence;" that is, the failure of either party to perform at or about the agreed day is fatal to his rights to enforce the contract; but in the case of real estate it is generally held that time is not of the essence of the contract unless it is either expressly so provided in the contract, or the circumstances of the case are such as to show that time was a matter of vital importance.

DESTRUCTION OF PREMISES.—Where personal property, which the owner has contracted to sell, is destroyed, the loss is the seller's provided the title is still in him, and the buyer has committed no default; but in most jurisdictions, if real estate is similarly destroyed, the buyer must nevertheless pay the price. In the absence of special provisions in a contract of sale, if a house on the premises sold has burned between the time of the contract and the time for its performance, without fault of the seller, the seller can compel the buyer to accept a deed of the land without the house and pay the full price. This rule has been much criticized, and it is not universally in force; for example, it is not the law of Massachusetts. In some other States the loss will not fall upon the buyer unless possession of the premises has been delivered to him under the contract, but in New York, and probably a majority of the States, even though the seller still has possession, as well as title, the risk of accidental loss rests upon the buyer. Where risk of destruction of the premises is thrown on the buyer, immediately after he has made a contract to purchase, it is of obvious importance that he should immediately insure the premises. The insurance of the seller, unless transferred to the buyer at that time with the company's assent, will not protect the buyer. Insurance is a contract of personal indemnity, and the seller's insurance only protects the seller's interest. The result is that if the premises are destroyed, the insurance company will not be obliged to pay the seller his insurance, since the seller, under the contract of sale, can recover from the buyer; and even if the insurance were paid to the seller, the buyer could not claim the benefit of it.

SPECIFIC PERFORMANCE.—In addition to the ordinary remedy for a breach of contract, namely an action at law for damages, another remedy, that of specific performance, is permitted in the case of contracts for the sale of land; that is, the court will actually compel one who has contracted to sell land to make a conveyance thereof on receiving the agreed price, and will similarly compel one who has contracted to buy to pay the agreed price on receiving a deed of the premises. Specific performance of such contracts is granted on the theory that money damages are an inadequate remedy, and that the nature of the situation is such that it is possible to compel the actual performance of the contract. In contracts for the sale of personal property, damages are generally considered adequate, but contracts for the sale of a painting or a race-horse would be specifically enforced. Sometimes the seller is unable fully to perform his agreed contract. He may not be able to give a title free from encumbrances, or he may have committed waste on the premises. In such a case, though the buyer need not carry out the contract unless he wishes, he can if he chooses get a conveyance decreed to him and an allowance deducted from the price commensurate to the injury caused by the encumbrance or waste. Specific performance will be granted not only against the seller, but if the seller in violation of his contract has conveyed the land to a third person who had notice of the contract or who did not give value in exchange for the land, the court will compel the grantee of the premises to convey them to the person who had the original contract to buy. If, however, one who has agreed to sell the premises actually sells and conveys them to another who is a purchaser for value without notice of the prior contract, such a purchaser gets an indefeasible title, and the person having the prior contract to buy must resort, for his only relief, to an action for damages against the seller. For this reason it is important to record a contract to buy or sell. This record operates as notice to all the world, and no purchaser subsequent to the record will have the rights of a purchaser for value without notice.

VENDOR'S LIEN.—In some States a seller of land who has not been paid the price is entitled to what is called a vendor's lien on the land. This enables him to compel a sale of the property to satisfy his claim for the purchase money unless the land has been conveyed, before proceedings are brought to enforce the lien, to a purchaser for value without notice that the original vendor is still unpaid. In many States, however, the seller has no vendor's lien and must take a mortgage back for any unpaid portion of the purchase price if he desires security for its payment.

DEFINITION OF MORTGAGE.—A mortgage is a transfer of property to a creditor to secure a debt. Unless there is a debt there can be no mortgage, and the original idea of a mortgage, still preserved in the forms of conveyance in many States, is that the mortgagor or debtor transfers the title to the mortgagee or creditor. In popular understanding the mortgagor owns the mortgaged premises but the mortgagee will take or sell them if the debt is in default. The theory of the common law, however, was that the mortgagee became the owner of the premises as soon as the mortgage was made, but that the mortgagor was entitled to re-acquire the ownership by payment of the debt at maturity. Indeed, early mortgages were often made by two separate instruments: (1) an absolute deed of conveyance to the mortgagee, and (2) an instrument called a defeasance which provided that on payment of the amount of the debt, on a given day, the property should revest in the mortgagor.

MODERN AMERICAN MORTGAGES.—At the present day in many jurisdictions a mortgage still remains, both in the form of the instrument and in the legal conception of the rights of the parties fundamentally, the same as under the early doctrines just outlined. In other jurisdictions, of which New York may be taken as a typical State, the theory is no longer that the mortgagee has title to the property, but that he has only a lien on it, which he may enforce if the debt is not paid. The difference in actual results under the two theories, however, is less than might be supposed. Where the mortgagee is still regarded as having the title, his power to make use of that title is limited so that he can only make use of it for the purpose of securing payment of what is due him. On the other hand where the mortgagee is regarded as having only a lien, the lien is a legal right against the real estate which enables the creditor to enforce his claim against it in practically the same way which he would do were he the owner of the real estate.

COVENANTS AND STIPULATIONS.—A mortgage of real estate ordinarily contains the same covenants of warranty as a warranty deed of real estate. Where a mortgage still has its common law effect of transferring title to the mortgagee, it is essential that the mortgage should contain a provision that until default the mortgagor shall be entitled to the possession of the premises. Covenants in regard to the payment of taxes by the mortgagor and the keeping of the premises insured for a certain amount, are usual and important provisions. There is also commonly contained in a mortgage a power of sale; that is an authority or agency given to the mortgagee to sell the premises free of the mortgagor's right of redemption in case default of payment is made, or in case such default continues for a certain specified time. In all States printed forms of mortgages are ordinarily used. These forms are prepared with care to suit the requirements of local law; and if you are sure that the printed form is prepared and sold for use in the State where the mortgaged land is situated, you may feel satisfied that the terms of the instrument are suitable to protect the rights of both parties.

EXECUTION AND RECORD OF MORTGAGE.—A mortgage of real estate must everywhere be executed with the same formality that is necessary for an ordinary deed of conveyance. Different forms are in use in different States, and it is always desirable to use the form of mortgage customary in the State where the land lies. It is important to ascertain whether a seal is necessary in that State, and the instrument must ordinarily be acknowledged before a notary public having a seal, or before a commissioner of deeds for the State in which the land lies. There is in every State a recording act by virtue of which unrecorded mortgages are made invalid against subsequent purchasers and sometimes against attaching creditors. Though an unrecorded mortgage is, as between the parties, as effective as if recorded, it is of vital importance promptly to record every mortgage in the Registry of Deeds in the county where the land lies.

SPECIAL CASES.—Where a mortgage is executed by an agent or by a corporation, it is essential that the agent or corporate officer have authority to act. In the case of a corporation it is necessary both that the corporation have power to make the mortgage in question and also that the particular officer or officers who attempt to exercise the power are authorized so to do. The principles here involved, however, are not different from those generally governing the acts of agents and corporations. The same may be said in regard to mortgages by husband or wife, by a partnership, or by trustees. In the case of mortgages executed by any such person it is necessary to take special precautions. A mortgage by husband or wife should generally be also executed by the other. A mortgage by a partnership should be executed in the same form in which the title is held by the partnership, and if the title is held by less than all the partners, it is desirable that the other partners should express their assent to the transaction either in the mortgage itself, or in a separate instrument executed with the same formality.

INTEREST IN PROPERTY.—Any kind of interest in real estate may be mortgaged and mortgages of property, not yet acquired by the mortgagor, have generally been held to attach to the property when acquired by the mortgagor, and then to give the mortgagee as full a right as if the mortgagor had owned the premises at the time he purported to mortgage them.

OTHER PARTICULARS.—The description of land in a mortgage should have the same exactness as is necessary in a deed. Unlike deeds, mortgages ordinarily state their consideration and must of course state the indebtedness which they are given to secure. A mortgage may be given to secure a past debt if the mortgagor, when he makes the mortgage, is solvent. If he is then insolvent, to give such a mortgage would be a preference, which is an act of bankruptcy, and subject the mortgagor to possible bankruptcy proceedings. If the mortgagee in such a case had reasonable cause to believe that the mortgagor was insolvent, the mortgage could also be set aside by a trustee in bankruptcy.

EQUITY OF REDEMPTION.—By the terms of the mortgage the mortgagor's right is ordinarily made dependent on payment of the debt on a fixed day, or of installments on fixed days. A day thus fixed in the mortgage is sometimes called the "law day." According to the terms of the instrument the only way in which the mortgagor can be revested with title to the property is by complying with the express terms of the mortgage and paying the debt on the law day. The result of this provision, if enforced, would be that if the debt is not paid exactly when it is due, the mortgagee remains the absolute owner of the mortgaged premises. Courts of equity, however, long ago limited the mortgagee's right, holding that the real object of the transaction is to secure a debt, and that if the mortgagee obtains his debt and interest he ought to be satisfied. Accordingly if the mortgagor was in default in the payment of the debt, he was allowed to redeem the property by payment of the debt and interest until the time of tender. If the mortgagee refused to accept his debt and interest, the mortgagor could bring a suit in equity to redeem the property and the court would order the reconveyance to him of the property on payment of the debt. Because of this right on the part of the mortgagor, his interest in the property came to be called an equity of redemption, and it is often so called at the present day. The position taken by courts of equity, permitting redemption, might work a hardship on the mortgagee because he could never feel sure of his title to the property, however long the debt might remain unpaid. This difficulty was met by allowing the mortgagee to bring a suit to foreclose the debtor's right of redemption. We speak of foreclosing a mortgage, but, strictly, it is the debtor's right to redeem which is foreclosed. When such a suit of foreclosure was brought equity would fix a time within which the debtor might redeem the premises by paying the debt and interest, and then the decree provided that if the debtor failed to pay within the named period, his right of redemption should be forever foreclosed. At the present time there are in practically all jurisdictions statutory rules, in regard to the foreclosure of mortgages, which we shall presently describe, but it is important to remember the fundamental nature of the mortgage transaction, and the original remedies of redemption and foreclosure.

A RECONVEYANCE IS NOT NECESSARY ON PAYMENT OF THE MORTGAGE.—If a mortgage is regarded as a mere lien to secure a debt, it is obvious that a payment of the debt discharges the lien, and the title already vested in the mortgagor becomes free from any incumbrance. On the theory of the common law, though the title passed to the mortgagee, it was subject to a condition subsequent which would revest the title in the mortgagor if payment of the debt was made at maturity. By mere operation of law, therefore, payment of the mortgage when due revested title in the mortgagor without reconveyance. After a default, however, a subsequent payment is not strictly a performance of the condition upon which the mortgaged deed provided that title should revest. Accordingly a reconveyance was necessary in such a case at common law, but at the present day it is generally not requisite even in case of payment after default.

THE MORTGAGOR IS LIABLE AS A DEBTOR.—The mortgagor is bound as a debtor ordinarily by a bond or promissory note in which he expressly agrees to pay the amount of his debt. It is perfectly possible that the debt secured by the mortgage should not be represented by such an instrument, but should rest merely in oral agreement or should be contained in a covenant in the mortgage deed itself, but it is usual and desirable to have a separate obligation. The fact that the debtor has given the mortgage does not in any way limit the rights of the mortgagee as an ordinary creditor. He may sue on the mortgage debt when it is due, in the same manner as if there were no mortgage. It is his option whether he will foreclose the mortgage, as a means of collecting his claim, or whether he will get judgment on the debt, and seek to collect that judgment in the same way that an ordinary judgment creditor would. This rule is changed by statute in California, and one or two other States, where by statute the mortgagee is required to realize from the mortgaged property what he can before seeking a personal judgment against the mortgagor. In many jurisdictions the creditor may, in a single proceeding, obtain foreclosure of the mortgagor's rights by sale of the property, and a personal judgment against the mortgagor for any deficiency which the proceeds of the property may leave. This is called a deficiency judgment.

RIGHTS OF MORTGAGOR AND MORTGAGEE IN MORTGAGED LAND.—Even though the mortgagor is regarded by the law as having no longer the legal title to the premises, but only an equity of redemption, his interest is regarded as real estate and descends on his death according to the laws governing real estate. The mortgagee's interest, on the other hand, is regarded as personal property since the debt which the mortgagee is intended to secure is personal property, and even a legal title to the real estate held by the mortgagee is held merely for security, and is an incident to the debt. So the mortgagor's interest in mortgaged property is subject to be seized on execution by his creditors while the mortgagee's interest can not be so seized. The mortgagee's creditors must reach his interest by means appropriate to realize upon the debt, not upon the land. The mortgagor's interest being regarded as real estate will give rise to the same estates of dower in favor of the wife of the deceased mortgagor or curtesy in favor of the husband of a deceased mortgagor, as are allowed by the law in the case of real estate generally. The mortgagor may, while in possession, deal with the property in any way in which an owner may, except that he will not be permitted to imperil the mortgagee's security by any kind of waste. The mortgagor may, subject to the mortgage, lease, sell or devise it. He may collect the rents and profits and use them as his so long as he is in possession. Where, however, the mortgagee is regarded as having the legal title to the premises, he may eject the mortgagor at any time from possession, even though the mortgage is not due, unless prohibited by statute or by the express terms of the mortgage deed. In fact he usually is so prohibited. Even when not so prohibited, it is not always well for a mortgagee to take possession because, if he does so, he is bound to account not only for all profits actually received from the premises, but also for all that might have been received. He becomes liable for any waste of the premises or any failure to deal with them in a reasonably prudent manner.

SALE BY MORTGAGEE OR MORTGAGOR OF REAL ESTATE.—Either the mortgagee or the mortgagor may assign his interest. The mortgagee in assigning his interest is in legal contemplation doing two things: (1) assigning the debt; (2) assigning the title or lien which he holds on the mortgagor's real estate as security for the debt. As to the assignment of the debt, the matter is governed by the same principles as govern the assignment of choses in action generally. That is, if the mortgaged debt is represented by a negotiable instrument, the instrument may be negotiated to the purchaser in the ordinary way, and with the ordinary effects of such instruments. If the mortgaged debt is not represented by a negotiable instrument, the assignment of the debt is an assignment of a chose in action. Where the common law view of mortgage still prevails, that the mortgagee has the legal title, he can only transfer it to an assignee by a deed executed with the same formalities necessary for the transfers of real estate. As, however, the law recognizes that it is the debt which is the essential feature of the relation between mortgagor and mortgagee, and that the mortgaged estate is held merely as security for a debt, a valid assignment of the debt is held to make the assignee equitably entitled to the mortgaged property as security. And, in effect, one who obtains the mortgage debt will secure the benefit of the mortgaged property even though the local law regards a mortgagee as having the legal title. Where the mortgagee is regarded as having merely a lien, the assignment of the debt involves a transfer of the lien.

INCIDENTS TO MORTGAGE.—If the mortgagor wishes to convey his interest, he transfers the estate by deed exactly as if it were unmortgaged, except that the conveyance is stated to be subject to a specified mortgage, and it is sometimes added "which the grantee assumes and agrees to pay." It is desirable for the seller that the grantee shall assume and agree to pay the mortgage while it is desirable for the buyer that he shall buy the premises merely subject to the mortgage without assuming it. The difference between the two transactions is this: In either event the grantee receives the premises burdened by a mortgage, the amount of which will be deducted from the consideration paid as the agreed value of the premises. In either event, if the debt is unpaid, the mortgagee will foreclose and the grantee will lose the premises. In order to save the premises, the grantee will have to pay the mortgage.

ASSUMPTION OF MORTGAGE.—The distinction is only seriously important when the mortgaged premises are worth less than the amount of the mortgage. In that event the mortgagee will be entitled to a deficiency judgment against the mortgagor. The mortgagor was the original debtor and cannot escape from his obligation to the mortgagee without the latter's assent. If the mortgagor is forced to pay, he cannot recover the amount from his grantee unless the latter assumed and agreed to pay the mortgage. If, however, the grantee did make such assumption, he will ultimately have to pay the deficiency. If the mortgagee, without foreclosing the property, should sue the mortgagor directly on the debt, the latter would be compelled to pay. Even if the sale to the mortgagor's grantee had been made merely subject to the mortgage, the mortgagor on paying the debt would be subrogated to the mortgage and would himself be enabled to foreclose the property. But if the property failed to realize enough to reimburse him for the payment of the debt, he would lose this deficiency unless the grantee had assumed and agreed to pay the mortgage. Whether the mortgagee may sue directly a grantee of mortgaged premises who has assumed and agreed to pay the mortgage, is a question which has been much litigated; but it is now held almost everywhere that the mortgagee may do so. Sometimes a succession of grantees, each in turn on buying the premises, assumes and agrees to pay a certain mortgage. The mortgagee, in such a case, is generally allowed to recover from any one of these grantees so far as is necessary to satisfy his claim; but the ultimate liability will rest upon the last purchaser who has assumed the debt. As against a grantee who has not assumed the debt, the mortgagee has no rights. He can deprive such a purchaser of his land, so far as is necessary to collect the debt, but he cannot hold him personally liable.

FORECLOSURE OF REAL ESTATE MORTGAGES.—According to the original theory of the law, the mortgagee became the absolute owner of the mortgaged premises by the failure of the mortgagor to pay the debt when due, and by the foreclosure or termination of the mortgagor's right of redemption. Foreclosure of this character is still possible in a few States, but in most States it has been wholly abolished, and everywhere the ordinary method of foreclosure is by sale of the mortgaged property. Frequently the sale is made by virtue of an authority or power of sale given in the mortgage itself, but sometimes it is made under authority of a decree of court in foreclosure proceedings. Where a mortgage contains a power to the mortgagee to sell on default of the mortgagor, he is acting not simply on his own behalf but as agent for the mortgagor in transferring title to the property. The proceeds will be applied first to the payment of the debt with interest and the expenses of the sale. Any surplus will be held by the mortgagee in trust for the mortgagor and must be paid over to the latter. The situation is entirely analogous to that created by a collateral note where stock or other personal property is transferred as collateral to secure a debt. The statutes of all States contain regulations in regard to the foreclosure of mortgages, which must be observed. They are aimed generally to protect the mortgagor from forfeiture of his property to any greater extent than is necessary to insure the payment of the mortgage debt. In any case of foreclosure the local statute and practice must be consulted.

DEEDS OF TRUST.—In some States what are called deeds of trust have been largely substituted for mortgages. The temptation to make such a substitution is greatest in jurisdictions which refuse to recognize the mortgagee as the legal owner of the premises. If the law denies the mortgagee this recognition, he can, by insisting, as a condition of his loan, that the premises shall be conveyed to a third person as trustee, achieve the result that the mortgagor at least is no longer the legal owner of the premises. Essentially the situation is the same under a deed of trust as under a common law mortgage. In both cases the legal title is held merely to secure the debt, and the court will secure to the debtor all the value of the property which can be realized from its sale over and above the amount of the debt. If the debt is paid of course the debtor is entitled to the return of the security whether it is real estate or personalty, and whether held directly by the creditor or by a third person as trustee.

THE TORRENS LAW.—The Torrens system of registration of land titles received its name from Sir Robert Torrens who drew the first Torrens law enacted in South Australia in 1858. The practice of searching titles has gone through this development. In country districts the person purchasing real estate frequently accepted the grantor's deed without any search of the title. Of course, if there were judgments against the grantor, or other claims against the real property, the purchaser or the grantee takes the property subject to these claims. Ordinarily, however, the careful purchaser employs a lawyer to make a search of the title before he accepts it and pays the purchase price. In New York City to-day, and in some of the other large cities of the country, most of the title searching has passed out of the hands of the lawyers into the hands of the title companies. The title company makes the search now, the same as the lawyer formerly did, with an added advantage. Suppose I am to buy Blackacre, and employ attorney Blackstone to search the title. He reports it as being free and clear. I take possession and pay the purchase price. Six months later the wife of the grantor appears on the scene. When the grantor conveyed, he stated in the deed that he was single. The wife establishes the validity of her marriage, and her husband's, my grantor's, death. She is, of course, entitled to dower. I am obliged to make some kind of settlement with her, and there is no way, probably, by which I can hold my lawyer for failing to find that the grantor was married, when he made the search for me. If the title to my property had been searched for me by a title company, it would have issued a title insurance policy in my name which would have protected me, in this instance, and I would have been reimbursed by the title company for the loss which I sustained in having to pay the dower claim of my grantor's wife.

ECONOMY OF TITLE SEARCHES. — Economically, the title company is a big step in advance of the former practice of having lawyers make a search. The title company can do it much cheaper. If Blackacre was sold, when lawyers alone were making searches, probably a different lawyer would be employed at each sale, and he would make a search back to the earliest deed. After a title company has made its search, the result is in its records and the next time it is on the same piece of property, the search would simply be what is called a continuation, which would carry the search from the last time the company was on the title down to the present time. This enables the title company to make its fee more reasonable than the lawyer, and we can now secure a title company's search and insurance policy frequently for less than formerly was paid to the lawyer for the search alone.

ESCHEAT. — However, the policies issued by the title companies are not absolutely satisfactory, and the next, and perhaps final, step is for the State to come in and guarantee the title. This is perfectly logical. The ownership of all land is in the State, theoretically, the same as under the English common law. The King, in those days, owned all the land. This is more than theory, even to-day. If a man dies, leaving no heirs and no will, his real property escheats to the State, this being based simply on the theory that the property goes back to its original owner, the State. If this is true, why should not the State insure the title? This is the theory of the Torrens' system.

EFFECT OF TORRENS LAW. — The first Torrens law, enacted in this country, was in Illinois, and similar acts have been passed in a number of the States, including New York. When such laws are on the statute books, generally the business of a title company will be legislated out of existence. For that reason, opposition to the passage of such laws has developed in some States. Perhaps the next fifty years may see them generally adopted throughout the country.

CHAPTER X

ESTATES AND TRUSTS

ESTATES.—When a person who owns property dies, the first question which arises is as to what becomes of his estate; who pays the bills, who takes charge of his business affairs, and what are the rules as to the division of his property. The first question a lawyer always asks is, "Did the deceased die testate or intestate?" that is, did he leave a will or not. If he left a will, probably he has named one or more executors in his will to settle his estate, in which case such person or persons will take charge. If he has not appointed an executor in his will, an oversight which rarely occurs, the probate court will appoint an administrator. If, on the other hand, the man died intestate, it will be absolutely necessary for the court to appoint an administrator. The executor will settle up the estate according to the directions contained in the will, but if no will was made, the administrator will settle up the estate according to the rules of the probate court, under which he is acting, and the property will be divided in accordance with the statutes of the State or States having jurisdiction over the estate.

CHARACTER OF PROPERTY.—It is very essential to distinguish carefully between the two kinds of property, real and personal, which the deceased leaves. Real property, as we have explained, consists of land with the buildings permanently attached to it, and all other property is personal property, although it may relate to real property. Thus, a mortgage on land is personal property, also the shares of stock in a corporation, although the corporation may be organized to engage exclusively in the ownership of real property, is personal property. Where a person dies leaving a will, his real property goes directly to the persons to whom he leaves it in the will. In the case where he dies intestate, his real property passes directly to his heirs at law, who are designated by statute. In neither case is any formality necessary, beyond the probate of the will, to vest the devisee of the testator or the heirs at law of the intestate with the title to the real property. The situation in regard to personal property is quite different. Where the deceased died leaving a will, his executor immediately has title to all the personal property. If he dies intestate, the administrator will take title as soon as appointed. The personal property is used by the executor or administrator to pay debts, and the real property, whether a man dies testate or intestate, is never used to pay debts unless the personal property is insufficient.

WILLS DEFINED.—The definition of Jarman is commonly used in defining a will: "A will is the instrument by which a person makes a disposition of his property to take effect after his decease, and which is, in its own nature, ambulatory, and revocable during his life." This definition is open to one criticism. It does not include oral wills which, as we shall see, are sometimes legal. We shall also use other terms in this chapter which must be defined. A testator is the man who makes the will, while the testatrix is a woman making a will. A codicil is a supplement to a will, made and executed with the same formality as the original will, and it becomes a part of the original will, adding to it, or altering it, as the case may be. A devisee is a person who takes real property under a will, while a legatee takes personal property under a will, and the real property passing under the will is called a devise, and the personal property a bequest. A legacy refers to money passing under a will. This is why the ordinary will uses this phrase: "I give, devise, and bequeath." It is not fatal, however, to make a mistake of having the will read, "I hereby devise," referring to personal property. It is more a mistake in the use of English, than a mistake in law to make a wrong choice of these terms which we have just defined. A holographic or olographic will is a will which is wholly written in the testator's or testatrix's own hand. The statutes of a few States recognize these wills as valid without the formal execution or attestation if they are wholly written, signed, and sealed by the testator's own hand. A nuncupative will is an oral will. While most wills must be in writing, in many jurisdictions the oral wills made by sailors at sea, and soldiers in actual service are recognized as valid without being reduced to writing and without any specified number of witnesses. It is perfectly apparent why these exceptions are made, because of the difficulty of securing the materials with which to make a written will by these two classes of people. Nuncupative wills are good only to dispose of personal property, unless a special statute has been enacted which provides otherwise, but this is not commonly done.

A WILL AND A GIFT CAUSA MORTIS DISTINGUISHED.—We have already referred to gifts causa mortis which are gifts of personal property made by the donor under apprehension of immediate death, coupled with the delivery of the property. The gift is defeated by the recovery of the donor. A gift causa mortis may be made orally, while, with the exception of nuncupative wills, all wills must be in writing. A gift causa mortis must be made under fear of pending death, whereas a will is ordinarily made with a view of the fact of death but not of its immediate happening. Again, delivery is necessary to make a gift causa mortis, whereas under a will delivery never takes effect until after the person dies, and then the legatee's title comes through the executor or administrator, and not directly from the testator. Real property is not the subject of a gift causa mortis, whereas a will may dispose of both real and personal property.

WHO MAY MAKE A WILL.—As a general rule, any person of sound mind and of the age of twenty-one years may make a will. In some States, a person eighteen years of age may make a will of personal property. Formerly a married woman could not make a valid will excepting in a few instances, but today, by statute, this common law disability has been either wholly or largely removed. The statutes of the particular State in which the married woman resides, or in which her property is situated should always be consulted.

TESTAMENTARY CAPACITY.—Another qualification is that the testator must have sufficient intellectual powers to enable him to be said to have "a sound and disposing mind, memory, and understanding." The case of Whitney v. Twombly, 136 Mass. 145, gives us as good a general statement as there is concerning the nature of testamentary capacity: "A testator has a sound mind for testamentary purposes, only when he can understand and carry in mind, in a general way, the nature and situation of his property, and his relations to the persons around him, to those who naturally have some claim to his remembrance, and to those in whom, and the things in which, he has been chiefly interested. He must understand the act which he is doing, the disposition which he wishes to make of his property, and the relation in which he stands to the objects of his bounty and to those who ought to be in his mind on the occasion of making his will." The ability to make a will is not necessarily gone because the testator is old, weak or ill, even practically at the point of death. The physical condition is simply significant in determining the mental condition, but of course a very weak physical condition does not necessarily mean a weak intellectual condition. Insane persons are not capable of making wills, but a person who is insane may still have a "lucid interval" during which time he is sufficiently restored to his normal condition to enable him to act with such reason as to make a valid will, although he may, very soon, relapse into his former insane condition. Ordinarily most peculiarities and eccentricities on the part of the testator do not affect his ability to make a will; neither do peculiar religious beliefs have any effect unless, in any of these cases, the person's mind is so completely controlled as to prevent the exercise of rational judgment in disposing of his property. His eccentricities must amount almost, in such cases, to a form of insanity to have this effect.

HOW A WILL MUST BE EXECUTED.—There are four requirements for the execution of a valid will:

(1) It must be in writing.

(2) It must be signed by the testator.

(3) The testator's signature must be made by the testator or the marking acknowledged by him in the presence of the necessary number of witnesses.

(4) It must be declared by the testator to be his last will in the presence of the necessary number of witnesses, who are present at the same time and who subscribe their names as witnesses in the presence of the testator.

OTHER FORMALITIES.—No particular form of writing is necessary. Probably typing is the most common form in use to-day. As a precaution, lawyers sometimes have the testator sign at the bottom of each typewritten page, where the will is of several pages, or the document is fastened together with silk, the two ends of which are carried to the last page and imbedded in a wax seal. The testator should sign the will himself unless he is unable to, from lack of education or feebleness, in which case, the statute generally makes provision for another form of signing. It is better practice for the testator to sign the will in the presence of his witnesses, acknowledge the signature, and then the testator should declare, in the presence of his witnesses, that this is his last will and testament. In many States, two witnesses are all that are necessary; a few States require three. Careful practice generally calls for three.

ILLUSTRATION.—A testator lives in New York. He has two witnesses to his will. His will is valid as far as his real property in that State is concerned, but should it happen that he also owns real property in a State where three witnesses are required, his will would not pass title to the real property in that State and, as far as that State is concerned, he would die intestate, and that real property would descend to his heirs in accordance with the laws of that State, which would quite likely not be what the testator intended to happen. By having three witnesses, his will is just as good in New York, where only two are necessary and the presence of the third witness makes the will good, and passes the real property situated in the State where three are required. It is always best to have the witnesses add their addresses to their signatures. This is not required by statute in many States, but after a person's decease, it may help in locating the witnesses by having addresses to which to refer. It is, of course, wise to use some care in the selection of witnesses, although almost any person is competent. Adults, of course, are preferable as witnesses, but an infant is a perfectly good witness, but he should possess sufficient intelligence to be able to appreciate the importance of the act he is witnessing. In view of the formalities to be observed in the execution of a will, and the technical niceties in the use of the proper word or phrase, often required to insure the expression of the testator's exact intention, the drafting of a will should never be left to a layman, but should always be entrusted to a lawyer.

THE FORM OF A WILL.—In our discussion it is well to keep in mind the form of a will. A simple will reads as follows:

IN THE NAME OF GOD, AMEN:

I, John Jones, of the Borough of Manhattan, City and State of New York, being of sound and disposing mind and understanding, do make, publish, and declare this my last will and testament, as follows:

First. I direct that all of my just debts and my funeral expenses be paid as soon after my death as conveniently may be.

Second. I give, devise and bequeath all the rest, residue and remainder of my estate, whether real, personal, or mixed, of whatsoever kind, character or description, and wheresoever situated, unto my wife, Emma Jones, for and during the period of her natural life.

Third. Upon the death of my said wife Emma, I give, devise and bequeath the said residue and remainder of my estate to my children, Alice Jones, Sarah Jones, and George Jones, to them, their heirs, executors, administrators and assigns forever, share and share alike, per stirpes and not per capita.

Fourth. This will shall remain in full force and effect notwithstanding children may hereafter be born to me.

Fifth. I nominate, constitute, and appoint my said wife Emma, and the Institute Trust Company, executors of this my last will, giving to them full power and authority to sell and convey any and all real estate, whereof I may die seized, at such times and for such prices as they may consider for the best interests of my estate.

Sixth. I hereby revoke any and all wills at any time by me heretofore made.

IN WITNESS WHEREOF, I have hereunto set my hand and seal this first day of July, 1921.

(Signed) JOHN JONES (L. S.).

Signed, sealed, published and declared by John Jones, the above-named testator, as and for his Last Will and Testament, in the presence of us, and each of us, and at the same time declared by him to us, and each of us, to be his Last Will and Testament, and thereupon we, at his request, and in his presence and in the presence of each other, have hereunto subscribed our names as witnesses, this first day of July, 1921.

RALPH ROE, 3921 Broadway, New York, N. Y.

JOHN DOE, 65 Fifth Avenue, New York, N. Y.

JAMES SMITH, 130 Post Avenue, New York, N. Y.

REVOCATION.—A will may be revoked at any time at the pleasure of the testator. The ordinary ways of accomplishing a revocation of a will are: (1) The testator executes a later will, and in express terms says, "I hereby revoke all former wills by me made." Even if such an expression is not put in the second will, if its terms are wholly inconsistent with the former will, this in itself, will act as a revocation. Again, a will may be revoked by mutilation, as by being burned, torn, or otherwise mutilated by the testator himself, or in his presence and by his direction. The mutilation of the will, however, if not accompanied by an intent thereby to revoke it, is of no effect. I think I am tearing up an old insurance policy, but because of poor eye-sight, discover later that I have torn my will. This would not amount to a revocation of the will. As has been said by a writer on the subject of wills, "No amount of cancellation or destruction without the intent to revoke, and no amount of intent without the actual destruction, will suffice to revoke a will. Both the intent and the actual destruction or cancellation must coexist."

Sometimes changes in the circumstances and conditions of the testator's life will work a revocation. For example, at common law, the marriage of a woman worked an absolute revocation of her will. This has now been changed in most States by statute. In a great many States, however, today, if a testator, having no children, should make his will, and after the execution of the will, a child is born, the will is revoked in toto, when no provision for such child is made in the will. However, as above stated, this rule is not uniform in all States, and local statutes should therefore be consulted on this point. Where a testator already has children, the birth of additional children will not affect his will except, that such after-born children will inherit the same as though he had left no will. These rules in regard to after-born children apply only where the will does not make any mention of possible issue, and for this reason it is well to insert the clause, in many jurisdictions, providing that the will shall remain in full force and effect notwithstanding the fact that children may thereafter be born to the testator.

PROBATE OF WILLS.—Every State has a probate court for the settlement of decedents' estates. Such a court is variously named as the probate court, the surrogate's court, and the like, according to the nomenclature adopted in a particular State. Before an executor named in a will has any authority to act, he must produce the will, and after the proper proceeding has been had, the will is admitted to probate, and he may then qualify under it by giving the necessary bond. If the deceased died intestate, the proper person will apply to the probate court for the appointment of an administrator, and after a hearing, the court will appoint the person entitled to receive letters of administration. The administrator will then qualify, give the necessary bond, and then proceed with the settling of the estate.

A testator may name anyone in his will as an executor. In the large cities, in recent years, it is becoming quite common to name a trust company as executor, because its facilities for handling estates render it more efficient than the average individual. If, on the other hand, the testator is unwilling to place the sole care of his estate in the hands of a trust company, he may name two executors, a trust company and his wife, if he is a married man, or a very close friend in whose judgment he has great confidence, and, together, the two act as executors. The fees which the executors receive are generally fixed by statute. If the deceased dies intestate, the letters of administration are granted by the court in accordance with a definite statute. While the law in the various States is not uniform, generally, the priority of the right to administration is arranged by statute something like this:

(1) On the estate of a husband:

    (a) To the widow, if there is any.

    (b) If there is no widow, or if the widow renounces, then to the children.

    (c) If there are no children, then to the issue of deceased children.

    (d) If no issue of deceased children, then to the nearest of kin.

(2) On the estate of a wife:

    (a) To the husband, who has an absolute right. If the husband for any reason does not desire to act as such administrator, he may select any fit person to administer the estate.

    (b) If there is no husband, then to the children.

    (c) If no children, then to the issue of deceased children.

    (d) If no issue of deceased children, then to the nearest of kin.

(3) On the estate of an unmarried child:

    (a) To the father, who has an absolute right. If for any reason the father does not wish to act, the court may select any fit person to administer the estate.

    (b) If there is no father, then to the mother and brothers and sisters, whether of whole or half blood.

    (c) If no mother or brothers or sisters, then to the nearest of kin in equal degree.

PER STIRPES AND PER CAPITA.—Where the subject of a testamentary disposition is directed to be "equally divided" or to be divided "share and share alike," or where similar words are used which indicate an equal division among a class of persons, the persons among whom the division is to be made take per capita, unless a contrary intention is discoverable from the will. Where the individuals of a class are specifically named, or are designated by their relation to some ancestor living at the date of the will, whether the testator or another, they take per capita, unless the context of the will shows an intention that they should take per stirpes. But where the gift is to an individual, or several named individuals, and to others as a class, the latter take per stirpes; unless the testator uses language indicating an intention that the members of the class shall share equally with the named individuals. A gift to a class of persons or on their death to their heirs or children will be distributed among such heirs or children per stirpes; but a gift to one person and the children of other deceased persons will be divided per capita, unless it appears from the context or circumstances shown by extraneous evidence that the testator intended a distribution per stirpes.

ILLUSTRATION.—A gift to children of testator, A. B. and C., or on their death to their heirs or children will be distributed, in the event of the death of C. before the testator, among heirs or children of C. per stirpes. (In other words, they will divide the share of their father between them.) But a gift to A. and to X. Y. and Z., the children of B. deceased, will be divided per capita.

THE CONSTRUCTION OF WILLS.—It sometimes happens that wills are not carefully drawn, and even if they are, their meaning is not always perfectly clear. Ordinarily, any person who is interested in the meaning of a clause of a will may bring a suit in the proper court asking for a construction of the will. Of course, each case is governed more or less, by its own facts, but there are certain general rules which the courts follow in trying to arrive at the testator's intent. For example, a will is ordinarily presumed to speak as of the time of the testator's death. Thus, reference in a will, to the arrival of the testator's youngest child at the age of twenty-five years, will apply to the youngest child at the time of the testator's death, although such child is born after the execution of the will. Ordinarily, a testator is presumed to have intended to dispose of all of his property, and if a will can be so construed, this will be done, rather than to adopt a construction which will make him testate as to part of his property and intestate as to another part. If there are two irreconcilable parts, the latter part is the one which prevails. Words are to be understood in their ordinary meaning, unless there is something to clearly show contrary intent. If, between two possible constructions, one of which would disclose a legal purpose, and the other an illegal purpose, the court will adopt the former.

DOWER.—Under the rules of the common law, a wife was entitled, on the death of her husband, to an estate for life in one-third of the lands of which her husband was seized of an estate of inheritance at any time during the marriage. This dower right still exists in most States, although it may differ in some particulars. For example, in Connecticut, a dower right exists only in the real property which the husband owns at the time of his death, and not, as at common law, in all the real property of which he was seized during the whole marriage. Therefore, reference to the statutes must be made in each State, to know the exact rule in a particular jurisdiction. Where the State adheres closely to the common law, this right, on the part of the wife, is a right of which her husband cannot deprive her; if the husband disposes of all his real property in his will to his friend, John Jones, such disposition is not valid and the wife would still be allowed her dower right by the probate court. It must also be borne in mind that dower refers only to real property. Generally, a husband may dispose of his personal property without any reference to his wife. Ordinarily, two things are necessary to establish the right of dower: (1) A legal marriage, and (2) seizin by the husband of an estate of inheritance in lands, or, in a layman's terms, the absolute ownership of a piece of real estate.

CURTESY.—Curtesy is the common law right which a husband has in the real property of his wife, and by it he is entitled to an estate for his life in all lands of which his wife was seized during marriage. Needless to say, women did not take part in law making when this law arose. To establish this right, three things are necessary: The two already mentioned in dower, and third, the birth alive of issue of the marriage. The right of curtesy does not exist in this common law form in as many States as does the right of dower. Where these two rights do exist, in their more or less modified form, you have the explanation of the fact that when a married man sells real property, his wife joins in the deed, or when a married woman sells real property, her husband joins in the deed. The act of either in joining, releases the dower or curtesy right and allows the purchaser to get a clear title.

CONFLICT OF LAWS.—We have already referred to this topic. It frequently happens that a person dies owning real property located in a number of States. It is almost certain that the laws covering real property will vary in these different States. If he was a resident of Philadelphia, his will will probably have been executed in accordance with the laws of Pennsylvania. The question arises whether such a will is valid to convey real property which he owns in New York, California, and Massachusetts. Insofar as the will affects real property, the mode of execution and its validity will be controlled by the law of the jurisdiction in which the real property is situated. If, then, the will had two witnesses only, as required by the Pennsylvania law, but three witnesses are required in one of the other States named, he would die intestate as far as the real property in the other State is concerned. Difficult questions sometimes arise in regard to gifts to charities. Some States limit the amount which a charitable corporation may receive as a gift under a will, and other States require that the gifts must be executed within a certain time before the decedent's death. Where there is a question of this character involved only a careful examination of the decisions and statutes in the States concerned can furnish the basis for any satisfactory answer. If there is personal property, the requisites of validity and construction of a will are controlled by the law of the testator's domicile. The question as to his domicile is sometimes quite difficult to determine and may require a court action. We have had a number of illustrations of that in connection with the inheritance tax laws, where the officers of one State have sought to establish the domicile of a particularly wealthy person, who has just died, within that State in order that they may secure the inheritance tax for the State, which would of course, be much larger if the person were adjudged a resident of that State than it would be if he were held to be a non-resident.

CONTRACTS TO MAKE A WILL.—It sometimes happens that one person may make a contract whereby he agrees to make a will in favor of another person. A, 75 years old, and of the proper mental capacity to make a will, makes a contract with Mary Jones, that, if she will live in his house and act as housekeeper as long as he lives, he will make a will and in it give her his house and $5000. He fails to make his will and dies suddenly at the end of the year after the making of this contract. It is generally recognized that contracts of this nature are valid. The general rules applicable to contracts apply here. There must be consideration, the contract must be certain in its terms, and as such contracts are not favored by the courts, because they are open to many forms of fraud, they must be proved by clear and convincing evidence, and the contract would have to be in writing under the provisions of the Statute of Frauds. In the illustration suggested, the further question arises, what is the remedy on the part of the housekeeper for a breach of contract. Ordinarily there are two proceedings open in such a case. The personal representative of the deceased might be sued at law to recover damages for a breach of contract, or one might proceed in equity to compel the parties who take the legal title to the house, in consequence of the failure of the decedent to make his will as he contracted to do, to convey the property which would have been conveyed by the will, had the will been made in compliance with the contract.

TRUSTS DEFINED.—In Bouvier's Law Dictionary, trusts are defined as obligations imposed, either expressly or by implication of law, whereby the obligor is bound to deal with property, over which he has control, for the benefit of certain persons of whom he may himself be one, and any one of whom may enforce the obligation. A trust arises when property has been conveyed to one person and accepted by him for the benefit of another. The person who holds the property and the legal title is called the trustee, and the person for whom it is held is termed the beneficiary or "cestui que trust." Trusts are created for a great variety of purposes. It is very common to create them by a will, the testator appointing a trustee to manage a trust fund which he sets aside for the maintenance and support of a certain person or a certain institution. A new device for creating a trust for the carrying on of a business, seems to be growing in popularity. The practice apparently began in Massachusetts with the creation of a trust for the operation of an office building and similar undertakings. Under this arrangement, a trust estate may have transferable shares, exemption of shareholder's liability, and frequently enjoys peculiar advantages in taxation matters. These organizations are sometimes spoken of as common law corporations. They are so comparatively new that the closest care should be exercised in operating a business under this form of organization. We shall now consider the powers and duties of trustees and include with them executors and administrators.

TRUSTEES, EXECUTORS, AND ADMINISTRATORS.—Trustees, executors and administrators may be classed together because they are alike in that they hold legal title to property which is held by them for the benefit of other persons. They hold the legal title. A trustee is the owner of the property, and any one who seeks a transfer of the legal title of the property must get it from the trustee. Executors have exactly the same powers as administrators, aside from powers that may be expressly given in the will. The difference in name is simply because an executor is appointed by the will of the testator, whereas an administrator is appointed by the court to take charge of an estate for which no executor has been named in a testator's will, or where the executor may have died or refused to act, or, the most frequent case, where the deceased died intestate.

THEIR APPOINTMENT.—Were it not for statutes, a trustee or an executor would become such simply because somebody had made him a trustee or an executor without any appointment or assistance from the court. But in the appointment of executors or trustees, under wills, the court is by statute generally required to make an appointment to give validity to a nomination or appointment in the testator's will. Administrators, of course, from their very nature, have to be appointed by the court. A trust, however, may be created between living persons without any appointment by the court, and frequently is. A real estate trust may be created by simply conveying property to trustees on the trust that they manage it and pay the income to the beneficiaries, and a great variety of trusts are constantly created without an appointment from the court. Wherever any question on a trust arises, or wherever the appointment of a new trustee is necessary, however, the court has jurisdiction, and any person interested in the trust can bring the matter before the court. When a testator dies the person named as executor in the will petitions for appointment, and unless there is some reason why he should not be appointed he doubtless will be appointed. If there is no executor, then the persons, or beneficiaries, interested in the estate, usually agree on someone to administer the estate, and a petition is filed for his appointment. The person who is next of kin, and competent to act, is generally appointed in the absence of agreement. These officers remain in office and retain their powers until their work is completed, unless they are sooner removed, which they may be at any time for cause.

THEIR POWERS.—What powers do these persons have? Do they have power to sell? We must first always look at the terms of the trust. If we are dealing with a trustee under a will we look at the will to see what powers the testator gave him. If we are looking at a question of a trust under a deed, we look at the deed, and the right of an executor to sell real estate similarly depends on whether any such power has been given him in the will. Aside from express power given in the instrument, a trustee has no power to sell either real or personal property unless the power is expressly given or unless the nature of the trust is such as necessarily implies the power, and courts are very slow in construing the existence of such power by implication. An executor, on the other hand, since his duty is to reduce the personal property of an estate to cash, and distribute it, has, in most States, implied power to sell personal property. He has, however, no power to sell real estate unless the will expressly gives such power. The court may authorize him to sell real estate, and will authorize him, if it is necessary to pay debts or legacies, but only in such cases unless a power is expressly given. Trustees, executors and administrators have no power to pledge property unless expressly given in the instrument under which they act. They have power to make such contracts as are necessary to carry out their trust, but only these, and even when they make such contracts they are personally liable upon them, having, however, a right of reimbursement from the estate which they represent. If they entered into an unauthorized contract they would be liable upon it personally and have no right of reimbursement.

THEIR DUTIES.—Their first duty is the care and custody of the property in their charge. A trustee, whose duty is to hold property, is bound to keep it invested so as to bring in an income, whereas an executor has no right to invest funds of the estate, except under the direction of the court; if he does so he will take the chance of loss, and the beneficiary can not only hold him liable for loss but can also take the profit should the investment prove profitable. The executor's duty is to reduce the property to cash and distribute it to the proper parties. All these officers owe the same duty of fidelity to their beneficiary that an agent owes to his principal. There is the same duty to execute the trust personally and not delegate authority, except in regard to ministerial or mechanical acts. There is the same duty to account, and furthermore, the accounts of these officers, if they are appointed by the court, must be filed in court. The trustee to carry out his trust will ordinarily distribute the income to the persons entitled, but, of course, trusts are of great variety, and not infrequently the object of a trust is to accumulate the income. Whatever the terms of the trust are they must be carried out. The duties of the executor and administrator are to distribute the estate by paying creditors first and the surplus to legatees or the next of kin legally entitled. They are allowed a fixed period, in many States two years, to settle an estate.

One of the most essential duties of any fiduciary is to keep the property he holds as a fiduciary separate and distinct from his own. This means that a trustee or executor receiving current income must keep a separate bank account as trustee or executor, and of course he should not draw checks on that fund for personal debts.

CHAPTER XI

CARRIERS AND WAREHOUSEMEN

CARRIERS WHO ARE PUBLIC SERVICE COMPANIES.—Common Carriers—that is, railroads, express companies, and other persons or corporations who carry goods for hire and hold themselves out to the public as engaged in the business of carrying goods for anybody for hire—are engaged in a public service. A man who owns a tramp steamer and gets cargoes as he can, is not engaged in a public service—he is not a common carrier or public carrier; but a person who has a line of steamers, or even one steamer, regularly engaged in plying between different places and taking goods as offered for hire, is engaged in public service.

DUTIES OF ONE ENGAGED IN PUBLIC SERVICE.—Now, being engaged in public service subjects a person or corporation who is so engaged to some special duties. Such a person cannot make any bargain he pleases with anybody he pleases, and refuse to make bargains with others, as an ordinary person can. It is the duty of any one engaged in a public service to give reasonable service to all who apply, without discrimination, and for reasonable compensation. Of course, carriers are not the only public-service corporations; electric light companies or gas companies or water companies are other illustrations; but common carriers, and especially railroads, are the most prominent public-service corporations.

RAILROAD COMMISSIONS.—Not only is there this common-law duty to serve all without discrimination and at reasonable prices, but both the States and the United States have established commissions to look after railroads and other carriers to see that they properly perform their duties. The Railroad or Public Service Commission in most States has a great variety of powers for compelling railroads to give proper service. The chief function of the Federal Interstate Commerce Commission originally, was in regard to rates, but its powers have since been enlarged by legislation. The Interstate Commerce Commission has the power concerning interstate commerce to say whether rates and practices are reasonable. A carrier is obliged to file with the Interstate Commerce Commission a schedule of its rates, and regulations concerning rates, and is also required to post these rates publicly in its stations. If anybody objects to the rates they must make complaint before the Interstate Commerce Commission. That is the only form of redress, and sometimes not an easy one for a person who is merely interested in a single shipment, because the expense and delay of proceedings before the Interstate Commerce Commission are such as to be prohibitive, unless the complainant's financial interest in the matter is considerable. It is common, therefore, for shippers' associations to take that sort of question up rather than to leave it for individual shippers. Any contract made by a carrier for either more or less than the scheduled rate is illegal and void.

CARRIER'S COMMON-LAW LIABILITY FOR GOODS.—A carrier, at common law, when he receives goods for transportation, is subject to a degree of liability beyond that imposed on any other person. An ordinary person who receives goods—a bailee, as he is called in law—is merely liable for the consequences of his negligence. A carrier, however, while goods are in course of transportation is liable, at common law, as an insurer against all kinds of accidents except those caused by act of God or public enemies. For instance, if goods were struck by lightning in transit that would be an act of God, and the carrier would not be liable; but if goods caught fire from any other cause, as from neglect of an outsider or the act of an incendiary, the carrier would be liable. Carriers, of course, dislike that and try to contract away their liability. They are allowed by law to do so, except that they are not allowed to contract for exemption from the consequences of their own negligence. It is largely this desire of carriers to free themselves from the extreme liability which the common law imposes on them, that induces them to give bills of lading. Bills of lading are often required by law, but carriers are pleased to issue them, as they can in that way contract to exempt themselves from this extreme liability, which lasts while the goods are in transit and until the consignee has had a reasonable time to remove them from the carrier's possession. If the consignee fails to remove them with reasonable promptness the carrier then becomes liable, merely as a warehouseman may, for its own neglect. The extreme liability of the carrier does not extend to damage caused by delay. The carrier is liable for delays in so far as they are caused by its own neglect, but otherwise is not liable. A carrier need not deliver the goods unless freight is paid, as it has a lien for freight charges.

THREEFOLD NATURE OF BILL OF LADING.—A bill of lading issued by a carrier for goods has a threefold character. In the first place it is a receipt. The importance of a receipt is as evidence of just what was shipped. It is important to the shipper as proof that the carrier received goods, of such a quantity and of such a description, in good order. It is important to the carrier as proof of the same thing, to prevent the shipper from claiming that he has shipped different kinds or quantities of goods from those described in the bill of lading. The second aspect of a bill of lading is as a contract. It is not only a receipt but a contract between the parties, the shipper and the carrier. It is as a contract that the stipulations it contains for limitation, of liability are important. Third, it is an order, when properly indorsed and surrendered, for the delivery of the goods.

CARRIERS CAN DELIVER GOODS ONLY TO HOLDERS OF ORDER BILLS OF LADING.—The thing that makes a bill of lading valuable, to buy or lend money on, is the fact that the carrier will hold the goods behind the bill of lading until the bill is itself presented and surrendered. If the carrier were to deliver the goods upon demand to anybody other than the holder of the bill of lading, it is obvious that there would not be much use in holding the bill of lading. The carriers have made a great contest on this question in the past. They have contended that they fulfill their duty if they deliver the goods to the consignee originally named in the bill of lading, whether that consignee continues to hold the documents or not. But that has been decided against them so far as order bills are concerned (that is, bills, which state that the goods are deliverable not simply to a consignee but to the order of a consignee) and these order bills have printed on them the provision that the bill itself must be surrendered before the goods will be delivered.

CARRIERS MAY DELIVER TO CONSIGNEE OF STRAIGHT BILLS OF LADING.—In a straight or flat bill, however (that is, one without the word "order") the carrier's contention has been upheld and the carrier is allowed to deliver the goods to the consignee, even though the consignee does not present the bill of lading and for all the carrier knows is not the owner of the bill of lading or of the goods.

BILLS OF LADING USED TO ENABLE SELLER TO RETAIN HOLD ON GOODS.—The ways in which bills of lading may be used, and are used, in the mercantile world, must be understood before the legal questions which arise, concerning them, can be grasped. The primary and original purpose of using bills of lading as symbols of the goods, was doubtless to secure the seller in his hold on the goods until he received the price, and that is still a vital purpose in the use of bills of lading. We have learned, in the case of the sale of goods, that unless credit is given, the delivery of the goods and the payment of the price are concurrent conditions. Now, when the parties reside at a distance there is difficulty in working out these concurrent conditions. If the seller ships the goods directly to the buyer, he loses his hold on the goods, and if the buyer does not keep his agreement to pay promptly, the seller will be unable to do anything about it. On the other hand, of course, the buyer does not want to pay in advance. Now, by means of bills of lading, the seller is enabled to keep his hold on the goods until he receives the price, and the buyer is enabled to secure possession of the goods as soon as he pays the price.

STRAIGHT BILLS TO BUYER GIVE THE SELLER NO HOLD ON GOODS.—The bill of lading may be used in various ways. Suppose, first, the seller when he ships the goods takes a straight bill to the buyer. That will not give the seller any hold, for the carrier will be discharged if without demanding the surrender of the bill of lading, he delivers to the consignee named. So we may cross off that as a possible means of protecting the seller.

STRAIGHT BILLS TO THE SELLER.—The second possibility is for the seller to take a straight bill, naming himself as consignee as well as consigner. If that is done the buyer cannot get the goods at once. Suppose the bill of lading was sent forward, even that would not of itself enable the buyer to get the goods, if the carrier wished to be technical, since in a straight bill the goods are deliverable not to the holder of the bill, but to the consignee named therein. There would have to be attached to the bill of lading an order from the seller, who is named as consignee in the bill, directing the railroad to deliver the goods to the buyer instead of to himself, the consignee named in the bill. That would be a perfectly feasible matter, but this method is not much used, and one reason why it is not much used is because the seller frequently wants to do something else besides keep control of the goods until the buyer pays for them. He oftentimes wants to get money from a bank in the meantime.

USE OF BILLS OF LADING BY SELLER TO OBTAIN LOANS.—When the seller is desirous of borrowing money from a bank, he takes the bill of lading to the bank with a bill of exchange drawn on the buyer, and he asks the bank at his home town to discount the bill of exchange, taking as security the bill of lading. If his home bank does this, it then sends the draft, with bill of lading attached, to its correspondent bank in the buyer's city, where the draft is presented to the drawee, who is the buyer, and if the buyer honors the draft then he is given the bill of lading. Now, banks would not do this, ought not to do it (occasionally they have), with a straight bill, even if the bill is drawn naming the seller as consignee, for the bank when it discounts the bill of exchange and gets the bill of lading as security gets no real hold on the goods. The railroad may deliver the goods to the consignee—the seller—without ever seeing the bill of lading, and without the bank, which holds the bill of lading, ever knowing anything about it; or the railroad may deliver to the buyer or some third person on a written order signed by the consignee. In other words, the railroad does not have to hold the goods until the bill of lading, properly indorsed, is presented to it.

STRAIGHT BILLS OF LADING GIVE NO SECURITY TO BANK.—The first and fundamental requirement, then, for any bank which may deal with bills of lading is never to have anything to do with straight bills. They give no security. A straight bill is readily distinguishable from an order bill on railroads in most parts of the country, at least, because uniform bills of lading are now in use, and the straight bill is always white and the order bill is always yellow. In foreign bills a greater variety of forms are used, and you may have to examine the terms of the bill before you can feel satisfied that it is of a sort that will give security. The vital words in bills of lading, as in negotiable paper, are the words, "order of" or "or order." If those are in a bill of lading it is all right as far as this matter is concerned. Therefore the third and fourth possible ways in which the seller may take the bill of lading to secure himself are the only ones which will enable him to finance the shipment at once.

BILLS OF LADING TO BUYER'S ORDER.—The third way which the seller may act in order to fulfill his purpose is to take an order bill of lading to the buyer's order. Although the bill of lading runs to the buyer's order, and although, therefore, title to the goods will pass to the buyer on shipment, the buyer cannot get the goods without that bill of lading. Therefore, so long as the seller retains the bill of lading nobody can get the goods from the carrier; and though the seller has parted with title to the goods, since he made the bill of lading run to the buyer's order, still he has retained control of them. Though it gives a security to the seller, and would give security to the bank, if the bank discounted a bill of exchange drawn on the buyer and took this bill of lading as security, it is not a desirable method for this reason: though the buyer cannot get the goods without the bill of lading, nobody else can get the goods without a lot of trouble, unless he has not only the bill of lading but the buyer's indorsement upon it. The bill of lading is drawn to the buyer's order, and if the buyer fails to pay and repudiates his contract, the bank or the seller will have trouble in getting back the goods. They will have to prove to the railroad that the buyer really has made default and that he no longer has any real interest in the goods.

BILLS OF LADING TO THE SELLER'S ORDER.—Accordingly, it is the fourth method which is in general use and which should be exclusively used. The seller takes the bill of lading to his own order and indorses it in blank; then he delivers it to his bank as security for a bill of exchange. If the bill of exchange is paid by the drawee on presentment at his city, he is given the bill of lading at once and he gets what he wants. On the other hand, if the buyer does not pay the draft on presentment, then the bank can realize on the security at once, if it wants to, because it has a bill of lading in its hands indorsed by the consignee to whose order it was drawn. If the bank proceeds against the seller as the drawer of the draft, when the latter pays and takes up the bill of lading he can similarly realize on the security, or get the goods back, because he will have a bill of lading in his possession which runs to his own order.

BILLS OF LADING TO "ORDER NOTIFY."—A slight modification of this form of bill of lading is made in order to let the buyer know when the goods arrive. When goods arrive at their destination it is a customary courtesy of railroads to notify the consignee; but if goods are consigned to the seller's order, the man who is really trying to buy the goods gets no notice, as his name does not appear on the bill of lading. To avoid that difficulty there is generally put on bills of lading, taken out to the seller's order when the goods are shipped in fulfillment of some contract or order, the words, "Notify X Y," X Y being the prospective buyer of the goods. Then when the goods arrive the railroad notifies X Y; he learns the goods are there and makes his plans accordingly. These bills of lading are often called "bills to order notify." The person who is to be notified is sometimes incorrectly called the consignee of the bill. The consignee is the person to whom the goods are deliverable, not the person who is to be notified necessarily; and where a bill is to the seller's order the goods are, by the terms of the bill of lading, deliverable to the seller and he is the consignee.

CROPS ARE MOVED BY USE OF BILLS OF LADING.—The various uses of bills of lading by sellers in order to insure concurrent payment by the buyer, and in order, with the aid of banks, to put themselves in funds while the goods are in transit, is a very important function of bills of lading. It is by such means the great crops of the country are moved, especially the cotton crop, which is moved almost wholly in this manner. The southern banks discount bills of exchange, which are customarily secured by bills of lading. The New York banks rediscount these bills of exchange and draw for a great part of the price of the cotton on English bankers. This use by sellers of bills of lading, however, is not the only mercantile use of bills of lading.

BILLS OF LADING TO BANKER'S ORDER.—Here is another method used, especially common in foreign commerce. A merchant in Boston wants to buy a cargo of goods from Europe, but he has not the money to do it. The seller in Europe does not know him and will not give him credit, so the merchant goes to bankers who have available foreign correspondents and states his case, and if he is in good credit with the bankers they say, "Order the goods from the man in Germany of whom you were planning to order them, and tell him to make the bill of lading out to us, and draw on us or on our correspondents in Berlin or London or Paris. On receipt of those bills of lading naming us as consignee we will pay, or cause to be paid, the bills of exchange attached thereto for the price." In this way the goods are shipped directly to the banker. In the cases mentioned before, the banker took an indorsed bill of lading, but in this mode of dealing the banker is himself the consignee, and on the faith of the consignment he pays the price of the goods. Then he delivers the bill of lading, indorsed, to the buyer, his customer, on the buyer's making a settlement or giving him security.

SURRENDER OF BILLS OF LADING FOR TRUST RECEIPTS. — There is one method of doing business in this connection which causes some risk to the bankers who engage in it. They frequently allow their customer, the buyer, to take the bill of lading, indorsed, for the purpose of entering the goods at the Custom House, or warehousing them, or even for the purpose of selling the goods, so that the buyer will be in funds to enable him to discharge his debt to the banker. The banker takes, when he does this, from the buyer to whom he delivers the indorsed bill of lading, what are called "trust receipts." These receipts state that the buyer has taken these bills of lading, that he holds them as a trustee, that they really belong to the banker, and that the buyer holds them simply for a special purpose, such as to enter them at the Custom House or to resell them and turn the proceeds over to the banker. If the buyer is honest, well and good; but if he should be financially pressed and dispose of that bill of lading, many courts, at least, would not protect the banker, but would protect the bona fide purchaser. What the banker ought to do is to stamp upon the bill of lading, if he delivers it to the buyer, that a trust receipt has been issued for certain specified purposes. In that case any purchaser of the bill of lading would have notice of the terms of the trust.

CHANGE OF ROUTING. — An analogous problem also may be supposed. A bank holds a draft for collection with bill of lading attached. It sometimes allows the drawee to take possession of the bill of lading and change the routing of the car. That is done because the buyer sometimes sells the goods before he receives them, and to save additional freight bills, he changes the routing on the original bills of lading. What risk does the bank run if it allows him to have possession of the bill of lading indorsed in blank? It runs the same risk as in case of trust receipts. The fact that the purpose was to change the routing of the goods is apparently immaterial. The change of destination does not do the bank any actual harm, except that the goods will be sent elsewhere, and perhaps to a point some distance from their original destination. The great risk involved is in allowing a man to have possession of a document which in effect is negotiable. If the bank does not get back its bill of lading it is in a bad position. If it did get back its bill of lading it would still have its security, only it would be subject to this difficulty, that the goods instead of coming to a place where the bank could conveniently get at them, have perhaps gone to a distant city, where it would be more trouble. If, however, changing the routing and the reselling involve a surrender of the old bill to the railroad and the issuing of a new bill of lading not only on a new route but with the purchaser from the consignee named as a new consignee, then the bank has thrown away everything, unless it actually obtains possession of the new bill, and even if it does it has only an inferior security.

ACCOMMODATION BILLS.—Let us now enumerate the risks which a purchaser or a lender runs in dealing with bills of lading, even with order bills, and consider how these risks can be obviated and how far they are inherent in the nature of the business. The first risk is that the bill may have no goods behind it, because it was originally issued without any goods. It has been quite a common practice, at some points where there is competition for freight, to accommodate customers by issuing a bill of lading for goods before the goods were received. Suppose a seller in Chicago deals with a man in Boston; what the seller normally ought to do is to buy goods, and ship them, getting a bill of lading, then take the bill of lading to a bank and get money on the faith of that bill of lading. You will see that that method requires the seller to have had money or credit in the first place, in order to buy those goods to ship. It would be very much more convenient for him if he could reverse the order and get the money from the bank first, then buy the goods and then ship them; and the kindness of the railroad agent frequently has enabled him to do that. The railroad agent, trusting to the seller's word that he will ship goods to-morrow, issues a bill of lading to him for the goods which the seller promises to ship. The seller dashes around to the bank, gets money and then buys the goods and ships them. He may carry on business in that way for a long time; no trouble occurs, nobody knows anything about it until the seller either goes bankrupt or becomes dishonest and fails to ship the goods after he has got the bill of lading, and then somebody finds himself with a bill of lading for which no goods have ever been received. Such bills have been called "accommodation" bills of lading, issued by the railroad for the accommodation of the shipper.

FICTITIOUS BILLS OF LADING.—In some cases the whole transaction is a fraud. In the case we have thus far been supposing, the railroad agent believed the seller was going to ship goods, and the seller intended to do so, only he wanted the bill of lading first; but money is so easily obtained, frequently, on bills of lading, that sometimes a shipper and a railroad agent put their heads together and say, "Let's make a few bills of lading," and as a pure fraud the agent writes bills of lading. These may be called fictitious bills. They are not exactly forgeries, you will see, since they are drawn by the regular agent of the railroad on the regular railroad form. One who took such a bill as this, however, would be protected if the carrier were liable. Railroads are generally, and other carriers are generally, financially responsible, and therefore the great question that interests the holder of such a bill is, are the railroads liable in damages because no goods are behind the bill of lading? It was held in an English case, seventy-five years ago, that in such a case the carrier was not liable on the ground that the agent who wrote the bill was acting beyond the scope of his authority in signing a bill of lading when no goods had been received. That decision has been much criticized, and justly criticized, because the carrier has put that agent in a position to determine when bills of lading shall be issued and when not. Of course, the agent ought to exercise his choice properly, but if the carrier has given him the power it ought to be responsible for the results. Nevertheless, in a majority of the States of this country, and in the Supreme Court of the United States, the English case has been followed; and the carrier would be liable neither on an accommodation bill nor a fictitious bill where no goods were shipped. There have been some attempts to change this rule by statutes, and in some States there is a statute, the Uniform Bill of Lading Act, so called, which provides among other things that the carrier shall be liable in the case supposed; but the trouble is that bills of lading dealt with in one State will not generally originate in that State. If a fictitious bill was issued in Chicago, although the bill named as a consignee a person in Boston, and was bought by a Boston bank, the liability of the carrier on that bill of lading would be determined by the law of Illinois. So, unless you have a satisfactory law where the bill originates, you will not be protected. Fortunately, the same statute has been passed in several States, and it is hoped that it will be in more. This, then, is the first risk, and the only way of obviating it is to have the law in satisfactory shape, passing a statute wherever it is necessary, so as to make the carrier liable for the wrongful act of its agent in issuing a bill of lading when no goods have been received.

GOODS BEHIND BILL OF LADING INFERIOR IN KIND OR QUALITY.—The second difficulty is somewhat analogous to the first. Suppose there are some goods behind the bill of lading but they are not of the quantity, quality or kind that the bill of lading specifies. This is a difficulty that cannot very well be wholly obviated. We may suppose that the goods originally were of defective quality and kind, or that they became so. Suppose, first, that a number of barrels of sand are delivered to a railroad and they are marked barrels of sugar, and the carrier issues a bill of lading for so many barrels of sugar. Now, the purchaser of the bill of lading finds, when he comes to realize on his security, that he has got barrels of sand with a freight bill against them for more than they are worth. What can he do? Of course, he has a right of action against the fraudulent shipper, but perhaps the shipper has run away or is irresponsible. Is the carrier liable here? The answer to this is, no. In the first place, the bill of lading says, "Contents and condition of contents unknown," so that the carrier has expressly guarded against promising that the barrels really contained sugar. And even aside from this clause, it has been held that the carrier is not liable for such a concealed defect. If, however, it was apparent when the carrier received the goods that they were not of the kind or quality named, then the carrier would be liable if it issued a bill of lading without specifying the difficulty. Thus, if the bill of lading called for 100 barrels of sugar and there were 95, the carrier would be liable for the missing five. It has admitted it received 100, and has promised to deliver 100; it must do so or be liable.

SHIPPER'S LOAD AND COUNT.—There is an exception to this last statement, however, in regard to one class of bills which are very common in some lines of trade; these are "shipper's load and count" bills. In many cases railroads build spur tracks to factories and run empty cars up to the factories, where the shipper loads the cars and himself writes out the bill of lading. An enormous fraction of the business of the country, consisting of the large shipments from factories, at any rate, is done in this way. The railroad agent simply signs a bill of lading as it is presented to him by the shipper who has made out the whole bill except the signature, and has loaded the car, the railroad agent seeing nothing of it. The railroad agent stamps across such a bill of lading, "Shipper's load and count." That means,

"The shipper loaded this car and counted the contents. We are not responsible, therefore, for the loading or the counting." The second great principle, in regard to lending money on bills of lading, is never to touch a shipper's load and count bill which obviously has not the responsibility of the carrier. You would have to rely wholly on the honesty of the shipper. The railroads, seeing that they are freed from liability on this form of bill, have sometimes, in some parts of the country, thought it would be a good thing to stamp every bill, "Shipper's load and count." That is an injury to the shipper, because the banks do not like to take such bills of lading, and yet not infrequently he cannot do much about it. In fruit shipments from California that sort of thing has been very common.

DESTRUCTION OF GOODS IN TRANSIT.—So much for defects arising at the time of shipment; but one may also have difficulties which arise after the shipment. Suppose the goods are absolutely destroyed in transit by any of a variety of causes. The owner of the bill of lading necessarily loses his security, unless under the bill the carrier is responsible for that particular kind of loss. But it may happen that the carrier is not responsible for that particular kind of loss. One may protect himself here, perhaps, by insurance of some kind. That would be the way to obviate this sort of risk, but if complete protection against this kind of risk is desired, the insurance ought to be not only against fire but against destruction, or really against deterioration in any form. Of course, goods which are likely to depreciate in transit are not as good security as goods which are more durable. A cargo of bananas is not as good security as a cargo of grain.

LACK OF TITLE IN SHIPPER.—A third risk, which any one who takes a bill of lading runs, is lack of title to the goods in the shipper. Suppose the shipper stole the goods and brought them to the carrier and demanded and received an order bill of lading. That looks like as good a bill of lading as any, and the goods may be all right, but the holder of the bill of lading cannot keep the goods. They still belong to the original owner from whom the shipper stole them.

SPENT BILLS.—A fourth risk is that the bill of lading may be a "spent bill," as it is called. A spent bill is one where the goods have been delivered by the carrier at destination, but the bill of lading has not been taken up. A bill of lading is unlike a note in this respect—it has no date of maturity. When you buy a promissory note you can guess whether it has been dishonored or not, by whether the time for performance has come or not; but if a bill of lading for a cargo of goods is offered to you, you have no means of telling whether the cargo arrived the day before or whether the goods have been removed. Of course, the carrier ought to take up an order bill of lading when the goods are delivered, and in the Uniform Bills of Lading Act that requirement is made, and the carrier is made liable on the bill if it is left outstanding and is purchased by a bona fide purchaser for value, who supposes that the goods are still in transit. This trouble with spent bills is not so likely to arise as a corresponding difficulty with what may be called "partially spent bills." It is not uncommon for partial delivery to be made and the bill of lading still left in the hands of the holder. Commonly, when all the goods are delivered, the bill of lading is taken up, but when part is delivered the carrier does not feel justified, and indeed is not justified, in demanding the surrender of the bill. What ought to be done, of course, is to indorse on the bill of lading the fact that part of the goods has been delivered, with a specification of the part. This also is required by the bill of lading statute, and a carrier is made liable for failure to indorse on a bill of lading the fact that part of the goods described therein has been delivered.

LACK OF TITLE TO BILLS OF LADING.—A fifth risk, which one who buys or lends money on bills of lading runs, is the chance that the person from whom he takes a bill of lading may not have title to it. This risk is the same that one runs in regard to negotiable paper. If an indorsement is forged, or if for any reason the holder of a bill of lading—or for that matter of a bill of exchange—cannot give a good title to it, one who purchases from him will not get a good title.

MEANING OF NEGOTIABILITY.—The extent of this risk depends somewhat on the degree of negotiability which is given to bills of lading, and requires an understanding of what negotiability means. Ordinarily, one who buys a contract right gets no better right than has the person from whom he buys it. On the other hand, though one who buys chattel property capable of delivery, like a horse or a book, does not get title if the person who sold it to him had no legal title, yet a purchaser does get a good title to such property if he buys, in good faith and for value, from a person who has legal title though not an equitable title. You will see this best by an illustration. If a fraudulent person has a contract right assigned to him by fraud, and then sells the contract right to a bona fide purchaser, the bona fide purchaser gets no greater right than the fraudulent person has; in other words, he cannot collect on the claim which he has obtained. On the other hand, if a fraudulent person has assigned to him, by fraud, a horse or a book, the legal title to which was in the assignor, he has acquired the legal title, and though he is subject to an equity, as the phrase is, and the horse or the book could be taken away from him by the defrauded person, if he could act quickly enough, yet a purchaser for value, without notice of fraud, will get an indefeasible legal and equitable title to the horse or the book.

Negotiable paper—like bills of exchange and promissory notes—is subject to the same rule as the horse or book, and is not subject to the same rule as ordinary contract rights; that is, a purchaser in good faith of an order bill of lading from a vendor having legal title thereto, will get title to it and to the goods behind it, in spite of the fact that the person from whom the bill of lading was bought had obtained title by fraud, and could have had the bill of lading, or the goods behind it, taken away from him by the person defrauded.

Another feature of negotiability is that the terms of the instrument, on the face and back, are regarded as definitely showing the title. If the instrument is made to A's order, A has power by indorsement to give a good title, whatever may have been the reason the instrument was made payable to A, and even though it was agreed by the original parties that A should be merely an agent and have no title or right to transfer. If the instrument is made out on its face to bearer, or is indorsed in blank by the person to whom it is made out on the face, anyone acting in good faith may treat the holder as the owner and acquire a good title from him, though in fact the holder may not have had a good title. Under the Uniform Bills of Lading Act, and under some other local statutes, bills of lading running to order are given full negotiability, but in many States they are only partially negotiable.

INDORSEMENT OF BILLS OF LADING.—Order bills of lading need, for their negotiation, indorsement by the consignee, just as a promissory note needs indorsement by the payee. But there is one difference between the indorsement of a bill of lading, it may be said in passing, and the indorsement of a promissory note. The indorser of a bill of lading incurs no liability by his indorsement. His indorsement is simply a transfer. If it turns out that the bill of lading is not honored by the carrier, the holder of an indorsed bill of lading cannot come back on the indorser in the way that the holder of a promissory note can come back on the indorser if the maker fails to pay.

FORGED BILLS OF LADING.—One final risk in regard to bills of lading is that the bill of lading may be forged or altered, and this has in practice proved the most serious risk of all. There have been, in times past, several sets of frauds created by forged bills of lading. One of the largest is known as the Knight-Yancey frauds which originated in Alabama. A cotton firm named Knight, Yancey & Co. forged a quantity of bills of lading and obtained a very large amount of money from banks. A circumstance that renders forgery easier in the case of bills of lading than in the case of any other valuable document, such as a check or a stock certificate, is the carelessness with which bills of lading have been made out. It is really incredible, the carelessness with which this has been done. Documents which represent a value of many thousands of dollars are scribbled hastily, in pencil sometimes, on forms that are accessible to anybody. The forgeries that have taken place have called attention to this evil, and at the present time there is more care exercised in making out order bills than was the case a few years ago; but even to-day an order bill of lading is made out with no special precautions against forgery. The forms can be obtained at any railroad station, and it is simply a question of copying writing, no devices of perforating or serial numbers or things of that sort being ordinarily used.

DEVICES TO PREVENT FORGERY.—In order to meet this risk several devices have been suggested. One which has been urged upon Congress is to pay the railroads a special small fee for issuing order bills with the precautions that a stock certificate is issued. The railroad would take the blank from a numbered book and would punch and stamp it in such ways and with such countersigning that it would be very difficult to forge. That method has not found much favor with shippers because they dislike the extra expense. They get their order bills of lading for nothing now, and they want to continue to do so. Another project is to make some sort of central clearing house to which shall be reported all order bills of lading as they are issued, so that it will be known whether there is outstanding a document corresponding to one that is offered to a bank for security. This method is to some extent in use.

ALTERATION OF BILLS OF LADING.—Alteration of a genuine bill may be as damaging as the out and out forgery of a new one. This case occurred in Maryland some years ago: a man who had always been in good repute had a line of credit at the bank, where he kept, as security, bills of lading. He was allowed to change these as he wanted to, putting in sufficient collateral always to cover what he took out. The railroad and steamboat lines with which he did business neglected in some instances to take up the bills of lading which he presented for shipments. They habitually did not take up the straight bills, and that is not required by law, and sometimes they did not take up the order bills. When this man got hard pressed he took some old order bills, which he still had in his possession, and changed the dates; then he took some straight bills which he had in his possession and changed the date of those, and also added the words "or order" to the name of himself as consignee. Then, after indorsing those they looked good. He took those altered bills to his bank and substituted them for genuine bills, and when the fraud was found out the bank found itself with about $100,000 of altered bills of lading. The carrier was held liable on the order bills, even though they had been altered, because it should have taken them up, but on the straight bills, which were a great part of the whole, the bank lost. Of course, they were still legally straight bills, although the holder had written "or order" on them. That fraud led to one protection being made in the uniform bill of lading recommended by the Interstate Commerce Commission. The uniform form of order bill has the words "order of" printed in front of the blank for the consignee's name, so that a straight bill cannot be made into an order bill by adding "or order." Moreover, the difference in color, between order and straight bills now gives a protection as to domestic bills; not as to foreign bills, however. If a bill is altered fraudulently the bill is worth just as much and just as little as it would have been worth if no alteration had been made; that is, the alteration, not the bill itself, is void.

ATTACHMENT OF GOODS IN TRANSIT.—There is one other risk in regard to bills of lading which no longer exists where the Uniform Bills of Lading Act is in force, and that is seizure by attachment for the benefit of some creditor. The bills of lading act provides that when there is an order bill outstanding, against goods shipped by a carrier, there can be neither attachment by a creditor nor stoppage in transit by the seller if unpaid. Where the uniform statute has not been passed, the matter is not so clear. Undoubtedly one who purchased for value or lent money on an order bill would be protected against later attachments by creditors of the former owner of the bill; but if creditors of the former owner had attached the goods prior to the transfer of the bill, the attachment would generally be held good, though the man purchasing or lending money on the bill knew nothing of the attachment.

WAREHOUSE RECEIPTS ARE SIMILAR TO BILLS OF LADING.—To what has been said in regard to bills of lading a few words in regard to warehouse receipts may be added. Warehouse receipts are entirely similar in character to bills of lading, and what has been said in regard to them is, in general, applicable to warehouse receipts. There is a Uniform Warehouse Receipts Act which is similar in its provisions to the Uniform Bills of Lading Act, and the Warehouse Receipts Act has been enacted in a majority of the States. Warehouse receipts may be, in form, order or straight. They are simpler in form, ordinarily, than bills of lading, because they do not have so many special stipulations and conditions, but in other respects they are practically identical. The risks that one who deals in them runs are the same in their nature as in the case of bills of lading. There is one circumstance, however, in regard to warehouse receipts that gives one a better chance to protect himself than in bills of lading. Warehouse receipts are generally used as collateral and for purchase and sale in the city where the goods are stored. It is therefore possible to telephone to the warehouseman or otherwise to assure oneself of the existence of the goods in a way that is not possible under the bill of lading, where the goods are in transit. The warehouse receipt, even less than a bill of lading, has a day of maturity. A bill of lading, as we have seen, has no particular day on which it is evident to a purchaser that it has finished its work, and that is even more true in a warehouse receipt. The fact that a warehouse receipt is pretty old does not necessarily show that the document is not a perfectly good document and that the goods are not there.

OPEN RECEIPTS.—There is one way of doing business with warehouse receipts which is different from anything that takes place with bills of lading, and which has been a subject of criticism, and which deserves criticism; this is the practice of issuing what are called open receipts. In an open receipt the warehouseman acknowledges he has received a certain quantity of things of a certain sort, and will redeliver that quantity of things of that sort; but not necessarily the identical things that were deposited. It is contemplated that the depositor shall have the right to substitute from time to time, for the goods originally deposited, other goods of like kind and quantity; that is, a receipt may be issued for 100 bales of burlap. The depositor who deals in burlap wants to use some of the bales that are in storage. He has pledged his warehouse receipt, which he originally received for the 100 bales of burlap, and he cannot surrender that, but he wants the warehouseman to let him take out 25 bales of the old burlap and put in 25 bales of new, and that is sometimes allowed. It seems a very unsafe practice. It is unsafe, for one who lends on warehouse receipts, to allow the depositor and the warehouseman to agree between themselves as to what shall be a sufficient substitution for goods which are the bank's collateral. Moreover, it is unsafe for the warehouseman, because if the holder of the warehouse receipt has not really consented to the substitution, or unless the form of warehouse receipt clearly shows that substitution is contemplated, the warehouseman would be liable to the holder of the receipt if the substituted goods turn out to be inferior to those which were originally deposited.

WAREHOUSEMAN IS A BAILEE FOR HIRE.—A warehouseman is a bailee for hire, and a bailee for hire is liable for neglect if the goods are destroyed or injured by his negligence. He is not an insurer. The ordinary bailee for hire is not subject to the extraordinary liability to which a carrier is subjected while goods are in transit.

SAFE DEPOSIT COMPANIES ARE BAILEES FOR HIRE.—There is one special kind of bailee, in regard to whom it may be worth while to say a few words particularly, and that is a safe deposit company. It has been questioned whether a safe deposit company is properly a bailee of the goods in the boxes to which the safe deposit company does not have access. It is simply in control of the general premises, and, furthermore, the holder of the boxes cannot have access to what is inside the boxes without the assistance of the safe deposit company. There is, therefore, a sort of joint possession. The safe deposit company and the depositor who hired the box have together the full control of the goods, but neither one of them alone has it. It has been suggested that the safe deposit company is merely a sort of watchman; that it is guarding property of which it is not in possession. But it is doing a little more than guarding, and it is generally held to be a bailee for hire; that means it must take reasonable care of the goods in its possession.

LIABILITY OF SAFE DEPOSIT COMPANIES FOR LOSS OF GOODS.—There are a number of cases, not a great many, but still some, where safe deposit companies have been sued for goods which were missing, or which the depositor swore were missing, from his box. If the court or jury is convinced that the goods have been lost from the box, the burden of explanation as to how it happened would be upon the safe deposit company. The safe deposit company is liable for the acts of its servants and agents. Of course, then, carelessness in regard to duplicate keys of any of the boxes might render a safe deposit company subject to suit if loss occurs thereby.

LIABILITY OF DEPOSITED GOODS TO GARNISHMENT.—One of the most important questions in regard to safe deposit companies is this: Are the goods in the safes subject to legal process? Suppose a safe deposit company is garnisheed (that is served with a trustee writ) in a suit against some one who has a box; can the company answer that it has no funds or goods of the defendant in its possession? Yes, it may; it cannot control the goods and it may answer, no funds. One case, however, must be distinguished, and that is where a bank or a safe deposit company has a separate trunk or box of a depositor in its possession. If it has that separate box, even though it is locked, and the bank has not the key, the bank cannot answer no funds; it must answer that it has a box the contents of which are unknown to it. A box, however, shut up in a safe deposit vault, that is, one of the regular tin safes, cannot be reached by the safe deposit company in the normal course of affairs, unless the depositor unlocks his lock. That is the reason for distinguishing between such a box and an ordinary box or trunk which is not itself enclosed in something, to which the bank or safe deposit company does not have access.

LIABILITY OF DEPOSITED GOODS TO ATTACHMENT.—Whether property in a safe deposit company is liable on a writ of attachment in a suit against the owner, is not so clear. It has been held in one case that it is so liable, and that the officer has a right to go in and seize the goods. This will not often be attempted, however, because the officer will not know in what box the debtor might have goods, and the safe deposit company will not tell him. The company is certainly under no obligation to help the officer. The regular way for a creditor to get at the goods of his debtor, concealed in the safe deposit box, is by first making the debtor disclose on examination in court what property he has, and then getting an order from the court that the debtor shall turn over what he has disclosed. This he must do or be imprisoned until he does. There is only one difficulty with this remedy, and that is that the debtor may have an infirm memory—in other words, he may commit perjury; he may have something in the box and not disclose the fact.

SEARCH FOR STOLEN PROPERTY.—If stolen property were sought, a search warrant describing the property might be presented to the safe deposit company, and it would have to permit the officer of the law to make the search for the goods described, but only for goods described in the search warrant. There is a case in New York where, on a search warrant for certain articles, the officer of a safe deposit company allowed the officer of the law to make a general examination of goods in its possession, and to remove some bonds which were not specified in the search warrant. The safe deposit company was held liable.

DEATH OF DEPOSITOR.—The question often arises: What is the situation on the death of the owner or renter of a safe? It is the same as in the case of the death of any bailor or depositor. The bailee must recognize the title only of the person who is appointed by law as the successor in interest to the deceased person. The safe deposit company has the right, and should exercise it, to demand proofs and identifications of persons who claim rights as representing deceased persons. Sometimes a dispute arises between joint owners of a box. In that case the only safe course for a safe deposit company would be to recognize the right of none until it had been passed on by the court. What is called a bill of interpleader, to determine which one has the right, should be filed in court, unless the conflicting interests can agree or one of them gives a bond to the company to insure its freedom from liability if it delivers the goods to him.

SAFE DEPOSIT COMPANY HAS NO LIEN.—A safe deposit company has no lien on the contents of a box for anything due to it. In that respect it is different from an ordinary warehouseman and a carrier, who have a lien on the goods in their possession for their charges. The reason is that a safe deposit company is not in such possession of the contents of a box as to give it a lien. If the renter of the box does not pay his bills, however, the company has the right to open the box and remove its contents, keeping them safe for the owner.

GIFT OF GOODS IN A SAFE DEPOSIT BOX.—It was held in a case, decided in the State of Illinois, that the gift of the keys of a safe deposit box amounted to a valid gift of property in the box when made with that intention. In order to make a good gift there must be a valid delivery, and it was held that the delivery of the keys amounted to a symbolic delivery of the contents of the box.

RIGHT OF SAFE DEPOSIT COMPANY TO SUE FOR GOODS WRONGFUL-LY TAKEN.—If goods are wrongfully removed from the box of a depositor, the safe deposit company has a right to reclaim them like any bailee, for it is the law that if goods are taken out of the hands of a carrier, warehouseman or other bailee wrongfully, the bailee may reclaim the goods from the wrongdoer, and bring an action at law for them, not as owner, but because the bailee has the right of possession to them while in his custody, and he may be liable if he lets them get into the hands of any one other than the true owner.

LIABILITY OF SAFE DEPOSIT COMPANIES UNDER INHERITANCE TAX LAWS.—One case in regard to the Illinois inheritance tax law indicates an imposition of some burden on the safe deposit company. The company is required to notify the Attorney-General ten days before it allows access by the representative of a deceased person to his box, and under certain circumstances the safe deposit company is required to retain, from the contents of the box, a sufficient amount to pay the tax, and is made liable if it fails to do so. This provision was held constitutional by the Supreme Court of Illinois.

CHAPTER XII
BILLS AND NOTES

HISTORY.—By the term "negotiable paper," we ordinarily mean promissory notes, bills of exchange and checks. The law governing negotiable paper originated among the customs of merchants on the continent of Europe. It was gradually introduced into England, and its principles grudgingly recognized by the common law judges. There is no branch of law where the desirability of uniformity is greater, as these documents pass from hand to hand like money, and travel from one State to another. Naturally, our first serious attempt at uniform legislation was made in this branch of law, and in the year 1896, the Commissioners for Uniform Laws prepared and recommended for passage the Uniform Negotiable Instruments Law. To-day, every State, except Georgia, has passed the Act, as well as the District of Columbia, Alaska, Porto Rico and the Philippines. For convenience in this chapter, we shall hereafter refer to this Negotiable Instruments Act as the N. I. L.

FORMS OF NEGOTIABLE INSTRUMENTS.—It is essential to carry in mind the customary form of the negotiable instruments we have just mentioned. A promissory note is defined by the N. I. L. as follows: "A negotiable promissory note within the meaning of this act is an unconditional promise in writing made by one person to another signed by the maker engaging to pay on demand, or at a fixed or determinable future time, a sum certain in money to order or to bearer."

A bill of exchange is defined by the N. I. L. as follows: "A bill of exchange is an unconditional order in writing addressed by one person to another, signed by the person giving it, requiring the person to whom it is addressed to pay on demand or at a fixed or determinable future time a sum certain in money to order or to bearer."

A check is defined by N. I. L. as "a bill of exchange drawn on a bank payable on demand."

Other documents may be negotiable in form, such as the ordinary bearer corporation bonds, liberty bonds, certificates of stock, and bills of lading. The principles discussed in this chapter would apply, ordinarily, to these documents, and are discussed more in detail in the chapters devoted to them which we have already considered.

WHAT IS NEGOTIABILITY?—Negotiability has been defined as that quality whereby a bill, note, or check, passes freely from hand to hand like currency. In fact, all of these documents are substitutes for currency, and so far as is practicable, it is desirable that they should pass as freely as currency. Negotiability applies only to this branch of the law, while assignability applies to ordinary cases of contract law.

SPECIMEN FORM OF PROMISSORY NOTE

SPECIMEN FORM OF DRAFT

Pa.____________19____

Pay to the

Order of

THE FIRST NATIONAL BANK

$________

____________Dollars,

Value received, and charge the same to account of

To________

NO PROTEST TEAR THIS OFF BEFORE PRESENTING

*Before the words "pay to" the time when the draft is due should be inserted—
as "at sight" or "30 days after date"*

SPECIMEN FORM OF CHECK

No. 1922

Statewood, Indiana, Sept. 14, 1921

THE INSTITUTE STATE BANK 17-81

Pay to Thomas R. Rice————————or order

Twenty-five and No/100————————————Dollars

$25.00

JOHN T. SMITH

ILLUSTRATIONS.—To illustrate the difference between the two: Jones worked for the Baltimore & Ohio Railroad Co. He presented his bill of $100 to the proper official, and a check was issued by the railroad payable to the order of Jones for that amount. Jones took the check, indorsed it, and with it paid his grocery bill. The grocery man deposited the check in his bank, and was notified shortly thereafter that payment had been stopped on the check by the Baltimore & Ohio. They claimed a fraud had been committed, that Jones was overpaid $50, and, therefore, they refused to honor the check. The grocery man, having taken this check in the usual course of business, is what we term a "holder in due course." The N.I.L. defines a holder in due course as:

Section 52. "A holder in due course is a holder who has taken the instrument under the following conditions: (1) That it is complete and regular upon its face; (2) That he became the holder of it before it was overdue, and without notice that it had been previously dishonored, if such was the fact; (3) That he took it in good faith and for value; (4) That at the time it was negotiated to him he had no notice of any infirmity in the instrument or defect in the title of the person negotiating it."

A holder in due course, then, would be entitled to collect the full $100 from the Baltimore & Ohio. This check is governed by the law of negotiability with the result which we have just indicated. Now change the facts a trifle. Jones presented his bill to the same officer of the Baltimore & Ohio as before. The officer says that checks are made out regularly on the first of the month. It was the fifteenth, and Jones did not feel able to wait until the first of the next month. He went to a friend and told him of his claim against the Baltimore & Ohio, and said: "I will assign this claim to you for $95, and then you can present the assignment, which I will draw up and sign, to the Baltimore & Ohio on the first of the month, and get the $100." His friend agrees and advances the money. When he presents the written assignment to the proper officer on the first of the month, he is told that the railroad has discovered that Jones' claim was really good for only $50, and that is all they will pay. Although his assignment reads for $100, he can collect only $50. This illustration is governed by the law of assignability, which applies to practically all contracts, apart from commercial paper. Under the rules of assignability, a person can assign no better claim than he has, or, as is sometimes said, the assignee stands in the shoes of the assignor. Jones really had a claim of only $50 against the Baltimore & Ohio, although he claimed it was $100. He could assign no more than he really had. These two illustrations show the great difference in the result of the application of the two principles, negotiability and assignability.

THE FORMAL REQUIREMENTS OF NEGOTIABLE PAPER.—There are certain formalities which all negotiable paper must have. It must be in writing, and signed by the proper person. No form of writing is specified in the Act, and lead pencil, or even slate pencil, is as good as ink, except that in the two latter cases the ease with which these forms of writing may be altered makes them most undesirable for use. But there is no law requiring the use of ink.

MUST CONTAIN A PROMISE.—Every negotiable instrument must contain words of negotiability. These words are, "to order," "to bearer," "to holder" or their equivalent. "I promise to pay John Jones, $100," and signed "John Smith," is a promissory note, but not a negotiable promissory note, because it lacks the words to "order" or "bearer," and is a document which would, therefore, pass by the law of assignability rather than the law of negotiability. In taking negotiable paper, therefore, it is always important to see whether these words are present. If they are not, the holder will lose the peculiar advantage and rights which the holder in due course acquires by the law of negotiability. A promissory note must contain a promise and a bill of exchange must contain an unconditional order. An I.O.U. for $100 signed "John Jones" is not a promissory note, because there is no promise contained in such a document.

UNCONDITIONAL PROMISE.—All negotiable documents must be payable without reference to any contingency. A note reads: "I promise to pay to the order of John Jones $100 when I attain my twenty-second birthday" and is signed by John Jones, now twenty-one. That is not a good note because the person may not live to be twenty-two. Even if he lives to become twenty-two the note is still non-negotiable, for when it was made the contingency existed. A bill of exchange, regular in form, but adding the expression, "If the Republicans win the next congressional election," is not negotiable. The one exception, as it might appear at first sight, is a negotiable document reading: "I promise to pay to the order of William White six months after death," etc. Such a promise is not contingent. Death will arrive at some time, although it may be uncertain just when. In the other illustrations the republicans might not win the congressional election, and the person might not become twenty-two. Again, all commercial paper must be made payable in money. "I promise to pay to the order of John Jones $100 worth of tobacco," is not negotiable. "I promise to pay to the order of John Jones $100 and fifty pounds of tobacco" is not negotiable. In both cases, the medium of payment is something other than money.

INCEPTION OF THE INSTRUMENT AS AN OBLIGATION.—In our discussion of contracts, we made the statement that a legal intention to make a contract was necessary. The same is true in commercial paper. A man must intend legally to issue a negotiable instrument in order to be liable on one as maker or drawer. Thus, in the case of Walker v. Ebert, 29 Wis. 94, the defendant, a German, unable to read and write English, was induced by the payee to sign an instrument, in the form of a promissory note, relying on the false statement that it was a contract appointing the defendant agent to sell a patent right. It was held that the defendant was not liable. The instrument, though complete in form, was not the defendant's note and the plaintiff acquired nothing by his purchase of the paper.

ILLUSTRATION.—We must contrast this with another situation. Suppose I hand you a paper with a promissory note printed on it, complete in every detail except your signature. I ask you to sign it. You sign the paper, without reading it over or knowing what it is, and give it back to me. I then transfer it to a person who takes it for value, in good faith, etc., or who is, in other words, a holder in due course. The question is, are you liable on such a document? The answer is, "Of course, you are." You may say, "I did not intend to sign a promissory note." The law answers you by saying, "You were careless in signing something which you did not read over, and one is presumed to intend the consequences of his own careless acts." Our German was in a different situation. He was not careless. He could not read English and was obliged to rely upon someone to tell him what the document was, and, granting that he used due care in selecting a responsible person to explain to him the nature of the document, he had done all the law required. Had he been imposed upon, on several previous occasions, by the same person who told him what the document was, and in spite of that, had relied on him to explain this document, then, undoubtedly, the court would have held otherwise and he would have been liable on the ground that he must have intended the consequences of his negligent acts, he being deemed negligent when he trusts a person who had not only misrepresented things to him but had actually defrauded him several times.

DELIVERY.—A note found among the maker's papers, after his death, imposes no obligation either upon him or upon his estate. In other words, in addition to the intentional signing of the document, to complete its validity, there must also have been what we call delivery. This is a passing out of the possession of the maker or drawer, of the document, into the hands of some third party. Delivery may be made in three ways: (1) By intention; (2) By fraud; (3) By negligence.

A VALID DELIVERY NECESSARY.—I hand you my promissory note and you take it. That, of course, is an intentional delivery. You tell me that you have a fine watch which I decide to buy, and I give you my promissory note in payment. Afterwards, upon examining the watch, I find that it is worthless and entirely different from your description. You have secured the note from me in that case by fraud, or there is, as we say, a delivery procured by fraud. I am sitting on a bench in Central Park, and I take out of my pocket a completed promissory note and look at it and place it upon the bench. When I leave I forget it and it stays there until someone comes along and picks it up. That is a delivery by negligence. All these forms of delivery are valid, making the documents good, some in the hands of all parties, others in the hands of the holder in due course only. The N. I. L. is so clear upon this matter that reference must be made to sections 15 and 16. For this reason both of these sections are reproduced here in full:

Section 15. "Where an incomplete instrument has not been delivered it will not, if completed and negotiated, without authority, be a valid contract in the hands of any holder, as against any person whose signature was placed thereon before delivery."

Section 16. "Every contract on a negotiable instrument is incomplete and revocable until delivery of the instrument for the purpose of giving effect thereto. As between immediate parties, and as regards a remote party other than a holder in due course, the delivery, in order to be effectual, must be made either by or under the authority of the party making, drawing, accepting or indorsing, as the case may be; and in such case the delivery may be shown to have been conditional, or for a special purpose only, and not for the purpose of transferring the property in the instrument. But where the instrument is in the hands of a holder in due course, a valid delivery thereof by all parties prior to him so as to make them liable to him is conclusively presumed. And where the instrument is no longer in the possession of a party whose signature appears thereon, a valid and intentional delivery by him is presumed until the contrary is proved."

DISTINGUISHING FEATURES.—It is very important to distinguish between these two sections. Let us take for illustration the famous case of Baxendale v. Bennett, 3 Q.B.Div. 525. Here the defendant wrote his signature as acceptor on several printed blank forms of bills of exchange and left them in a drawer of his desk. The blanks were stolen, filled out, and negotiated to the plaintiff, an innocent purchaser. It was held that the plaintiff could not recover. The reason for this decision is that the document was incomplete and as the Act says: "Where an incomplete instrument has not been delivered it will not, if completed and negotiated, without authority, be a valid contract in the hands of any holder, as against any person whose signature was placed thereon before delivery." On the other hand, if I leave in my safe, checks which I have signed and made out in full and they are payable to bearer, although a thief breaks in and steals the checks from the safe, those documents will be valid in the hands of a holder in due course. The reason here is that although there has been no delivery, either by intention or by fraud or by negligence, nevertheless, the Negotiable Instruments Act has extended this theory of delivery, even further than the law went before the Act was passed, and says that when the document is in the hands of a holder in due course, a delivery is conclusively presumed.

CONSIDERATION.—Another essential in the inception of the instrument is consideration. We have already discussed this topic in the chapter on contracts. We made the statement at the beginning of this chapter that the law of negotiable paper came from the continent of Europe and was grudgingly received by the courts of England. The law of negotiable paper on the continent of Europe did not have any idea of consideration, and this is one reason why the law was reluctantly admitted to the English common law and explains the reason now why we have the doctrine of consideration in negotiable paper. It would not be safe for the student to accept all we have said in regard to consideration in the chapter on contracts and apply it to negotiable paper. The difference is at once apparent when you read Sections 24 and 28 of the Negotiable Instrument Act which read:

Section 24. "Every negotiable instrument is deemed prima facie to have been issued for a valuable consideration; and every person whose signature appears thereon to have become a party thereto for value."

Section 28. "Absence or failure of consideration is a matter of defence as against a person not a holder in due course."

So, we see, that in the general law of contracts, consideration is absolutely essential to a binding contract but in the law of negotiable paper, consideration is not absolutely essential except when you are dealing with the immediate parties. An illustration will explain this. I wish to make you a present on your next birthday which is January 12. To-day, September 15, I give you my promissory note due on your birthday for $50. This is to be my present to you. You take the note and then hold it until your birthday arrives and I do not pay it. Then you sue me on the note. You cannot recover anything because there was no consideration for the note and the absence of consideration is a perfectly good defence between you and me, whom the law calls the immediate parties. But, suppose, instead of doing this, you had kept the note about six weeks and then had taken it to your bank and asked them if they would discount the note for you and they had done so, taking it in absolutely good faith. They know me to be a responsible party, so they are willing to accept my promissory note. They knew you and they presumed that you had taken the note for a valuable consideration although, as a matter of fact, it was a gift to you. Under the circumstances, the bank is a holder in due course and when the note becomes due, if I do not pay, the bank will sue me and will collect from me because, as the Act says, "the failure of consideration is a matter of defence as against any person not a holder in due course." But the bank is a holder in due course.

ACCEPTANCE OF BILLS OF EXCHANGE.—The holder of a bill of exchange will take it, soon after receiving it, to the drawee, the person upon whom it is drawn, for his acceptance. The drawee will accept it by writing across the face of it "Accepted," signing his name and perhaps adding "Payable at the First National Bank." A form of bill of exchange, duly accepted, will be found elsewhere in this chapter. The Act provides that the acceptance must be in writing and signed, either on the document itself or on a separate piece of paper attached to the document. As soon as the drawee accepts the bill, he then becomes known, not as the drawee but as the acceptor and he is the party primarily liable on the bill, that is, he assumes responsibility for its payment. The holder has a right to demand an acceptance for the full amount of the bill and may refuse to take an acceptance for a less amount. It is not always possible for the drawee to know whether he has sufficient funds to justify an acceptance, and so the Act gives him twenty-four hours within which to make up his mind. During that time the holder is obliged to wait without taking any further action. Just as a conditional promise to pay money is not a good promissory note, just so a conditional acceptance is not looked upon as an acceptance which a party is obliged to take. There are, however, occasionally times when a person is willing to take a conditional acceptance. For example, I hold a bill of exchange for $1,000. There are three or four indorsers upon it and I take it to the drawee to have him accept. He will not accept for more than $500. Now I feel that the drawer and all of the indorsers are financially irresponsible and I would rather have the acceptance of the drawee for $500 than nothing. I am willing to take it. The question comes up as to the effect of this upon the other parties, the drawer and the indorsers. The Act covers that fully and it is important that it be kept in mind:

Section 142. "The holder may refuse to take a qualified acceptance, and if he does not obtain an unqualified acceptance, he may treat the bill as dishonored by non-acceptance. Where a qualified acceptance is taken, the drawer and indorsers are discharged from liability on the bill, unless they have expressly or impliedly authorized the holder to take a qualified acceptance, or subsequently assent thereto. When the drawer or indorser receives notice of a qualified acceptance, he must, within a reasonable time, express his dissent to the holder, or he will be deemed to have assented thereto."

NEGOTIATION.—If negotiable paper is a substitute for money, it follows that its most distinguishing characteristic is the fact that it may be transferred from one owner to another. This transfer is made in one of two ways. It may be by operation of law, or by act of the parties. By operation of law, we refer to such a case as where a person dies and his commercial paper then becomes the property of his administrator or executor. In other words, the law transfers the paper to the deceased person's legal representative. The other case, the transfer by the act of the parties is, of course, the ordinary case and the one we shall consider here. The sections in the Negotiable Instruments Act which discuss this matter are so clear that we can do no better than insert them in full at this time:

Section 30. "An instrument is negotiated when it is transferred from one person to another in such a manner as to constitute the transferee the holder thereof. If payable to bearer it is negotiated by delivery; if payable to order it is negotiated by the indorsement of the holder completed by delivery."

Section 31. "The indorsement must be written on the instrument itself or upon a paper attached thereto. The signature of the indorser, without additional words, is a sufficient indorsement."

Section 32. "The indorsement must be an indorsement of the entire instrument. An indorsement which purports to transfer to the indorsee a part only of the amount payable, or which purports to transfer the instrument to two or more indorsees severally, does not operate as a negotiation of the instrument. But where the instrument has been paid in part, it may be indorsed as to the residue."

NEGOTIATION BY INDORSEMENT.—Reference should be made to the several kinds of negotiation by indorsement. We have first the blank indorsement. There the person to whom the document is payable simply writes his name on the back in the same way as it appears on the front. That is, if John Jones is the payee, he writes his name across the back of the instrument "JOHN JONES." Next, there is the special indorsement. John Jones, in this case, is the payee and wishes to transfer the note to John Wanamaker. He writes across the back, "pay to the order of John Wanamaker" and signs his name, JOHN JONES. A restrictive indorsement is one where the further negotiation of the instrument is limited or restricted altogether. For example, the payee writes across the back "Pay to the order of John Jones only." That restricts the further negotiation of the instrument. Another form that is commonly used is in depositing checks in the bank in your own account; usually you indorse "for collection" and sign your name, or you indorse "for deposit only" and sign your name. This form of indorsement simply constitutes the bank your agent to make collection, but not for any other purpose except that the Act now authorizes a bank to begin suit to collect on a document indorsed in that way. Another form of indorsement, known as the qualified indorsement, is frequently used in the case where you wish to indorse without incurring the usual liability of the indorser. This is done by adding under your name the expression "without recourse." This does not mean, as is commonly supposed, that you are free from all liability as an indorser. We shall refer to this later.

THE HOLDER IN DUE COURSE.—As we have seen, the distinguishing feature of the law of commercial paper is negotiability as distinguished from assignability. The principles of negotiability are designed very largely for the protection of the person whom we call the holder in due course. It is essential then to bear in mind the condition under which a person becomes such. Section 52 of the Act defines a holder in due course as follows:

Section 52. "A holder in due course is a holder who has taken the instrument under the following conditions: (1) That the instrument is complete and regular upon its face; (2) That he became the holder of it before it was overdue, and without notice that it had been previously dishonored, if such was the fact; (3) That he took it in good faith and for value; (4) That at the time it was negotiated to him he had no notice of any infirmity in the instrument or defect in the title of the person negotiating it." Section 57 defines what the rights of this holder in due course are:

Section 57. "A holder in due course holds the instrument free from any defect of title of prior parties, and free from defences available to prior parties among themselves, and may enforce payment of the instrument for the full amount thereof against all parties liable thereon."

It is clear, then, that by this section, the Act means that the holder in due course takes free of personal defences, although he does not take free of absolute defences. It simply remains for us to consider briefly what is meant by a personal defence and what is meant by an absolute defence. We have already illustrated this in one of our cases where the note was a present. In this case, there was no consideration for the note. The boy to whom it was given could not recover, whereas when he transferred it to an innocent third party, a holder for value, he could recover. Thus we say, failure of consideration is a personal defence. Again, some person steals my check book, fills out a check, and forges my name. The check is then taken and finally gets into the hands of a person who is strictly a holder in due course. He could not recover on it, however, because forgery is a real defence. That is, no one can hold me liable on my forged check. The ordinary illustration of real or absolute defences are infancy, lunacy, illegality and sometimes fraud. Other defences are generally personal defences and do not affect the holder in due course. To put it another way, a real defence is good against the whole world; a personal defence is available only against such as are not holders in due course.

LIABILITY OF PARTIES.—The parties primarily liable on negotiable documents are, on a note, the maker; on a bill of exchange, the acceptor; and on a check, the drawer. The liability of these three parties is most concisely stated in Sections 60, 61, 62, as follows:

Section 60. "The maker of a negotiable instrument by making it engages that he will pay it according to its tenor, and admits the existence of the payee and his then capacity to indorse."

Section 61. "The drawer by drawing the instrument admits the existence of the payee, and his then capacity to indorse; and engages that on due presentment the instrument will be accepted or paid, or both, according to its tenor, and that if it be dishonored and the necessary proceedings on dishonor be duly taken, he will pay the amount thereof to the holder, or to any subsequent indorser who may be compelled to pay it. But the drawer may insert in the instrument an express stipulation negativing or limiting his own liability to the holder."

Section 62. "The acceptor by accepting the instrument engages that he will pay it according to the tenor of his acceptance; and admits: (1) The existence of the drawer, the genuineness of his signature, and his capacity and authority to draw the instrument; and, (2) The existence of the payee and his then capacity to indorse."

INDORSERS' LIABILITY.—We have not yet considered the question of the liability of persons who transfer negotiable documents. Indorsements may be made, as we have said, in two ways: either by indorsing the document, or if it is payable to bearer, by delivering it without indorsement. The liability of these two parties is stated in the Negotiable Instruments Act in Sections 65 and 66 in the following language:

Section 65. "Every person negotiating an instrument by delivery or by a qualified indorsement, warrants: (1) That the instrument is genuine and in all respects what it purports to be; (2) That he has a good title to it; (3) That all prior parties had capacity to contract; (4) That he has no knowledge of any fact which would impair the validity of the instrument or render it valueless. But when the negotiation is by delivery only, the warranty extends in favor of no holder other than the immediate transferee. The provisions of subdivision three of this section do not apply to persons negotiating public or corporation securities other than bills and notes."

Section 66. "Every indorser who indorses without qualification, warrants to all subsequent holders in due course: (1) The matters and things mentioned in subdivision one, two and three of the next preceding section; and (2) That the instrument is at the time of his indorsement valid and subsisting. And, in addition, he engages that on due presentment, it shall be accepted or paid, or both, as the case may be, according to its tenor, and that if it be dishonored, and the necessary proceedings on dishonor be duly taken, he will pay the amount thereof to the holder, or to any subsequent indorser who may be compelled to pay it."

QUALIFIED INDORSEMENT.—Section 65 speaks of delivery by qualified instrument. You will remember that we have already mentioned the indorsement in the form "without recourse." This is a qualified indorsement. The kind of liability a person incurs who indorses in that way is set forth in Section 65. This is important because the layman assumes that in indorsing "without recourse" one means to incur no liability as indorser. Such is not the case. Reread section 65, which covers the indorsement without recourse. There is liability for the things mentioned therein. Then in section 66, the last paragraph, you will notice that every indorser, who indorses without qualification "engages that on due presentment, it shall be accepted or paid, or both, as the case may be, according to its tenor, and that if it be dishonored, and the necessary proceedings on dishonor be duly taken, he will pay the amount thereof to the holder." This does not mean that the indorser will always pay, but only if the necessary steps are taken. We shall consider what these necessary steps are when we take up the subject of "protest."

CHECKS.—A check is simply a bill of exchange drawn on a bank and payable on demand. Therefore, the general principles which we have been laying down, in regard to bills of exchange and other negotiable paper, apply to checks, although, of course, the check is a more recent development in the law of commercial paper than the other two forms, namely, the promissory note and the bill of exchange. Section 186 of the Act reads: "A check must be presented for payment within a reasonable time after its issue or the drawer will be discharged from liability thereon to the extent of the loss caused by the delay."

HOLDER OF CHECK.—It is important to remember that the holder of a check has no right against the bank. Thus, if I hold John Rockefeller's check, drawn on the Institute National Bank, and I present it to the bank and the bank refuses to pay it for no reason at all, or for a purely arbitrary reason, I cannot sue the bank. The only thing I can do is to seek to get the money on the check from Mr. Rockefeller personally. This is because the drawing of a check is not the assignment of so much money to the payee named in the check. Of course, Mr. Rockefeller might sue his bank for failure to honor his check if it refuses to pay it to me for no valid reason. One further fact is important. When a holder of a check procures it to be certified by the bank, that releases all indorsers and also the drawer. And so, if I have a check drawn by Mr. Rockefeller and indorsed by six millionaires and I take that to the bank and have them certify it and then the bank fails, I have lost everything if the bank never pays anything to a depositor. By getting it certified I release Mr. Rockefeller and all of the indorsers.

THE MEANING OF PROTEST.—Protest is often used broadly to signify any dishonor of a negotiable instrument, but, of course, properly it means presentment by a notary, and his certification that an instrument has been presented for payment and has been dishonored. Protest is only necessary in regard to foreign bills. A foreign bill is one which is drawn in one State and payable in another. For this purpose the different States of the Union are foreign to each other. A bill drawn in New York payable in Boston is as much a foreign bill for this purpose as one drawn in England payable here.

WHAT MAY BE PROTESTED.—Though protest is not necessary for any other negotiable instrument except foreign bills of exchange, including foreign checks, it is convenient frequently to protest other negotiable instruments. The law provides that protest may be made of other negotiable instruments, and the certificate of protest is evidence in such cases, as well as in the case of foreign bills of exchange, of the facts which it states, namely, that the instrument has been duly presented and notice given. Statements in a certificate of protest, however, whether of foreign bills or of other instruments, are not conclusive evidence of the facts which they state. They are some evidence, but it may be shown by other evidence that the instrument was not presented, or was not presented at the time the certificate asserts, or that the notice was not given as therein asserted.

SUGGESTIONS FOR DRAWING NEGOTIABLE PAPER.—Very few suggestions are necessary in drawing checks. We almost always use the printed form. The only thing to be careful about is to draw lines through the blank spaces so that a check written for $70 may not have something else written before the word seventy, thereby raising the amount to, say, One thousand seventy, and the figures, because they are not near the dollar sign, correspondingly raised. The promissory note is frequently drawn by the parties without any printed form. In order to be negotiable, the note must bear the words "or order," or "bearer"; otherwise, it would not be negotiable, and would pass by the law of assignability without any of the advantages accruing to negotiable paper. The draft, or bill of exchange, is the document which the average layman is the least familiar with, and before drawing one, a printed form should be secured or a book on negotiable paper be consulted.

NEGOTIABILITY.—Care should be taken in the indorsement of any negotiable paper. The indorsement in blank, that is, simply writing your name upon the paper on the back, is the one commonly used, but is a dangerous one to use, if there is any possibility of the paper being lost or stolen. For example, A has a promissory note payable to his order, and he simply writes his name across the back and mails it to a person who has agreed to accept it in payment of a bill A owes him. The letter is lost, gets into the hands of X, who opens it and takes the note. Of course, the note is no good to X. X, however, takes the note to someone and persuades that person to discount the note for him. That person does it in good faith, believing X came by the note rightfully. The discounter is therefore a holder in due course, and he would be able to collect on the note. What A should have done, when he sent the note to his friend John Brown, was to have indorsed it specially, "Pay to the order of John Brown, A." Again, a person who is collecting some money for his friend receives a check payable to his order. He wants to turn the check over to his friend, and indorses it by a special indorsement. When the friend tries to collect on the check, it is returned "no funds." The friend now may hold the person responsible who indorsed the check, because an indorser guarantees the payment of the instrument if the proper steps be taken to fix his liability. Ordinarily, of course, we wish an indorser to assume this liability, but in this particular case there was no reason why this man should have indorsed the check in that way. He could have indorsed it, and added to his signature the words "without recourse," which would have relieved him from paying the instrument if the drawer did not pay it.

CHAPTER XIII

TORTS AND CRIMES

TORT, CONTRACT, AND CRIME DISTINGUISHED.—We have already discussed contracts in detail. The fundamental idea of contracts is that the obligation of a contract is voluntarily assumed. Although it might be difficult, at least theoretically, I may take the position that I will not enter into any contractual relationship with anyone for a month. I could do this legally, if I were willing to put up with the annoyance which I would probably suffer. But suppose I take the position that I will assault Jones and I will not pay him any damages for the injuries occasioned by my assault. My position would be wholly untenable. The contract obligation is voluntarily assumed. The law imposes the obligations or duties which exist in torts, and I must observe those duties whether I wish to or not. Similarly, one must observe all of the criminal law of the jurisdiction where he is, whether he will or not. In fact, ignorance of the law is no excuse. A man may even commit a crime, although he did not know there was a law prohibiting the act. Again, in the definition of a tort, we shall find the expression, "breach of duty imposed by law." A man arrives home late at night. He finds a person suffering from exposure at his front door. The person asks to be taken in and lodged for the night, but the householder refuses to take him in, and the man contracts pneumonia from exposure. In this case the householder is not liable. There is no duty imposed by law to be your brother's keeper. There may be a moral obligation in the case just cited, but not a legal one.

JURISDICTION.—There is another way in which a criminal action is sometimes different from an action in contract or an action in tort. A suit on a contract may be brought in any court where jurisdiction over the parties may be secured. For example, A and B make a contract in New York. The contract is broken, and six months later, A and B are both in Galveston, Texas. Either party could sue the other in the Texas court on the broken contract. The same is true in regard to most tort actions. A slanders B in New York. A little later both are in San Francisco, California. B could sue A in a California court for slander. A criminal prosecution, however, must always be brought in the State where the crime is committed, and generally in that very county of the State. Hence, if A murders B in Kings County, New York, the trial could not, under any circumstances, be held in Essex County, New Jersey, for no New Jersey court would have jurisdiction over an offense committed in New York, because the wrong is done to the people of the State of New York, and not to the people of the State of New Jersey.

TORT DEFINED.—It has been stated by the Court of Appeals of New York that no satisfactory definition of a tort can be found. It is easier, perhaps, to explain to the layman the meaning of the term "tort" by simply enumerating such things as are torts. For example, assault and battery is a tort, and so are libel, slander, false imprisonment, malicious prosecution, fraud, deceit, and negligence. Bigelow's definition is perhaps least objectionable of all of the definitions. He defines a tort as a breach of duty imposed by municipal law, for which a suit of damages will lie. Every tort involves the violation of a duty owed to the individual. For example, A owes to B the duty not to attempt with force to harm his person, or to hit him, or to touch him intentionally, or recklessly. The violation of this duty to B, by A, constitutes the tort of assault and battery. Again, A owes to B the duty not to injure B's reputation, either by spoken word or by written word, so long as B has done nothing to forfeit this right to a good reputation. The violation of this duty, on the part of A, constitutes the tort of libel or slander. So, then, it is easy to see why libel, for example, is a tort. It is a breach of duty which the law imposes upon A for which B may sue and recover damages if he is injured. The same with assault and battery, and the various other torts.

CRIME DEFINED.—A tort, as we have indicated, is a breach of duty owed by A to B. A crime is also a breach of duty, but in this case, A is an individual citizen, and B is a sovereign State. C murders D. When C is prosecuted, the action will read, "The people of the State of New York against C." In other words, the crime is a wrong to the State, and so a crime has been defined as an act or omission which is forbidden by law, to which a punishment is annexed, and which a State prosecutes in its own name. Murder, manslaughter, arson and forgery are all crimes. We may correctly also add assault and battery, thus suggesting the fact that the same act may be both a crime and a tort, because the assault is a wrong against the individual and against the State. The individual will sue in a civil court, to recover pecuniary damages, in an ordinary suit of tort, while the State, for the same offense, through the district attorney's or prosecutor's office, will criminally proceed against the guilty party. We shall now consider briefly some of the more important torts and crimes.

ASSAULT AND BATTERY.—Assault is an attempt, real or apparent, to do injury to the person of another. Battery is a completed assault. It is not necessary that a person have the actual ability to carry out the threat to constitute an assault. For example, to point an unloaded revolver at a person is an assault. While the definition might convey the impression that force was necessary, this is not strictly true, because deception sometimes may be the equivalent of force. For example: Assault and battery is committed where a person administers a drug to someone under the belief that he is taking an entirely different kind of drug. Certain assaults, although technically such, are excusable or justifiable. Formerly a school teacher had the right of corporal punishment without being liable for assault and battery. By statute this right is generally taken away now. A parent, however, may inflict corporal punishment on his child without any civil liability. Courts generally assign as the reason for this, the fact that it would not be conducive to the welfare of the family to have children sue their parents, and the further fact that the child's rights are protected by giving him the right to have his parent arrested and punished criminally for an assault. While it was held formerly that a husband had the right to beat his wife, no modern court has upheld this view.

SELF-DEFENSE.—Another case where assault is justified is in the case of self-defense. It is common saying that a man's house is his castle, and the right of self-defense is founded on the right of self-preservation. So that it follows that a man may use force in protecting both himself and his property. A greater amount of force is ordinarily permitted in the protection of the person than of property. In using force, however, such force only as is reasonably necessary may be used. For example, a man attempts to take my watch from my pocket. I strike his arm to prevent it, and do so successfully. Thereafter, as soon as the man's back is turned, I jump on him and assault him, injuring him severely. I would be liable in this case because more force than is necessary for the protection of my property was used.

LIBEL AND SLANDER.—These two terms are frequently combined under the one term of defamation which is defined as a false imputation upon one's character or reputation. Slander is oral defamation, and libel is written defamation. The action of slander is very technical. Perhaps there is no better summary than that given by the United States Supreme Court in the case of Pollard v. Lyon, 91 U. S. 225, as to what statements are slanderous per se. "Slander," the court says, "may be divided into five classes, as follows: (1) Words falsely spoken of a person which impute to the party the commission of some criminal offense involving moral turpitude, for which the party, if the charge is true, may be indicted and punished. (2) Words falsely spoken of a person which impute that the party is infected with some contagious disease, where, if the charge is true, it would exclude the party from society; or (3) Defamatory words falsely spoken of a person, which impute to the party unfitness to perform the duties of an office or employment of profit, or the want of integrity in the discharge of the duties of such an office or employment. (4) Defamatory words falsely spoken of a party which prejudice such party in his or her profession or trade. (5) Defamatory words falsely spoken of a person, which, though not in themselves actionable, occasion the party special damage." A libel is any writing, picture, print or effigy which tends to hold one up to the contempt, scorn, ridicule, or disgrace of his fellow men. We see then, that many statements which would not be slanderous would be libelous.

PRINCIPLES COMMON TO BOTH LIBEL AND SLANDER.—Certain principles are common to both libel and slander. There must be a publication in either case. To say to a school teacher, in a room where he and the speaker are the only persons present, that he is a fool, would not be slanderous. There is no publication. To write a letter to a minister calling him a thief and a crook would not be libelous because there would be no publication. After he had opened the letter and read it, should he show it to any of his friends, he would have made the publication, and impliedly have consented to its publication. Whether to send statements like this on a postal card constitutes a publication or a libel is an open question, as also is the question whether the dictation of false statements to a person's stenographer constitutes publication to some third person.

PRIVILEGE.—Certain clearly slanderous or libelous statements may, nevertheless, not be actionable, because they are absolutely or qualifiedly privileged.

Such is the case of any speech made by a member of Congress, or a member of the State Legislature on the floor of the legislative hall. Such statement, however, made from the stump during a political campaign, would not be privileged. The first is what we call an absolute privilege. There is a certain class of privilege which we speak of as qualified privilege. Newspapers, for example, are permitted to comment by way of criticism on any matters of current interest, provided a reasonable limit is not exceeded. It would not be permissible for a newspaper to pick out John Jones, a wholly retiring and inconspicuous citizen of a town, and make statements about him which hold him up to ridicule, because the public welfare does not call for such action. However, were John Jones running for public office, it would be proper for a newspaper to make comment upon his record, and such statements would have a qualified privilege, although subjecting him to ridicule. A member of the legislature on the floor of the legislature could make statements concerning the same John Jones and never be liable because of his absolute privilege. We must assume, that, with each case mentioned, the statement made is false, in order to have it constitute libel or slander. In other words, truth is a defense to an action for defamation. A person has no right to a false character, and to speak the truth about him does not, therefore, constitute a tort.

FRAUD OR DECEIT.—In order to establish the tort of fraud, it is necessary to prove the following five allegations: (1) that A makes a false statement of a material fact; (2) with knowledge of its falsity; (3) with the intent that it should be acted upon; (4) that the other party believed it to be true; and, (5) acted upon it to his damage. The absence of any one of these five elements will prevent the action of fraud from existing. The action of fraud is most important not only in torts, but also it plays a large part in the law of contracts, and the law of sales, as to both real property and personal property. A stock broker says to Mr. Jones: "My house is offering the best bargain in oil stocks which has been on the market for five years. Aetna Oil Mining Stock at $5 a share is the best buy on the curb to-day. There is no doubt the company will pay 10% in dividends in the first year." Green, relying on this representation, purchases 100 shares of the stock. The stock, thereafter, steadily declines, and never pays a dividend. Has he cause of action for fraud? Clearly not, because there has been no false statement of material fact. These statements about the future earning capacity are seller's talk, or the salesman is merely puffing his wares. Both these expressions are common in the reports and for a mere statement of opinion, no action of fraud lies. It must be a statement of fact. Supposing the same broker had said to his customer, "Aetna Oil Company has paid 10% dividends for the last ten years," and such statement afterwards was found by the purchaser to have been false. An action of fraud would lie, because the dividend record of a company is in the past, and it is not opinion, but fact. Again, suppose the statements to have been the same as in the second illustration, and that they were altogether false, but within three months, through a sudden change in conditions, the affairs of the company were greatly improved, the stock went up in value, and began to pay large dividends. Again, there would be no cause of action, because the fifth element, that of damage, would be lacking. Again, suppose the purchaser, after learning from the broker about the past dividend record, should say, "I will give you my answer to-morrow." Meanwhile, he looks up in a financial paper the dividend record and discovers the statements to be false. He then purchases the stock. Here he would have no cause of action, although he might be damaged, for the reason that by making his own investigation, he has clearly shown that he has not relied on the statement made by the broker, and the fourth element of the action of fraud is missing. In all of these situations, the court assumes that it is dealing with a person of ordinary intelligence, and it does not require the very highest degree of caution on the part of the person claiming to be defrauded, nor will it aid the defrauded person if he does not exercise an ordinary degree of care in safeguarding his rights and forming his judgment in the particular transaction. In laying down this rule, the court does not require that a person must make his own private investigation ordinarily, but he may rely upon the statement made to him. For example, in a Massachusetts case, a real estate broker, in selling a piece of property to a purchaser in a suburban town adjoining Boston, told him that forty trains per day stopped there. The statement was false, the purchaser could have easily inquired at the railroad ticket office, which was only a short distance from the real estate agent's office, but he did not do so. It was held that he could recover in an action of fraud. Were it not so, the courts would, in practice, be laying down the rule that one must assume everyone a liar. On the other hand, had this same purchaser been defrauded by the same real estate dealer a half-dozen times before, then he would not be acting as a reasonably careful man in relying on a statement of this kind. Under these circumstances, the ordinary prudent man would make his own investigation.

FALSE IMPRISONMENT.—A person under ordinary conditions, enjoys the full right of freedom of locomotion. The invasion of that right we call false imprisonment. It is immaterial how trivial the imprisonment may be, for merely locking a person in a room for five minutes as a joke would be enough to give rise to cause for action. The amount of damages which the jury might allow under the circumstances would, of course, be another matter. Many of the principles mentioned in assault and battery are applicable in this tort. Certain persons have a right to imprison other people, and it is not false imprisonment. The sheriff of the county, with a warrant for my arrest, may imprison me, and, of course, I have no action for false imprisonment. He is acting under regular process from the court. A man commits a serious crime in my presence. I lock him in a room until I can call an officer. This is not false imprisonment. The right of a private citizen to make an arrest and not be liable for false imprisonment is stated as follows in Section 183, of the New York Code of Criminal Procedure:

A private person may arrest another: (1) For a crime, committed or attempted in his presence; (2) When the person arrested has committed a felony, although not in his presence.

This is typical of the rule as it exists, with slight modifications, in most of the States. While mere words alone will not constitute an assault, it has been held that mere words will constitute false imprisonment. While a person may be justified in arresting someone else, yet, for the abuse of that privilege, the same as using greater force in self-defense than is necessary, the action of false imprisonment will lie. The man whom I arrest for committing a very serious crime in my presence, I lock in my house and keep there a month, feeding him on bread and water. I am guilty of false imprisonment because while I had a right to arrest him, it was my duty to turn him over to the proper authorities just as soon as possible. In a case, such as this, a month is, of course, an unreasonable time.

NEGLIGENCE.—To say that negligence is failure to use due care is a poor attempt at definition, but it is practically all that can be said. The common law maxim, "sic utere tuo ut alium non laedas" (so use your own as not to injure another), is at this basis of the law of negligence. At the outset, we must be careful to distinguish between "accident" and "negligence." I am walking on a street and slip on a banana skin, and in falling, knock down a passing pedestrian. This is an accident. With my office window overlooking the street, in a banana-eating contest, I eat fifteen bananas, and throw the skins out of the window on the sidewalk. The street is not well lighted. A passerby falls and is injured. This is negligence, and I would be liable.

CONTRIBUTORY NEGLIGENCE.—Negligence must be proved in order to entitle the injured party to recover. The court will not presume negligence merely because an injury takes place. Again, I repeatedly warn a motorman and conductor on a trolley car that I wish to get off at a certain station. Both parties forget the request, and the car goes by the station at the rate of fifteen miles an hour. I think I can get off safely, and attempt to do so. In doing so, I slip and break a leg. Although the two employees of the trolley company were negligent, for not attending to their business, I am guilty of contributory negligence in trying to get off a rapidly moving car, and cannot recover. Contributory negligence is a bar to recovery.

STANDARD OF CARE.—The standards of care to be applied in negligence vary from time to time. What would have been due care on the part of a railroad company fifty years ago, would probably, in few cases, be held to be due care today. This is so, because of the improvements which have been made in mechanical devices in the past fifty years. Again, in order to make a cause of action for negligence, there must be some causal relation between the negligent act and the injury. Granting that the man who slipped on the banana skin, which I threw from my office window, had sued me for damages because of his broken leg, it would not follow that I would be liable to the same man five years later, for the reason that an insurance company denied him a policy because of stiffness in the same broken leg, caused by the fall on the banana skin. The law looks not at the remote, but at the proximate, cause of the injury.

ILLUSTRATION.—The owner of lands owes a duty to persons coming upon that land, and the failure to perform that duty is negligence. Here, again, we have to consider who the person is. I enter Wanamaker's store to make a purchase. In going from the second to the third floor, I trip on a defective nosing on the stairway. This has been out of order for some time, and the floor walker was aware of that fact. I have a cause of action against Wanamaker's store for failure, on their part, to exercise due care in having the premises reasonably safe for the use of customers. Suppose, in making a purchase in that same store, in the basement, I see an open door leading into the engine room where the heat generator is located. Being interested in heating appliances, I go into the room, although there is a sign above the door "no admittance." I fall in an unguarded hole in the floor, which has been open for a long while, and the existence of this hole is known to the management. I cannot recover because I am a trespasser. I am in a place where I had no right to be, and, as to trespassers, the owner of property owes no duty, except to refrain from wilful attempts to injure such a person. I may not set a trap in my back yard to catch a trespasser, although I owe no duty to him to have the back yard safe for his use. A peculiar variation in this rule has been made by some States, in the so-called turn-tables cases. Railroads maintain turn-tables in their yards for the purpose of reversing locomotives and other cars. While children, coming upon the premises, are trespassers, nevertheless, many courts have held that such things are what might be called "attractive nuisances," and in such cases the owner of property is under special duty to use care even as to trespassers, to see that they are not injured. These are merely a few of the general principles of the law of negligence as applied by the courts.

CAPACITY OF PARTIES IN TORT ACTIONS.—We discussed the question of the capacity of parties in making a contract. There is not as much qualification upon a party's liability for tort as for contract. To-day, generally, a married woman is liable for her torts, the same as any one else. A corporation is liable for its torts committed by its agents or servants in the scope of their employment. An infant is held responsible for his torts. It is sometimes said that a person is liable for his torts from the cradle to the grave. This is not strictly true. If a baby two years old puts his finger in my eye, injuring it, he would clearly not be liable. But a person of tender years is liable for his torts, whenever he has sufficient intelligence to know what he is doing. Some courts place the age at seven years, while others consider each individual case and the degree of intelligence possessed by the infant.

THE CRIMINAL LAW.—A crime is a wrong which the State recognizes as injurious to the public welfare, and punishes in a criminal action in its own name. There are certain leading principles of the American system of criminal law which must be kept in mind.

(1) A man is presumed to be innocent until the contrary is shown, and a jury, to be justified in bringing in a verdict of guilty, must be satisfied beyond a reasonable doubt, of the guilt of the accused. The rule in civil cases is that the jury must find for the plaintiff or defendant by a preponderance of evidence. Thus, it is possible for a person to secure a verdict in a civil action for damages for assault and battery, while with the same evidence, a jury would not be justified, in a criminal action in convicting the defendant.

(2) In general, no person may be tried for a criminal offense, of any magnitude, until he has been indicted by a grand jury. The grand jury is generally twenty-four men, and hears the case against the prisoner only as presented by the prosecutor or district attorney. If the grand jury believes the evidence to be sufficient to warrant a trial before the petit jury, they bring in a true bill, and then the trial takes place before the petit jury of twelve men, in open court. The prisoner is entitled to counsel, at the State's expense, if he is not able to furnish his own.

(3) The prisoner may not twice be put in jeopardy for the same offense.

(4) A person may not be tried under an "ex post facto" law.

An "ex post facto" law is one which makes an act, which was innocent when committed, a crime. Such laws are unconstitutional. This term is never used in civil law, but the term "retroactive statute" expresses the same idea. Thus, a statute passed January 15, 1920, providing that all contracts made since January 1, 1919, must be witnessed by three witnesses, would be a "retroactive statute" and not valid.

CRIMINAL RESPONSIBILITY.—As a general rule, if a person, when a crime is committed, has sufficient mental capacity to understand the nature of the particular act constituting the crime, and the mental capacity to know whether it is right or wrong, he is liable criminally, whatever may be his capacity in other respects. As in contracts, or torts, there is a special rule in regard to infants. The English common law, which is pretty generally followed in this country, is that a child under the age of seven is conclusively presumed incapable of committing a crime. This is because of the fact that at common law, a criminal intent was necessary in all crimes, and an infant under seven was presumed not sufficiently advanced to be able to form a criminal intent. Between the ages of seven and fourteen, there is a presumption of incapacity to commit a crime, the presumption being very strong near seven, and rather weak near fourteen. Between the ages of fourteen and twenty-one, the presumption is that the infant is capable of committing a crime. As a general rule, one person is not liable for the crimes of another, unless he participated in them, directly or indirectly. A partner, therefore, is not liable, criminally, for the acts of his partners, merely because they are his partners. Neither is a principal or master liable for the criminal acts of his agent or servant, merely because the relationship is that of principal and agent or master and servant. We will consider briefly a few of the more important crimes.

HOMICIDE.—Homicide is the killing of a human being, and is divided into excusable, felonious, and justifiable homicide. The distinction between excusable and justifiable homicide is very slight and perhaps of little utility. Where either exists, a homicide takes place under such circumstances that the party cannot strictly be said to have committed the act wilfully and intentionally, or if he does commit it with full intention, under such circumstances of duty as to render the act performed not a felonious homicide. A felonious homicide is committed wilfully and under such circumstances as to render it punishable. Murder is the wilful killing of any person with malice aforethought. In some States, by legislative enactments, murder is divided into degrees, as murder in the first degree and murder in the second degree. The penalty for murder in the first degree is death, or in a State where capital punishment is abolished, life imprisonment. There are various other distinctions between these two forms of murder which must be ascertained from the statutes themselves.

MANSLAUGHTER.—Manslaughter is the unlawful killing of another without malice, either express or implied. Manslaughter is also frequently divided into different degrees, and the punishment varies accordingly. A reference to the State statutes is necessary, as in murder, to know what the local law is.

BURGLARY.—Burglary, as a common law offense, is the breaking and entering of a dwelling house of another, in the night time, with the intent to commit a felony therein, whether the felony be actually committed or not. But in most jurisdictions the offense has been extended by statute so as to include breaking and entries which were not burglary at common law. Unless changed by statute, it must be committed in the night time, and there must be both a breaking and an entering. Breaking a window, taking a pane of glass out, or bending the nails, is a breaking. Cutting a wire netting on a screen door is also a breaking. In such cases a screen door is not to be considered as a mere protection against flies and mosquitoes, but as a part of the building. As to whether opening a door or a window, already partly open, constitutes a breaking, the cases are in conflict. Without the intent to commit a felony, breaking and entering is a bare trespass, which would not be a crime. The felonious intent must exist at the time of the breaking and entering. Hence, if it can be proved satisfactorily to a jury, that a man broke into a house for a night's lodging only, he would not be guilty of burglary. As in homicide, reference must be made to the local statutes for the actual definition of burglary and its punishment in that jurisdiction.

FORGERY.—Forgery is the false making of an alteration of a writing to the prejudice of another man's right. Forgery may be committed of any writing, which, if changed, would operate as the foundation of another man's liability. Hence a check may be forged, an assignment of a legal claim, an indorsement on any negotiable document, an acceptance of a bill of exchange, a letter of recommendation, a railroad pass or railroad ticket. The penalty for forgery and various other acts of which it may consist, are so purely statutory as to make any further comment useless.

LARCENY.—Larceny is the felonious taking of the property of another, without his consent and against his will, with the intent to convert it to the use of the taker. The taking must be with criminal intent, but not necessarily for the sake of gain, although the property must be of some value, however slight. The taking must be against the consent of the owner, and if the consent is given, although obtained by fraud, the crime is not larceny. Larceny relates only to personal property. Hence the statement made falsely concerning A: "you are a thief. You stole my marle" (marle being a kind of earth), is not slander, because it is not a charge of a crime involving moral turpitude, as real property is not the subject of larceny. Larceny is generally divided into petty larceny and grand larceny, the difference between the two being generally the amount involved, which varies with the local legislation.

ROBBERY.—Robbery, at common law, is the taking, with intent to steal, of personal property in possession of another, from his person or in his presence, by violence or by putting him in fear. In a majority of jurisdictions, statutes have been enacted defining robbery substantially in accord with the common law. It is not necessary that the property taken should be the property of the person from whom it is taken. As in other crimes, there must be a criminal intent, and so where, in an indictment, the offense was charged as robbery, but as proved was, at most, an improper and rude act, and intended only as a joke, it was held that no robbery had been committed.

CHAPTER XIV

MISCELLANEOUS

INSOLVENT DEBTORS—"GRAB LAW."—When a debtor is insolvent there are several things that he may do. In the first place he may do nothing. He may let his creditors try to get any money out of him if they can, and in general let the creditors take the laboring oar. Where there is no bankruptcy law prevailing, either State or Federal—and that was the situation in many of the States of the Union prior to the passage of the present National bankruptcy law—a debtor might get along that way for a long time. That is one thing he might do.

COMPOSITION WITH CREDITORS.—The second thing the debtor may conceivably do is to try to make a composition with his creditors. Though it is the law that receiving a smaller sum will not discharge a liquidated and undisputed debt for a larger amount, even if it is so agreed, an exception is made in the case of a composition where a number of creditors agree that each of them will take a smaller sum for his claim. The debtor may try to get his creditors to do that, and occasionally he succeeds.

GENERAL ASSIGNMENTS.—A third thing which he may do is to make a general assignment of all his property to trustees in trust to pay his creditors ratably. Such an assignment is not valid in Massachusetts, though in most States it would be, if free from fraudulent incidents. In Massachusetts it would not prevent his creditors, or any one of them, from attaching his property just as if it had not been assigned, but if creditors assent to the assignment then, to the extent of their claims, the assignment becomes valid. In other States the assent of creditors is presumed if the assignment is not fraudulent, and therefore without any actual assent the situation is the same as in Massachusetts after assent of all the creditors.

FRAUDULENT INCIDENTS IN GENERAL ASSIGNMENTS.—In every State a general assignment under certain circumstances will be regarded as fraudulent against creditors. Such a conveyance may be treated as void by the creditors, and the property conveyed seized by them as if the debtor had made no conveyance. Some of these incidents which may make a general assignment fraudulent may be noted. If the assignor was solvent when the conveyance was made, the transaction is fraudulent, for if he has sufficient assets to pay his debts, the only object the assignment can have is to prevent them from being paid at once, and compel the creditors to wait until the assignees under the deed realize upon the property, that the debtor holds, at better advantage than if a forced sale were made at once. If the assignees are given unlimited power to continue business it is also fraudulent, since the business would in effect be carried on at the risk of the debtor. The debtor being insolvent will lose nothing if the business proves unprofitable whereas if profitable there may be a surplus after the payment of the debts. A provision authorizing continuance of business so far as is necessary to dispose of property on hand, or to work up raw material on hand, is generally upheld. A provision authorizing sales upon credit is often, though not uniformly, held fraudulent, since it permits the assignees to defer the settlement of the estate. The most important provisions likely to be attacked as fraudulent, however, are provisions in regard to preferences. Aside from bankruptcy statutes, it is lawful for a debtor who has insufficient means to pay all of his creditors, to pay some in full, though this results in the total exclusion of others. Accordingly a general assignment of a debtor's property on a trust, that the assignees shall pay in full certain named creditors and pay the remaining creditors ratably out of the residue, has generally been upheld though statutes in some States have altered the law in this respect. A kind of preference which is generally deemed fraudulent, however, is one which is made conditional on the creditors giving the debtor a discharge. A general assignment, unlike a bankruptcy law, or a composition, does not free the debtor from liability for so much of his debt as remains unpaid. Debtors have sometimes sought to avoid this result by making a general assignment of their property in trust for ratable distribution among such creditors as should give the debtor a full release and discharge of all claims. Such a provision, attempting, as it does, to impose as a condition of a creditor's sharing, that he should take his share in full satisfaction of his claim, is almost universally held to make a general assignment fraudulent. Under the bankruptcy law, a general assignment may within four months be set aside by bankruptcy proceedings; but a creditor who has once assented to a general assignment cannot thereafter join in a bankruptcy petition against that debtor.

BANKRUPTCY.—The fourth and most important way, however, now, of settling the estates of insolvent persons is provided by statute. The Federal Constitution gives Congress power to pass uniform laws on the subject of bankruptcy throughout the United States, and the Supreme Court has held that when the Federal Government has not taken advantage of this privilege given by the Constitution, States have power themselves to enact bankruptcy laws. In some States there were such laws, but in many there were not. The Federal law now supersedes all State laws on the subject. It was passed in 1898, and under that law the debtor may either become a bankrupt by his own voluntary petition, or his creditors may petition him into bankruptcy if he commits what is called an "act of bankruptcy." This is true, at least, if the debtor is an individual, or is a moneyed business or commercial corporation (except railroads, insurance companies, and banking corporations). When corporations of the excepted class become insolvent, their affairs are settled by still a fifth method—receivership. A special privilege, also, is given to wage earners and farmers. They may, if they choose, become voluntary bankrupts, but are not liable to involuntary proceedings.

PETITIONS IN BANKRUPTCY.—Suppose a debtor wishes to become bankrupt himself. He files a petition in the United States District Court, which is the court of bankruptcy jurisdiction, and is immediately adjudicated a bankrupt. If his creditors want to make him a bankrupt it is necessary that three of them, having claims amounting to not less than $500 in the aggregate, should join, unless there are less than twelve creditors in all. In that event one creditor only may petition. This petition must set forth (1) the creditors' claims, (2) the fact that the debtor has committed an act of bankruptcy, and (3) the fact that he owes debts aggregating $1,000 or more. However slight his indebtedness, if he cannot pay it, a man may be a voluntary bankrupt, but he must owe at least $1,000 to be liable to involuntary proceedings.

ACTS OF BANKRUPTCY—FRAUDULENT CONVEYANCES.—Now what are the acts of bankruptcy which render a debtor liable to a petition by his creditors? In the first place a fraudulent conveyance is an act of bankruptcy. Reference to a fraudulent conveyance by general assignment has been made; but there are many kinds of fraudulent conveyances. If a debtor who is insolvent, or who is made insolvent through a gift made by himself, should give away a portion of his property, that would be a fraudulent conveyance, irrespective of the debtor's intent, because the necessary effect of the gift would be to hinder, delay and defraud his creditors. It would be a fraudulent conveyance for a debtor to seek to conceal his property from his creditors by putting it in the hands of some kind friend to hold for him until his creditors should cease to be so troublesome as at the present time. It would be a fraudulent conveyance for a man who is pressed by creditors to turn himself into a corporation for business purposes, and assign all his property to that corporation. This transfer to a corporation, even though done openly, would necessarily hinder and delay his creditors.

PREFERENCES.—As has already been said, paying one creditor to the exclusion of others is not a fraudulent conveyance, but it is a preference, and a preference is a second act of bankruptcy. Either for the debtor to give a preference himself or to allow a creditor to get a preference, by legal proceedings, is an act of bankruptcy. Any transfer made by an insolvent debtor, to pay or to secure in whole or in part a previously existing debt, is a preference.

GENERAL ASSIGNMENTS.—A general assignment, whether fraudulent or not, is an act of bankruptcy. The consequence is, therefore, that if a debtor makes a general assignment, his creditors have the choice of letting it stand and having the estate settled under the general assignment, or of setting it aside and having bankruptcy proceedings.

RECEIVERSHIPS.—Still another act of bankruptcy is the appointment of a receiver on account of insolvency. There, also, the creditors virtually have an option of letting the receivership stand and having the receiver take charge of the distribution of the assets, or of petitioning the debtor into bankruptcy and having the bankruptcy court take charge.

ADMISSION OF INABILITY TO PAY DEBTS.—One further act of bankruptcy is an admission by the debtor of his inability to pay his debts and his willingness to be adjudicated a bankrupt. An act of bankruptcy can form the basis of a petition only within four months after its commission.

INSOLVENT DEBTORS USUALLY COMMIT ACTS OF BANKRUPTCY.—

Now an insolvent debtor cannot very well avoid committing one of these acts of bankruptcy. He can avoid making a fraudulent conveyance, but he will find it pretty hard to avoid making a preference. He need not, it is true, pay any of his debts, and it is not a preference to pay money out for present consideration, or to transfer property for present consideration, as to make a mortgage for a new loan; but it will be hard for him to prevent creditors from getting a preference by legal proceedings, at least if the debtor has any assets at all; for if the debtor does not pay any of his creditors, some of his creditors will sue him, get execution, and endeavor to levy it on the debtor's property.

PROCEDURE AFTER ADJUDICATION.—If a debtor has once been adjudicated a bankrupt, it makes no difference whether it was on a voluntary petition or an involuntary petition; the matter goes on in both cases the same way. The first thing, after the adjudication, is, that the referee, a sort of subordinate judge, requires the bankrupt to submit schedules of his assets and of his creditors. The debtor is induced to make these schedules as complete as possible, for the following reasons: if the schedule of assets is knowingly incomplete, the debtor is committing a crime and is likely to be shut up in jail. If the schedule of his creditors is incomplete, any creditor who is left out or whose address is so incorrectly given that the creditor does not get notice of the proceedings in time to prove his claim, is not affected by the discharge; and as the debtor wants a discharge from as many debts as possible, he, of course, will make his schedule of creditors as complete as possible. From this schedule of creditors, the referee sends notices out to all the creditors to meet and choose the trustee. The creditors meet and choose a trustee, who then endeavors to collect the assets of the estate, and under the direction of the court, pays dividends from the assets to the creditors.

PROPERTY WHICH THE TRUSTEE GETS.—The question may be asked: "What property does the trustee get?" He gets all tangible property that the debtor could transfer at the moment of his bankruptcy. He gets intangible property, patents, trademarks, copyrights, seats on the stock exchange, and good-will of a business, with the exception that the debtor still retains the right to carry on his old business himself, in the future, in his own name. The trustee gets rights of action of the bankrupt, except personal rights of action, as they are called. These consist of rights of action for personal injuries, as for assault, or for personal injury by negligence. A right of action for breach of promise of marriage also would not pass to the trustee in bankruptcy. Not only does a trustee get this tangible and intangible property, but he gets also a right to recover any property fraudulently conveyed by the bankrupt, which is not in the hands of a bona fide purchaser, even if the fraudulent conveyance was made years before, provided the statute of limitations has not completely run against it. Any preference, also made within four months before the filing of the petition in bankruptcy, may be recovered from the preferred creditor, if he had reasonable cause to believe, when he received it, that he was getting a preference, but not otherwise. The trustee in bankruptcy gets the debtor's life insurance policies, except in so far as they are made exempt by statute. Life-insurance policies, in favor of a beneficiary other than the insured himself, are exempt, though if the premiums were paid by the debtor while insolvent, the premiums so paid within the past six years may be recovered, and the beneficiary would in effect have to pay those premiums back in order to hold the policy. Even if the policy runs to the insured himself, in his own name, he has the privilege, under the bankruptcy act, to redeem it from the trustee in bankruptcy by paying its cash surrender value. Property acquired by the bankrupt, after the beginning of bankruptcy proceedings, does not pass to the trustee. The bankrupt's property passes free of attachment or judgment liens, secured by creditors within four months prior to the beginning of bankruptcy proceedings. This has no bearing on a case, where, prior to bankruptcy, money has been actually collected by legal proceedings, but only to cases of seizure under legal proceedings which are still pending at the time the petition is filed. If a debtor becomes bankrupt, within four months after his property is attached, the attachment is dissolved. If the debtor does not become bankrupt until after four months, the attachment is a valid lien on the property attached, and so far as the property is sufficient to pay the creditor, he can collect his claim from it, even though the debtor becomes bankrupt before the creditor finally gets judgment and collects his claim.

PROOF OF CLAIMS.—The trustee collects all this property and tries to reduce it to cash, as fast as he can, and while this is going on, creditors will also be proving their claims. It is only claims which exist at the time of filing the petition which are provable, but the debts need not be due at the time of the bankruptcy; it is only essential that they shall be in existence. Interest is added or rebated, as the case may be, to the date of filing the petition. That is, if you have a non-interest-bearing note falling due July 1, and the debtor becomes bankrupt May 1, the face of the note will be proved less a rebate of two months' interest to May 1, because the present value of the note on May 1 is what is provable. On the other hand, if the note had been due on April 1, interest would be added up to the date of filing the petition, and if the note was an interest-bearing note, of course the interest would be provable up to May 1, even if the note did not fall due until July 1 or later. Debts, arising subsequently to the date of filing the petition, must be enforced against the bankrupt's assets acquired after his bankruptcy. Claims for tort are not provable, that is, claims for injuries to person or property not arising out of contact. But a judgment for tort, obtained before the filing of the petition, is provable. There has been a good deal of trouble in regard to what are called contingent claims. The commonest instance is the indorser's liability on a note which is not yet due when the indorser becomes bankrupt. At the time of filing the petition, the indorser's liability is contingent on the possibility that the maker may not pay the note at maturity, and that notice of dishonor will be given to the indorser. Creditors, who have received a preference, cannot prove claims unless they have surrendered, within four months of the bankruptcy, any preference which they have received with reasonable cause to believe that it was a preference. Secured creditors can realize on their security and then prove for the balance of their claims. A few claims are given priority over others and paid in full before any dividend to other creditors. The most important claims of this sort are the wages of workmen, clerks or servants earned within three months of the bankruptcy and not exceeding the sum of $300.

LEASES.—Leases belonging to the bankrupt pass to the trustee in bankruptcy, if he wants them, but the trustee in bankruptcy need not take any kind of property which seems more burdensome than beneficial to him, and as a trustee would have to pay, the rent under a lease in full, if he took it, he frequently will prefer to abandon it. The landlord can prove for rent, which is already accrued, but he cannot prove for rent which has not already accrued, even though part of the period for which the rent is claimed has elapsed, unless there is a special covenant in the lease. If the trustee in bankruptcy assumed the lease, then, of course, the landlord would look to the trustee for the rest of the term. If the trustee did not assume the lease, the landlord would have his option of doing either of two things: he could leave the bankrupt in the premises and have a right of action against him for the rent, from time to time, as it accrued, or he could eject the tenant; but if he ejected the tenant he could not hold him for rent. Generally he would eject a bankrupt tenant rather than let him stay.

SET-OFF.—Set-off may be made by a debtor of the estate who also has a claim against the estate. He does not have to prove his claim, taking a dividend on it and then paying, in full, the debt which he owes to the estate. He may set one off against the other, but he is not allowed to acquire claims for the purpose of set-off within four months prior to bankruptcy. Otherwise, one owing money to an insolvent debtor, could buy up at a discount claims against the debtor, equal in amount to his indebtedness to the bankrupt.

EXAMINATION AND DISCHARGE OF BANKRUPT.—The bankrupt may be examined by any creditor with a view to the disclosure of his assets. This is a most important right. Finally, if in every respect, he obeys the bankruptcy law, the debtor gets a discharge. Grounds for refusing him a discharge are, that he has made a fraudulent conveyance; that he has obtained credit by false representation; that he has failed to keep books of account for the purpose of concealing his financial condition; that he has committed an offence punishable by the bankruptcy law, as making a false oath or refusal to disclose his property or to submit to examination; and finally a debtor who has already been discharged in bankruptcy within the previous six years cannot, as a voluntary bankrupt, again obtain a discharge. These are reasons for refusing a discharge altogether, but even though a discharge is granted, certain liabilities are not discharged. Claims for obtaining property by false pretences, or for false representations, are not discharged. Claims for defalcation or embezzlement, as a public officer or as a fiduciary, and claims for wilful and malicious injury to the property of another, are not discharged. Nor are taxes or claims for alimony or for the support of a wife or dependent children.

COMPOSITION IN BANKRUPTCY.—At common law it was necessary to have the consent of all a debtor's creditors in order to make the composition operative as against all of them. In bankruptcy there is a special provision for composition, and with the approval of the court, a composition may be declared binding, not only as against those who have assented to it, but as against all creditors having provable claims, if a majority in number and amount of the creditors, taking part in the bankruptcy proceedings, assent to the discharge.

INSURANCE.—Insurance is a contract whereby, for an agreed premium, one party undertakes to compensate the other for loss on a specified subject from specified perils. Policies of insurance are as various as the contracts which they cover. In 1779, Lloyd's adopted a standard form of marine policy, which, with some changes, is in practically universal use in the British world. A standard form of fire policy has been adopted by many of the fire insurance companies in the United States.

POLICY PROVISIONS.—Certain terms occur frequently in insurance law, with which one should be familiar. A valued policy is one upon which a definite valuation is put, by agreement of both parties, on the subject matter of the insurance written on the policy; for example, a policy "insuring the S.S. George Washington, valued at $1,000,000." An open policy, on the other hand, is one in which a definite sum is written on the face of the policy, but instead of agreeing as to the value of the property insured, indicates the limit of recovery in case of the destruction of the property. Floating policies are such as cover articles which cannot be designated with certainty, as for example, a constantly changing stock of goods. In life insurance there are many kinds of policies. Probably the most common is the regular life, under which the insured pays certain fixed premiums throughout life, and the beneficiary receives the amount of the policy only upon the death of the insured. Life insurance policies in which the investment feature is prominent, are generally called endowment policies, and they require the insured to pay a certain premium, annually, for a certain number of years. If the insured dies before premium payments cease, under the terms of the policy, the beneficiary receives the full amount of the policy. If the insured lives beyond the stated period, he is entitled to receive the amount written on the face of the policy or he may be allowed to receive a paid-up policy for some specified sum. A policy of reinsurance is simply a contract made by one insurance company with another, whereby the first reinsures with the second some individual risk which it has itself accepted and insured.

ELEMENTS OF CONTRACT.—In order that the contract of insurance shall be valid, it must possess all the essential elements of the ordinary contract. Although there is a certain element of chance in an insurance contract, it is always held that it is not in the nature of a gambling contract. A peculiar feature of this contract is that it is one of the utmost good faith, and requires that each party shall disclose to the other all material facts in his knowledge that may affect the making of the contract.

INSURABLE INTEREST.—An essential element in the law of insurance is that of insurable interest. By this term we mean that interest of the insured, which is exposed to injury by reason of the peril insured against. Such interest does not necessarily need to be a legal right, but only such as to justify a reasonable expectation of financial benefit, which will be derived by the continued existence of the person or property insured. While it is difficult to define accurately an insurable interest in property, Section 2546 of the California Civil Code defines it thus: "Every interest in property, or any relation thereto, or liability in respect thereof, of such a nature that a contemplated peril might directly damnify the insurer, is an insurable interest." In life insurance, an insurable interest is requisite, but this interest, if existing at the time the policy is issued, is sufficient, although such interest subsequently terminates. Every person has an insurable interest in his own life, or he may procure insurance on the life of another, when so related to that other, either by reason of blood, marriage, or commerce, that he has well-grounded expectation of deriving benefit from that other's life, or suffering detriment through its termination. It is well settled that a creditor has an insurable interest in the life of his debtor. The courts are not clear as to just how much this interest is, but it will not be allowed to greatly exceed the sum of the debt. The relationship between the insured and the insurer is governed, to a very large extent, by the law of agency.

SURETYSHIP AND GUARANTY.—Suretyship has been defined as an accessory agreement by which one binds himself for another who is already bound. A surety is a person who is liable to perform any act, that his principal is bound to perform, in the event that his principal fails to perform as agreed. Where there is more than one surety, the parties are known as co-sureties. The distinction between the contract of suretyship and that of guaranty is not altogether clear, and frequently not observed by the courts. So far as the distinction can be defined, we may say that if the parties undertake to pay money, or to do some other agreed act, in case the principal fails to perform his part, then they are sureties. On the other hand, if they assume performance, only in the event that the principal is unable to perform, then they are guarantors. The principles which apply to both, are, in many respects, similar. The terms used by the parties are not necessarily conclusive as to whether it is a suretyship or guaranty relationship. For example, in the case of Saint v. Wheeler, etc., Mfg. Co., 95 Ala. 362, where a contract was under seal by which the parties "guarantee," along with one of their number, to pay absolutely and irrespective of solvency or insolvency, all damages which might result, etc., it was held that the contract was one of suretyship, and not of guaranty, although they had used the express term "guarantee" in the language of the contract.

QUALIFICATION OF A SURETY.—A surety may be distinguished from an indorser in that the undertaking of the surety is absolute, whereas that of the indorser is conditional. The Negotiable Instruments Act provides that a general indorser "engages that on due presentment, it (the instrument) shall be accepted or paid, or both, as the case may be, according to its tenor, and that if it be dishonored, and the necessary proceedings on dishonor be duly taken, he will pay the amount thereof to the holder, or to any subsequent indorser who may be compelled to pay it." Hence, if an indorser is not notified, or if the instrument is not protested, if that is necessary, he is discharged.

PRINCIPAL AND SURETY.—Ordinarily, the relationship of principal and surety is entered into under the terms of a contract, the chief object of which is the creation of the relationship. As a general rule, any person who is capable of making a contract may be surety. Formerly, it was sometimes said that an infant was absolutely unqualified to make a contract of this kind, but now his contracts of suretyship are held to be voidable, the same as his other contracts. In some states a married woman is still prevented by statute from becoming a surety for her husband. Like ordinary contracts, a contract of suretyship must be supported by sufficient consideration. It is ordinarily a collateral engagement to pay a debt of another, and hence, comes under the section of the Statute of Frauds which requires a contract to answer for the "debt, default, or miscarriage of another," to be in writing.

SURETYSHIP LIABILITY.—The general extent of the suretyship liability is measured by the contract of the principal, which he guarantees. If no cause of action can be maintained against the principal on the contract, it follows necessarily that the surety is not liable. The tendency of the courts is to favor the surety. His obligation is ordinarily assumed without any pecuniary compensation, and it is accordingly said that his liability is "strictissimi juris," (strictly construed by the law). A surety has the right, then, to insist upon the very letter of his contract, and if there is a reasonable doubt as to whether his contract requires the doing of certain acts or not, that doubt should be resolved by the court in favor of the surety. Consequently, a surety will not ordinarily be held liable for any default of the principal, which occurred prior to the surety's contract to be such. The death of the surety does not necessarily terminate his liability, and his personal representatives will be responsible for the carrying out of his contract, especially where the contract reads that the surety "binds his heirs, executors and administrators."

SURETY'S OBLIGATION UNDER NEW CONTRACT.—It frequently happens that the principal's contract is not completed, and a renewal is necessary. The question arises whether the surety's obligations are continued under the new contract, the same as under the old. The principle which the courts apply is that if the renewal amounts to an entirely new contract, then the surety's obligation is at an end. But if the renewal is simply a part of the original contract, and does not call for any new contract, his obligation continues under such renewal. As the contract between the principal and surety is of a more or less confidential character, the law requires, as we have mentioned in insurance, the exercise of the utmost good faith on the part of the principal. Hence, if a surety, before entering into his contract, applies to the principal for information about any material matter pertaining to the contract, the principal is bound to give full information as to every fact within his knowledge, and if he does anything to deceive the surety, he vitiates the contract. Another application of the same principle is found in the rule that the principal must not do any act injurious to the surety or inconsistent with his rights. Consequently, if the principal makes any arrangement with his principal debtor, by which the risk of the surety is materially increased, or the terms of the contract are altered or varied or the time of payment is extended, the surety in any of these cases would be released from any liability unless he is consulted and gives his assent to such changes in his contract. It is necessary that the new contract, which the principal makes, be a valid contract in order to release the surety. Hence, if the principal makes a contract extending the time of the payment on the obligation six months, and that is all there is to the contract, such extension agreement would be invalid because of lack of consideration, and the surety in such case would not be discharged from his liability under the old contract. If the obligation which the surety undertakes to pay is a promissory note, an agreement by the principal to extend the time of payment, would not, of itself, release the surety, there being no consideration. A part payment made by the maker, before the note was due, for which an extension of time to pay the remainder is granted, would be binding, because such part payment, before a note is due, constitutes good consideration for an agreement to extend the time to pay the balance, and consequently the surety is discharged.

NEGLIGENCE OF THE CREDITOR.—It is generally true that the creditor is under no obligation to be diligent in the pursuit of the debtor. Consequently, a mere negligence of the creditor, to sue or otherwise attempt to collect a claim against his debtor, although there is a surety for the creditor, does not relieve the surety of his liability. Mere delay, then, in proceeding against the principal debtor, does not release the surety, unless there is between the creditor and principal debtor a valid and binding agreement, under which a delay does prejudice the surety.

DISCHARGE OF SURETY.—A surety is discharged by the payment or performance, by the principal, of the condition in the agreement. It is even held that the surety is discharged if a tender of payment has been made to the principal, after the debt is due, and it is refused by him. In such a case, the tender amounts practically to a payment of the debt and a new loan creating a new contract. It sometimes occurs that the creditor has collateral security for the payment of the debt, or secures control of money or property of the debtor and which he may lawfully apply to the debtor's obligations under certain circumstances. The principal may voluntarily surrender or dispose of these securities. In such a case, the surety is discharged from liability to the extent of the value of the securities disposed of or surrendered. Of course, the surety is not discharged where the principal takes additional securities, or if some securities are given up and sufficient are retained by the principal to pay the debt, the surety is not relieved and cannot complain, for the reason that he has not been injured.

RIGHTS OF SURETY.—It is a well established rule of law that where the surety is obliged to make good on his contract he is entitled to relief, the law implying a promise on the part of the principal to reimburse the surety for any damages which he suffers. Of course, this assumes that the surety was legally bound to pay the debt. If he pays it because it is a moral obligation or for any other reason which the law does not recognize as legally binding, he is not able to compel the principal to reimburse him.

RIGHT OF CONTRIBUTION.—One of the peculiar remedies, which the courts of equity have developed, is that of contribution. This right is frequently used in the law of suretyship. When one of two or more sureties, for the same obligation, has paid more than his share of the debt, he is entitled to be reimbursed for the excess by his co-sureties. This right is known as the right of contribution. As has been said before, a surety, if he pays when he is not legally bound to do so, must stand the loss himself; and the same is true where he is one of several co-sureties. Thus, if one co-surety pays a debt, which is barred by the statute of limitations, he would not, in that case, be entitled to contribution from his other co-sureties.

SURETY COMPANIES.—Surety companies conduct such a large business at the present time that a word should be said about them in connection with this topic. The surety company is a corporation, and its powers are, of course, defined by its charter, and the laws of the State in which it is incorporated. In general, surety companies are authorized to guarantee performance of contracts and to execute bonds and undertakings required by the courts. One tendency is noticeable in recent years. The kind of suretyship, we have been referring to, is generally that in which the surety is an individual, who undertakes his task for no consideration, and for that reason, as we have said, the courts construe the contract of suretyship strictly in favor of the surety. More and more, now, the practice of the individual becoming a surety is decreasing, and in his place the surety companies offer their services in a more satisfactory manner, under modern business conditions, but with the striking difference, that the surety company offers its services only for pay, which will net the company a profit. Hence, the rule that the contract should be construed strictly in favor of the surety does not fit the case of the surety company which is paid for its services. In the case of the American Surety Co. v. Paulu, 170 U. S. 133, and in many other cases, the rule is laid down, that the contract will be construed against the surety company and in favor of the indemnity which the obligee has reasonable grounds to expect. So, it has been held that a surety company will not be relieved on its contract, by an extension of time to the principal, and that there is no presumption that the surety was injured by the extension unless the injury is actually proved.

PATENTS.—The policy of encouraging monopolies, while generally frowned upon, finds two exceptions in the law of patents and copyrights. Consequently, the Federal Constitution gives the exclusive right to Congress to "promote the progress of science and useful arts by securing for limited times, to authors and inventors, the exclusive right to their respective writings and discoveries." The patent office is located in Washington, and here the Commissioner of Patents has his official office, and applications for all patents are made through him, and he is authorized to establish regulations for the granting and issuance of patents. The duration of a patent right depends, of course, upon the statute. At the present time, the period is seventeen years, and at the end of that time, the person holding the patent must yield up his monopoly and all that pertains to it. A patent is in the nature of a contract, and the United States Supreme Court has said "The true rule of construction in respect to patents and specifications, and the doings generally of inventors, is to apply plain and ordinary principles to them, as we have endeavored to on this occasion, and not, in this most meta-physical branch of modern law, to yield up to subtleties and technicalities, unsuited to the subject, and not in keeping with the liberal spirit of the age, and likely to prove ruinous to a class of the community so inconsiderate and unskilled in business as men of genius and inventors usually are." A distinction is usually made between pioneer patents, and patents which are merely improvements on one already issued. The former are always given a liberal interpretation, while the latter should be strictly construed.

ELEMENT OF NOVELTY.—It is the element of novelty which gives rise to the right to a patent. It is not possible to discuss in this limited space, the countless decisions upon this point. A thing may be novel and entitled to a patent, although very old. Some lost art of the Egyptians is re-discovered by an American. Although the idea is several thousand years old, to all practical purposes it is new, and the inventor would be entitled to a patent. Like any other property, an inventor's right may be lost by abandonment. Thus, where an inventor taught a large number of people, with no suggestion that the thing was an experiment, and received pay for his instruction, the court held that this constituted an abandonment of his claim, and he was not entitled to a patent.

INFRINGEMENTS.—A suit may be maintained by the owner of a patent against one who infringes, and as this is a matter under the United States laws, all patent suits are tried in the Federal courts. A patent right is personal property, and upon the death of the owner, goes to his personal representative. Patent rights, like other personal property, may be assigned and sold.

SALE OF PATENTED ARTICLES.—In recent years, many cases have arisen over the question whether the manufacturers of patented articles are entitled to impose conditions respecting the use of their manufactured articles by purchasers. Early cases seem to support the view that, as the theory of a patent was that of a monopoly, these conditions would be upheld even after the patented articles came into the hands of a purchaser. Decisions of the United States Supreme Court, however, have tended the other way. So, attaching a notice to a patented article, stating that the article is licensed for sale and use at a specified price, and that the purchase is an acceptance of these conditions, and that in the case of a violation of this restriction, all rights revert back to the patentee, cannot convert an otherwise apparently unqualified sale into a mere license to use the invention. In Bauer v. O'Donnell, 229 U. S. 1, the Supreme Court said: "The right to vend conferred by the patent law has been exercised, and the added restriction is beyond the protection and purpose of the act. This being so, the case is brought within that line of cases in which this court, from the beginning, has held that a patentee, who has parted with a patented machine, by passing title to a purchaser, has placed the article beyond the limits of the monopoly secured by the patent act."

COPYRIGHTS.—A copyright is the exclusive privilege of printing, or otherwise multiplying, publishing and selling copies of literary or artistic productions. The nature of a copyright is thus defined by the United States Supreme Court, in the case of Caliga v. Newspaper Co., 215 U. S. 158: "Statutory copyright is not to be confounded with the common law right. At common law, the exclusive right to copy existed in the author until he permitted a general publication. Thus, when a book was published in print, the owner's common law right was lost. At common law, an author had a property in his manuscript, and might have an action against any one who undertook to publish it without authority. The statute created a new property right, giving to the author, after publication, the exclusive right to multiply copies for a limited period. This statutory right is obtained in a certain way, and by the performance of certain acts which the statute points out. That is, the author having complied with the statute, and given up his common law right of exclusive duplication, prior to general publication, obtained by the method pointed out in the statute an exclusive right to multiply copies and publish the same for the term of years named in the statute. Congress did not sanction an existing right; it created a new one."

PROPERTY RIGHT IN IDEAS.—The doctrine that a person has a property right in his ideas has never been recognized, either by common law or by statute. To illustrate: If A, in the course of a conversation with B, gives his idea of what would be a brilliant thought to work up into a detective story, and B, possessing some literary ability, takes the idea and writes a successful detective story, he is entitled to the profits secured from the sale of the book, and there is nothing that A can do about it. The idea which A handed to B has been put by B into such form that it is practicable to allow B to copyright it, and protect his property right in the story. There is no practical way to protect a mere idea.

EFFECT OF COPYRIGHT STATUTES.—One must bear in mind the effect of copyright statutes on common law rights. At common law, an author has a property in his manuscript, and may obtain redress for any attempt to deprive him of it, and the copyright act provides that nothing in the act shall limit the right of the author, at common law, or in equity, to prevent the copying, publication or use of an unpublished work, without his consent and it gives him the right to damages should this be done. At common law, the author of any literary composition had an absolute property right in his production, and he could not be deprived of it so long as it remained unpublished. Interesting questions have arisen in regard to the nature of the property rights in letters. The question as to the rights of the sender and the recipient are frequently troublesome. The rights of the writer consist in the power to make or restrain a publication by the recipient, but he cannot prevent a transfer. The rights of the recipient are those of unqualified title in the material on which they are written. He has the right to keep them, to read them, and show them to a limited circle of friends, somewhat in the same way as a family picture album might be used.

PROPERTY RIGHT IN INFORMATION OR NEWS.—Another interesting question is as to whether there can be any property right in information or news which has been collected at great expense by the Associated Press or some similar organization. The most important case on this question is that of the International News Co. v. the Associated Press, 248 U. S. 215. The Associated Press, organized in New York, is a corporation created for the purpose of collecting news and distributing it to about 950 newspapers at an annual expense of about $3,500,000. The International News Service was a corporation organized in New Jersey to collect and sell news to a chain of newspapers. The complaint was made by the Associated Press that the International News Service was engaged in pirating its news in three ways: (1) By bribing employees of newspapers, published by complainant's members, to furnish Associated Press news to defendant, before publication, for transmission by telegraph and telephone to defendant's clients, for publication by them; second, by inducing Associated Press members to violate its by-laws and permit defendant to obtain news before publication; and, third, copying news from early editions of complainant's newspapers, and selling it, either bodily or after rewriting it, to defendant's customers. The court held that news should be regarded as quasi-property, and that it was unfair competition in business for the International News Service to take from newspapers, which are members of the Associated Press, news furnished by it, and refused to modify the injunction issued by the District Court restraining any taking or using of the Associated Press news, either bodily or in substance, from bulletins issued by the Associated Press, or any of its members, or from editions of its newspapers, until its commercial value to the complainant and all of its members had passed away.

APPLICATION FOR COPYRIGHT.—The formality of securing a copyright is comparatively simple. The register of copyrights, in the library of Congress at Washington, furnishes a blank which the applicant fills out and returns, giving the required information, and on or before the first day of publication, the applicant must send two copies of the copyrighted book to the library of Congress. The copyright is good for twenty-eight years, with a right to renewal. The works for which copyrights may be secured may be classified as: (a) Books, including composite and cyclopedic books, directories, gazetteers, and other compilations; (b) periodicals, including newspapers; (c) lectures, sermons, and addresses, prepared for oral delivery; (d) dramatic or dramatic-musical compositions; (e) musical compositions; (f) maps; (g) works of art, models or designs for works of art; (h) reproductions of a work of art; (i) drawings or plastic works of scientific or technical character; (j) photographs; (k) prints and pictorial records. There are certain things, which, while technically they are under the classification we have given, are not subject of copyright. The opinions handed down by the judges of all of our courts, although they are in the form which would ordinarily permit copyright, are not subject of copyright because of the general principle of law that a judge receives a stated annual salary and cannot, therefore, have any pecuniary interests in the fruits of his judicial labors. This does not mean, however, that the opinions of the United States Supreme Court, for example, are not to be found in a copyrighted book. The Supreme Court Reporter, which is one of the systems of reporters published by the West Publishing Co. as a purely commercial enterprise, is copyrighted by that company. This is because of the fact that the editorial staff of the West Publishing Co. prepares a syllabus for each opinion, an exhaustive index in each volume, and a table of cases, and all of this matter arranged by that company, is subject to copyright, and they have the right to use the opinions of the Supreme Court the same as any other publisher would have. Again, a copyright might be refused on the grounds that the book on which the copyright was sought was an immoral or obscene writing, and therefore not entitled to protection of the copyright law. The word "Copyrighted" accompanied by the name of the copyright proprietor should appear on the page opposite the title page, or if the article copyrighted is a picture, the act provides that the device, accompanied by the initials or the symbol of the copyright proprietor, shall appear on the article.

SUBJECTS OF COPYRIGHT.—In the classification we have just given, mention is made of lectures, sermons, etc., as being the subject of copyright. It is held, however, that a lecture, delivered orally to a class of students, is not published to the extent that the instructor loses his right to it, although the students may be allowed to make notes for their own use. In the same way, the artist does not lose his common law copyright by an exhibition of his pictures in his studio or in a public gallery where they are placed for sale. Similarly the public presentation of a dramatic production does not deprive the owner of his rights in it. The reason for this is that at common law the public performance of a play does not mean an abandonment to the public generally.

TRADE MARKS AND TRADE NAMES.—A trade mark or trade name is a mark or symbol which the tradesman puts upon his goods, so that they may be identified and known by the public generally. A trade name differs from a trade mark in that it is descriptive of the manufacturer himself, and involves the individuality of the maker. Statutes will be found covering the registration of trade marks and trade names, but the protection which the law affords the owner of these is not confined to a statute alone. It is generally held that a trade mark, subject to some qualifications, arises without the aid of any statute.

SUBJECT MATTER OF TRADE MARK OR TRADE NAME.—The question as to what is the subject-matter of a trade mark or a trade name, can only be determined by a careful reading of the cases. A trade mark may consist of a name, a symbol, a letter, some arbitrary form, or a newly-coined word. Pictures of animals, coats of arms, and the like, are frequently used. No trade mark can be obtained by the mere use of a color or generally a geographical term, nor can a trade mark be obtained from the form of a package in which goods are packed, and generally, mere letters and numbers cannot form a trade mark, although the arbitrary combination of numbers, such as "Babbitt's 1776" may be a valid trade mark.

NAMES NOT VALID TRADE MARKS.—Generic names, and merely names of articles, are not valid trade marks, as "Extract of Wheat," and "New York Cough Remedy." A trade name of a firm, a corporate name, or the name of a publication, although they are not strictly trade marks, are, nevertheless, of the same nature as a trade mark, and will be protected in the same manner.

UNFAIR COMPETITION.—The most common way in which trade marks and trade names become the subject of litigation, is in connection with unfair competition. By this term we mean, ordinarily, the imitation by one person, for the purpose of deceiving another, of the name, device, or symbol used by a business rival. The courts act in such cases upon the theory that the public should be protected, and should not have other goods pawned off on it in place of something else which a person thinks he is getting. This matter of unfair competition is the subject of much litigation in the courts, and one or two illustrations will show how the question arises. For example: In an English case, decided in 1897, the plaintiff had manufactured and sold a relish which was made under a secret recipe and was sold under the name "Yorkshire Relish." The defendant then put a sauce on the market resembling it, and sold it under the name of "Yorkshire Sauce." The court held that the plaintiff was entitled to an injunction. In the case of the International Silver Co. v. the Rogers Co., 66 N. J. Equity 119, the court enjoined the use of the word "Rogers" in the corporate title of the William H. Rogers Corporation, on the ground that its use was a part of the proceedings by which the public were deceived. In this case a manufacturer of silverware, in Plainfield, N. J., was attempting to trade upon the reputation of the "1847" brand of plated silver made by the Rogers Company of Connecticut, which company was at the time of the action, a constituent part of the International Silver Co. The Connecticut Company had built up a large and good reputation by a long period of sales of its silverware to the public under its trade devices, and the use of its business name. The New Jersey Company was simply attempting to trade on that reputation, which is almost always the case in unfair competition.

CONFLICT OF LAW.—Although we have referred to the uniform legislation in the various topics of commercial law which we have been considering, there is still much in the subject of conflict of law which concerns the student of commercial law. International law is commonly divided into two branches, public and private. Public is that which regulates the political intercourse of nations with each other; private, that which regulates the comity of States in giving effect in one to the municipal laws of another relating to private persons. Conflict of law is one division of the broader subject of international law and is frequently called private international law. In the sense in which we are now using the term, the various States of the Union are considered as foreign to each other. The problems embraced in this topic and their bearing on commercial law may be more fully appreciated if we take a simple illustration. A stock broker with offices in New York City seeks to sell the stock of a new oil mining company to a purchaser in Indiana. The sale is one which is not allowed by the Indiana "blue sky" law. New York has no such law. The sale is effected by means of circulars and correspondence between the New York broker and the Indiana purchaser. Is this transaction to be governed by the law of Indiana or of New York? Its validity will depend upon our answer to that question and this is the type of question one has to answer on the subject of conflict of law. With approximately forty different "blue sky" laws in the country at present, and the great number of stock transactions carried on between the States, the importance of this topic may be appreciated. Again, even where we have a uniform act as, for example, the Uniform Negotiable Instruments Act, there are still differences in the law in some States. Each statute must be interpreted by the courts, and although the judges are sincere in their efforts, it can not be expected that we will always have a uniform interpretation of the same act by the courts in each and every jurisdiction of the United States.

FUNDAMENTAL PRINCIPLES.—There are several fundamental principles we should keep in mind before we turn to the specific branches of commercial law as affected by our topic. The term comity is one of common use in conflict of law and is defined as the recognition which one nation or State allows within its territory to the legislative, executive, or judicial acts of another nation or state. Comity is not a matter of right, but a courtesy, and one country may exercise its right and prohibit citizens of other countries from suing in its courts. Of course the various States of the United States are not as completely free in this matter as separate countries, because of the provision in the Federal Constitution guaranteeing to the citizens of each State all the privileges and immunities of citizens in the several States. There are still many questions which are not affected by the Federal Constitution. For example, a suit is brought in New Jersey upon a contract of suretyship made in New York by a wife for her husband. There is a statute in New Jersey prohibiting a married woman from doing this. New York has no such statute. Shall the New Jersey court enforce the contract which the parties made in New York but which they could not have made in New Jersey? Under the principle of comity a New Jersey court has held valid such a contract. Again, it is entirely conceivable that a person living in Turkey might make a binding contract to marry three women at the same time. Suppose the Turk before the time for performing the contract arrives, comes to New York and then refuses to marry the three women. Could they sue him for a breach of contract in the New York court? Clearly not. Here they would be asking the New York court to enforce a contract which while admittedly valid, when made in Turkey, is decidedly against the public policy of any monogamous country. Comity being a courtesy, not a right, would not require a New York court to recognize the Turkish contract. In our illustration of the wife acting as surety, no question of public policy was involved and hence there was no impropriety in New Jersey recognizing as valid her contract, although such a contract could not have been made within the State of New Jersey.

CONFLICT OF LAW AS RELATING TO THE STATUS OF PROPERTY.—As we have pointed out heretofore, property is divided into real property and personal property. Reference should be made to the distinctions between these two kinds of property as described in a preceding chapter. Suppose A dies intestate in Texas owning real property in New York. The law relating to the descent of real property is different in Texas from that in New York. A's heirs wish to know by which law this New York real estate will be governed. It is almost universally recognized that all matters concerning the title and disposition of real property are determined by what is known as the lex loci rei sitae, that is, the law of the place where the property is situated. Accordingly the heirs in Texas would be governed by the law of the State of New York and, similarly, if A had also owned property in Illinois, that property would be governed by the Illinois law. Suppose, also, A had owned $50,000 worth of stock in various corporations and he kept one-half of this stock in his safe deposit box in Galveston and the other half in New York City. While the dominion of a State over personal property within its borders is complete, nevertheless by virtue of the principles of comity, the rule has been recognized almost from time immemorial that personal property is governed by the law of the domicile of the decedent at the time of his death. Hence A's stocks (and bonds for that matter) would be divided according to the law of Texas whether they were in his safe deposit box in Galveston, New York City, or Chicago. It follows, when no rights of creditors intervene, that the law of the domicile of the testator will control in regard to his will of personal property, and the law of the place where the real property is situate will control in regard to it.

CONFLICT OF LAW AS RELATING TO CONTRACTS.—It is a general principle of contract law that the construction and validity of a contract is governed by the lex loci contractus, the law of the place where the contract is made. When the contract is made in one jurisdiction and is to be performed in another, the question becomes more difficult. The Supreme Court of the United States, in Scudder v. Union Nat. Bank, 91 U. S. 406, has laid down the following rules in reference to the law governing contracts in cases in which the place of making and the place of performance are not the same. "1. Matters bearing upon the execution, interpretation and validity are determined by the law of the place where the contract is made; 2. Matters connected with the performance are regulated by the law of the place where the contract by its terms is to be performed; 3. Matters relating to procedure depend upon the law of the forum (i. e., the court where the case is heard)." These three general rules have been adopted and applied by many jurisdictions in a long line of cases involving every conceivable kind of contract. But perhaps it is even more generally stated, when the contract is to be performed in a place other than the place where it is made, that the law of the place where the contract is to be performed will determine the validity, nature, obligation and effect of the contract, or, in other words, in case of conflict the lex loci solutionis (the law of the place of performance) will prevail over the lex loci contractus. Although these statements at first seem somewhat contradictory, we may always apply another rule which is a sound test for the determination of the proper law to be applied. We may properly say that the intention of the parties should control and it is generally agreed that the law of the place where the contract is made is, prima facie, that which the parties intended to govern the contract, and in the absence of a contrary intention ought to control. It frequently happens that a contract made in one State is sued upon in the courts of another State. The law governing the procedure in the trial of this case will be the law of the forum, that is of the State where the case is tried, regardless of what the law may be on the same matter in the State where the contract was made. There may be, for example, a peculiar rule as to a wife's being able to testify on the contract in question. This rule will be enforced by the court although no such rule existed in the State where the contract was made. There is no great hardship in the application of such principles because the courts of the State where the contract was made are open to the parties, and if they wish to avail themselves of the services of a court in a different jurisdiction they must take it as they find it with its rules of procedure.

ILLUSTRATION.—There is another type of contract which involves the question of conflict of law to which attention should be called. The facts in the case of Fonesca v. Cunard Steamship Company 153 Mass. 553, illustrate this point. A passenger on one of the steamships of the Cunard Steamship Company bought a ticket in Liverpool for Boston and on the ticket was a clause providing that the steamship company should not be liable for any damage to a passenger's baggage during transit, regardless of whether the steamship company was negligent in handling the baggage. When the passenger arrived in Boston, and her trunk was delivered, it was found that the contents had been damaged by sea water due to the steamboat company negligently leaving a porthole open. The passenger sued, and the Massachusetts court held there could be no recovery for the damage, for, although such a clause exempting a carrier for his negligence was not valid under the Massachusetts law (and in fact the law of practically all American jurisdictions), nevertheless, since the law of England permits such a clause, and this was an English contract, the ticket having been bought in Liverpool, the passenger was bound by the terms of her contract. There are many kinds of contracts of transportation of baggage, of passengers and of telegraph messages, involving the carrying out of such contracts in many different States. Not all of the decisions in the various States of this country are harmonious. We must expect to find many such problems in business and the answer is often one that requires most careful study on the part of a lawyer.

CONFLICT OF LAW AS RELATING TO NEGOTIABLE PAPER.—There is not so large a field for questions of conflict of law to come up in negotiable paper as in some of the other topics we have been considering. Forty-seven States have now passed the Uniform Negotiable Instrument Law. But, as we have pointed out, the interpretation of this law in the various States is not invariably uniform. Suppose a promissory note has six indorsers. Every indorsement is governed by the law of the State where it was made, and should there be a different law in this matter, we would at once have a question in conflict of law. Again, in determining the negotiability of a document made in one place and payable in another, we have a further question in conflict of law. The authorities do not agree here although perhaps we may say the majority hold that the law of place or payment controls. These problems will be considered in the text-book on Negotiable Instruments.

CONFLICT OF LAW AS RELATING TO INTEREST AND USURY.—We find a variety of usury laws throughout the United States. Some few States allow the lender to charge any rate of interest. Others allow a fixed rate, usually 6%, and provide that the lender forfeits both principal and interest if he charges more. Still others allow a fixed rate and provide that interest only is forfeited if a higher rate is charged. It is easy to see that a contract made in one State may be sued upon in another State and the usury laws of the two States may be entirely different. We may say as a general rule that usury laws do not offend any principles of public policy. There is nothing wrong in asking a New York court, where the legal rate of interest is 6%, to enforce a contract made in a State where a higher rate is allowed. On the other hand, no New York court would allow citizens of New York simply to date a contract Boston, Massachusetts, and provide for a 10% interest rate, thereby hoping to evade the New York Usury law, when, except for the date on the contract, it was in reality wholly a New York contract.

INDEX

A

D

E

J

K

L

M

Q

R

S

W

Lector House believes that a society develops through a two-fold approach of continuous learning and adaptation, which is derived from the study of classic literary works spread across the historic timeline of literature records. Therefore, we aim at reviving, repairing and redeveloping all those inaccessible or damaged but historically as well as culturally important literature across subjects so that the future generations may have an opportunity to study and learn from past works to embark upon a journey of creating a better future.

This book is a result of an effort made by Lector House towards making a contribution to the preservation and repair of original ancient works which might hold historical significance to the approach of continuous learning across subjects.

HAPPY READING & LEARNING!

LECTOR HOUSE LLP
E-MAIL: lectorpublishing@gmail.com